MAN AND SOCIETY:

THE SCOTTISH INQUIRY OF THE
EIGHTEENTH CENTURY

MAN AND SOCIETY:

The Scottish Inquiry
of the Eighteenth Century

By Gladys Bryson

REPRINTS OF ECONOMIC CLASSICS

AUGUSTUS M. KELLEY · PUBLISHERS
NEW YORK 1968

This book is for

ALICE GARDNER HOYT

FOR these larger [general philosophical] ideas within the scope of which social theorizing has been carried on, have as a rule been derived, consciously or tacitly, from some comprehensive view of the universe and man. Here is an enormously rich field of research. There are but few works known to me that trace the philosophical origin of the ideas which have in the past so largely governed special social studies by means of studying the intellectual framework within which the latter are carried on. The philosopher has not as a rule traced the ramifications of his ideas in economics, politics, the writing of history, jurisprudence, or the development of educational theories; workers in the latter fields have often taken current ideas ready made, and omitted to ask for their source in prior philosophic speculation, and to consider the degree in which they are affected— or infected—by that origin.

JOHN DEWEY

FOREWORD

IT is with genuine pleasure that I acknowledge the assistance which several friends, colleagues and institutions have given me in the preparation of this book. The volume has been a longer time in the making than I had anticipated, and it is quite likely that several of the persons whom I wish to thank may, with the peculiar generosity which characterizes the academic world, wonder what help it was they rendered me. But I remember, and I wish to thank them again now that the study is completed. It goes without saying that they may not approve, in part or as a whole, the interpretations to which their conversations and correspondence have contributed; I can only hope that I have not done violence to their opinions as they shared them with me.

The first to be mentioned, in order of time and of the greatness of my indebtedness, is Frederick J. Teggart, Professor Emeritus of Social Institutions in the University of California, Berkeley. It was he who first stimulated me to such intellectual activity and independence of judgment as I may now possess; more specifically, it was he who first opened up to me that comparatively unexplored field in which comprehensive philosophical ideas are to be seen as the "generalized ancestors" of particular social theories. To have studied and taught with Professor Teggart was an experience not to be forgotten. Marjorie Nicolson, formerly Dean of Smith College and now Professor of English in Columbia University, has been of great help to me. From her vast knowledge of the idea-complexes of the seventeenth and eighteenth centuries she gives freely, always, to other students of those centuries. In this and in other ways the generosity she has shown me has been beyond itemizing. For reading and criticism of the entire manuscript I am greatly indebted to Professor Howard Becker of the University of Wisconsin, Professor Frank H. Hankins of Smith College and Professor Louis Wirth of the University of Chicago.

Professor Wirth gave additional advice and help of several kinds which have been most valuable.

For clarification of particular points I wish to acknowledge the aid of Professor George Plimpton Adams of the University of California, Berkeley, the late Professor Nicholas J. Spykman of Yale, Professor Douglas Clyde Macintosh of Yale, Professor Philip Wiener of the College of the City of New York and Smith College and Dr. Panos Morphopoulos of Johns Hopkins University. I am especially indebted to Arthur O. Lovejoy, Professor Emeritus of Philosophy in Johns Hopkins University, for a personal letter in which he sets forth the issues with reference to the conceptualizing of society on which eighteenth-century opinion was divided; in Chapter VI of this book I quote his formulation of those issues. Mr. W. Fraser Mitchell of Reading, Berks., has given me a glimpse of the limitations under which all of us work who deal in the slightest way with Lord Monboddo. I look forward to reading his projected study of the crotchety Laird for almost certain corrections of some points in the interpretation of Monboddo's theories which I have offered here. Professors Katherine G. Hornbeak and Edna Rees Williams of Smith College have freely responded to my requests for advice on specific matters of form and structure. For her meticulous care in the preparation of the manuscript for the press and for her warm personal interest in its fortunes I thank Miss Mildred O'Brien, also of Smith College.

In the early days of this study a University Fellowship at the University of California, Berkeley, and a Sterling Fellowship at Yale made possible freedom from other obligations so necessary for such widely flung research. Along the way many librarians have been helpful, especially those in Smith College, Yale, Columbia, Princeton, Harvard and the British Museum. Dr. L. W. Sharp, Librarian to the University of Edinburgh, and Dr. H. W. Meikle, Librarian of the National Library of Scotland, were wonderfully generous in their friendly aid, as were the Keepers of the Library of the Writers to the Signet. For a personal introduction to the latter I am indebted to Mr. James Watt, of Edinburgh, himself a Writer to the Signet. At the conclusion of the work President Herbert Davis and the Trustees of Smith College joined with the American Council of Learned Societies in a grant-in-aid-of-publication, and to both of these groups I am deeply grateful.

Permission to quote passages from books or articles under copyright is acknowledged at appropriate points in the Notes. The editors of the *Sociological Review* (London) should be mentioned here for their courtesy in allowing me to reprint in Chapter VI a substantial portion of a paper published in their journal, Vol. xxi, No. 4 (October 1939), entitled "Some Eighteenth-Century Conceptions of Society." The passage by John Dewey quoted on the page facing the Foreword is from his chapter, "Philosophy," in *Research in the Social Sciences*, edited by Wilson Gee (New York, 1929), pp. 257-58, by permission of the publishers, the Macmillan Company.

I do not want to close this acknowledgment of the cooperation which has been given me without speaking warmly of the staff of the Princeton University Press. The Director, Mr. Datus C. Smith, Jr., and Miss Jean Mac Lachlan in their correspondence somehow manage to convey an impression of infinite leisure and ease of procedure at the Press which is, of course, illusory, but which is, nevertheless, very pleasing to the person at the other end of a chain of letters.

GLADYS BRYSON

Smith College,
Northampton, Mass.
August 23, 1944

CONTENTS

I

INTRODUCTION

THE history of efforts to formulate the problems and methods of social science has not yet been completely written and probably never will be. Chapters in that history we have had: chapters dealing with the development of the now separated and segmented sciences, or with selected ideas dominant through the centuries, or with selected social theorists in logical or chronological order. Most of these treatments leave the student aware that much has been omitted. What is often presented is an account of a series of individuals who have held this idea and that. Or, again, an idea is traced from some point in time to another, and its variations noted, but without much connection being made with other related ideas. Now ideas are not isolated and atomic; rather, they come grouped, in patterns, complexes, or configurations—if we may use current terminology. When we isolate one for study we usually see it out of its right relation and function, and our procedure is analogous to that of the older anthropologists who isolated and traced the dispersal of culture traits, while ignoring the complex cultures from which the traits have been abstracted. No wonder that, as a result, both idea and trait often seem cold, formal and meaningless.

The aim of this book is to provide only another chapter dealing with the development of social science, but a chapter of a different kind. We shall be concerned here with the efforts of the eighteenth century to establish an empirical basis for the study of man and society. We shall focus our attention on a group of Scottish writers of moral philosophy who were absorbed in that empirical enterprise, even though they gave expression to "mixed modes of thought." The choice of this Scottish group can be completely justified. In the first place, the authors were so closely connected by ties of friendship and by the relation of teacher and pupil that we may fairly speak of them as composing a school—a school of high order, too. In them we shall see a group of scholars working at the same set of problems over a period of a century. Standing head and shoulders above them all was David Hume, pivot and provocation to the group. It was due only to the orthodoxy of the Town Council of Edinburgh, and not to his own desire, that Hume was not in a university chair. But the academic succession is clear: from Francis Hutcheson through Adam Smith, his pupil, to Thomas Reid, Smith's student and successor in moral philosophy in the University of Glasgow; Adam Ferguson, student at St. Andrews, student and professor at Edinburgh, to Dugald Stewart, who was the prize pupil of both Ferguson and Reid. With Hume, outside the ranks of the professors, were his kinsman, Lord Kames, who was to the group patron, critic and jester; and, with Kames in the same Court of Session, Lord Monboddo, "the most learned man in all of Scotland save Sir William Hamilton."

Second, although they thus stand as a connected group of scholars, mutually influencing one another, they were not an ingrown, isolated group carrying on a type of pursuit peculiar to Scotland. On the contrary, they were closely in touch with the movement of thought on the continent and some of their procedures were typical of what was being carried on in France, and toward the end of the century in Germany also. We shall not be guilty, then, of false perspective in looking to them for knowledge of the eighteenth century's best efforts toward a science of man; and we shall be filling in a gap too long unattended in the history of social theory.

Third, they were an influential group. Kant himself said that he owed his intellectual awakening to the reading of Hume's *Enquiry Concerning Human Understanding*. It is probable, too, that Germany might have been less prolific in doctoral dissertations but for the problem of reconciling Adam Smith's discussion of sympathy with his discussion of self-interest. John Hill Burton was probably correct in saying that no third person writing in English in that period has had so much influence on the opinions of men as either Hume or Smith. The ovation granted the school, particularly Reid and Stewart, by the French is written large in the works of Royer-Collard, Jouffroy and Cousin. What is not so widely recognized is the degree to which the Scottish thought was spread in the United States. At first it was popularized chiefly by way of President John Witherspoon of Princeton and Princeton's increasing influence in the new nation, and later by way of President James McCosh of Princeton and President Noah Porter of Yale. Until well past the middle of the nineteenth century the texts named in the catalogues of the Eastern universities were over and over the works of Hutcheson, Smith, Ferguson, Reid and Stewart. Hume, as accepted text, was anathema, but as a target he was everywhere used. More recently we have had the admission of William McDougall that his psychology of instincts or propensities mirrors the psychology of this group; the statement of the sociologist Franklin Giddings that the organizing principle of his system of sociology, "the consciousness of kind," he derived from Adam Smith's *Theory of Moral Sentiments*; and we have had Albion W. Small, in his lifetime called the dean of American sociologists, recalling sociologists to the vantage position occupied by these same moral philosophers.

Our purpose in focusing attention on this group will not be that of recalling any twentieth-century social scientists to the positions so loved of the eighteenth, nor of tracing this idea or that of our day back to an earlier exponent. We shall be concerned chiefly with the effort of the earlier group to lay the foundations for an empirical science of man, a goal which we have not yet completely achieved. In fairness to the eighteenth-century writers and to ourselves we shall have to find their empiricism as it expressed itself in their more "comprehensive view of the universe and man," as Professor Dewey phrases it; for it was a comprehensive view which their framework of thought required. From the time of Socrates until the emergence of the separate social sciences in the nineteenth century, moral philosophy offered the most comprehensive discussions of human relations and institutions which were available. Today we are likely to think of it too entirely as the equivalent of abstract ethics, without realizing that in most of those centuries the scope of its interests was bounded only by the limits of the activities of men.

There is real point, then, in our reviewing the scope and method of this older discipline, especially in its typical form in a period immediately preceding the emergence of the separate social sciences. It is strange that historians of social theory have so long neglected a detailed analysis of it, when the opening of any book of the general title of "moral philosophy" reveals discussions of human nature, social forces, progress, marriage and family relationships, economic processes, maintenance of government, religion, international relations, elementary jurisprudence, primitive customs, history of institutions, ethics, aesthetics— all, even the last, topics of import in the social sciences of our day. This old moral philosophy displays itself, even to cursory examination, as the matrix of the social sciences. Within the social sciences, moreover, there is great need for work in the field of research indicated by John Dewey in the quotation presented at the beginning of this essay: we need to know more about the comprehensive views of the universe and man within which special social theories have been developed; we need to know the intellectual framework within which the social studies are now carried on; we need to abandon the bad practice of taking current ideas ready-made without asking for their source in prior philosophic speculation and the influences of that source. And, in our day, devoted to empirical procedures, it may be useful to take account of an earlier effort in the same direction, to be sure that we are not "infected"— John Dewey's word again—by false notions carried over unexamined and unsuspected. For both of these objectives, seeing freshly earlier comprehensive views and examining the outreach toward empirical science, the old moral philosophy will serve us well.

The members of this Scottish group who, as moral philosophers, were among the precursors of twentieth-century social scientists, were at home in the intellectual climate of the late Enlightenment when secular interests once again commanded attention and when inquiries were related to the business of living with one's fellows rather than to the "metaphysics of the schools." It was the rare analyst who did not begin his investigations with "Experience" instead of with some large a priori afforded by "Reason." Largely because of that, philosophical speculation grew in popularity; as Victor Cousin writes, "Philosophy acquired . . . a public condition and became an established thing . . . ,"[1] freed from the cloak of theology and made the possession of common men. By philosophers themselves the study of philosophy was advocated as "the great antidote to the poison of enthusiasm and superstition."[2]

It was a notable period for Scotland and its intellectual life. We may well remind ourselves when we are inclined to think of the country as under the power of a harsh, theocratic Calvinism that, even so, there was a long tradition of Scottish lawyers, doctors and preachers going abroad for their education and for travel; not every Scot was a rustic Davie Deans. It was to this "constant influx of information and of liberality from abroad" that Dugald Stewart attributed that "sudden burst of genius, which to the foreigner must seem to have sprung up in this country by a sort of enchantment, soon after the rebellion of 1745."[3]

Scottish Calvinism itself was being modified, though the Moderates, even, were afraid of being thought heretical. What they did was simply to shift the emphases in their preaching and let time do its work; their religion had "less dogma and more morality than of old; and if their sermons lacked unction, they had no fanaticism and much sanctified good sense."[4] Miss Elizabeth Mure said of the new school of theologians, "They taught that who-ever would please God must resemble him in goodness and benevolence, and those who had it not must affect it by politeness and good manners."[5] Moreover—moderates, se-ceders and conservatives alike—they were all Scots before they were preachers, and in their irritation at the govern-ment, both before and after the union of 1707, they made common cause. Perhaps Buckle was right in holding that it was this daily rebellion against the government which was the salvation of the people from the tyranny of their kirk. It kept alive their energy and acuteness, whereas in Spain the church had acquiesced in the government's pro-gram and the tyranny of the Inquisition was unmitigated.[6]

Trade, industry and improved methods of farming added greatly to the prosperity of the country in the course of the century. Particularly after the '45, agricul-ture experienced real advances. We note men like Lord Kames, at the age of eighty, writing his *Gentleman Farmer* to spread abroad new ideas of farming, and undertaking the drainage of three thousand acres of marshland; Lord Monboddo experimenting with new crops; and James Hut-ton, the geologist, bringing ploughmen from Dorset to teach his workmen the use of the two-horse plough and the newer methods.[7] The Highlands, however, were not at once prosperous. The abolition of clan chieftainship after the '45 dispossessed many Highlanders; it is estimated that between 1763 and 1775 thirty thousand of them emi-grated to America, many came down into the Lowlands to work at whatever opened up, and thousands of others turned soldier and sailor. Before the close of the century, however, the section was being opened up by roads and waterways, and there came an end to the isolation and backwardness of the people there.[8]

In this period of change and increasing material pros-perity Scotland's enlightenment took place. Sir Henry Craik, in giving an account of the groups and circum-

stances involved, speaks a number of times of the variety
and richness of the types of the people, who, gathered together upon a narrow scene and sharing common traditions, were yet not weighed down with the burden of social
convention:

> The mingling of pride and poverty, of high notions of aristo-
> cratic dignity with an almost ludicrous simplicity and quaintness
> of social habit, of national exclusiveness with a strain of cosmo-
> politan experience, imparted a keen intellectual stimulus to the
> Scottish society of that day. . . . It is this combination of a
> fundamental conservatism, with intellectual freedom which con-
> stitutes the chief interest of Scottish history during the next gen-
> eration.[9]

In the towns especially there was opportunity for the
mingling of these types in all sorts of clubs and societies.
As a rule each group met regularly at a favorite tavern.
Much conversation went on, much French claret was con-
sumed—as well as stronger beverages—and whatever the
members had to offer in the way of philosophy, science or
belles-lettres was augmented, criticized and further inspired by these gatherings of friendly competitors. Truly,
as Graham writes, "It may indeed be said that in taverns
Scots' modern literature was born, and the first public it
addressed was in a public house."[10]

As in the sixteenth century under Buchanan and Mel-
ville, so now again in the eighteenth century the universities took on new life. This was both product and, in part,
the source of the new intellectuality. Early in the century
the University of Edinburgh became famous as a school of
medicine, the inspiration of which was John Monro, and
his son Alexander (1697-1767) who was a pupil of Boer-
haave. It had been one of the universities early to establish a chair of chemistry and it had always excelled in
mathematics. One David Gregory at Edinburgh and his
brother, James Gregory at St. Andrews, publicly taught
the philosophy of Newton "before it was able to supplant
the vortices of Descartes in that very university [Cam-
bridge] of which Newton was a member." A successor of

Gregory's, Colin Maclauren, friend and interpreter of
Newton, shared honors with Bernoulli in a prize of the
French Academy for his *Essay on Tides*[11]; another later
mathematician, John Playfair (1748-1819), as professor
of Natural Philosophy helped to popularize James Hut-
ton's new theory of the earth. All the Scottish colleges had
their share of substantial scholars. John Theodore Merz
calls attention to the fact that these men of science in Scotland were affiliated with the universities, whereas the English universities were not yet organized to accommodate
their activities. It was indeed the "eclipse" period of both
Oxford and Cambridge.[12] After attending Balliol College,
Oxford, from 1740 to 1746 as Snell exhibitioner, Adam
Smith decided that all the benefits were planned there not
for the students, but for the masters, many of whom had
given up all pretense of teaching.[13]

It is generally agreed that the personality most responsible for the new spirit of enlightenment in the Scottish universities was Francis Hutcheson, the earliest of the group
of philosophers with whom we shall deal. A charming lec-
turer, a liberal in religion and politics, he so opened the
world of learning to the lads who sat under him that they
came to care more for it than for the world to come. "I am
called New Light here," he wrote soon after taking up his
duties at Glasgow. He was referring simply to the nomenclature of one of the religious sects of the period, but in
ways other than sectarian the phrase has been applied to
him ever since. He and his friend, the Reverend William
Leechman (1706-1785), the principal of Glasgow,[14] did
"put a new face on theology" as they set out to do, and
also a new face on the whole of Scottish learning and interests.

The new era in university teaching was certainly not to
be attributed to the material equipment and organization
of the colleges. The buildings for the most were exceedingly shabby and inadequate; teachers were overworked
and so poorly paid in salaries and fees that they resorted to
taking students as boarders into their homes. Lectures were

in Latin, until Wodrow and Simson, Rosse and Hutcheson began about the same time to address their classes in English.[15] It was English of the Scots' variety, we may be sure. The lecture system, then as now, produced some very certain results, as evidenced in Andrew Lang's amusing account of a conversation between a professor and a student who was not scribbling violently: "Have you notes of the lecture, Mr. —?" the professor asked. "Yes, sir." "Whose notes?" "My grandfather's, sir." Lectures and notes were necessary in the eighteenth century, however, as until 1730 books were chained and padlocked to library shelves.[16] The most serious handicap to learning, the regenting system, was overcome in the course of the century. Under this system a regent, or tutor, would take a class of youths, entering at the tender age of eleven, twelve or thirteen, and carry them through the college course, teaching them all he could of every subject. The plan was abolished at Edinburgh in 1708, at Glasgow in 1727, at St. Andrews in 1747 and at Marischal College of Aberdeen University in 1757, but King's College, Aberdeen, retained it until the end of the century.[17]

From available accounts we gather that the curriculum was not particularly inspiring—Latin and Greek,[18] logic, moral philosophy and natural philosophy. Yet here and there within the organization of studies there were opportunities to acquire something more than formal and antiquated knowledge. We have to remind ourselves of the continental influence on these Scottish schools, particularly that of Paris and Bologna, which meant among other things a tendency to keep in touch with practical affairs, with law and public concerns. The field of moral philosophy itself led straight into politics and law. There was, for example, a professorship at the University of Edinburgh in 1759 named the chair of the Law of Nature and Nations. This recalls the original chair of that title created for the Baron Samuel Pufendorf by the University of Heidelberg in 1661. The Scottish chair was not held continuously and when, after a long vacancy, it was revived in 1858, it was rechristened the chair of Public Law.[19] In our day of almost too practical studies it is interesting to discover that the University of Edinburgh in 1790 established the first professorship of agriculture in the British Empire, and that in 1794 at Glasgow, John Anderson, professor of natural philosophy, invited working men to attend his courses in experimental physics at the university, and at his death in 1796 left his property to found an institution which would further the application of science to industry.[20]

In such a system of education, then, the Scottish students of the eighteenth century acquired their learning. It was not a costly affair for them in money. A visitor among them in the early days of the nineteenth century wrote back to his kinsfolk that any young man who could afford a decent coat, and live in a garret upon porridge or herrings could pass through his academic career creditably; that the majority had seldom more than thirty or forty pounds a year and many got along on little more than fifteen or twenty.[21] Of the universities it could truly be said, in the translation offered by Sydney Smith as a motto for the *Edinburgh Review*, "Tenui musam meditamur avena—we cultivate literature upon a little oatmeal."[22]

Fully participant in the life of the period and part of its variety, its conservatism and its freedom of thought, was the group of moral philosophers: Hutcheson, Hume, Smith, Ferguson, Reid, Stewart, and their jurist friends, Lord Kames and Lord Monboddo. They are often called the Common Sense School, from the ready solution offered by most of them to the problem of knowledge on a common sense basis, in opposition to the epistemological idealism of Berkeley and Hume. At other times they are called the Moral Sense School, because of the belief held by most of them that man is possessed of a faculty of immediate moral perception and judgment comparable to his faculty of seeing or hearing. Sometimes they are called the Sentimentalists, because of their insisting that sensation and feeling together are far more determinant of man's action than is his rational nature. By whatever name we call them as a group, it is evident that they all took their stand on "the permanent good sense of humanity."[23] If, in their effort to refute Hobbes and Mandeville, they "made human nature too lovely,"[24] it was because they felt they had to supply some hopeful and, as they felt, certain guarantee that the world would not go to moral wrack and ruin now that God's dicta were no longer the only foundation of morality, and now that rationalism could no longer be counted on to provide an eternal and immutable code of ethics.

We could speak also of George Turnbull, of John Pringle, of David Fordyce, of Archibald Campbell, of Alexander Gerard, but on the whole their contributions mirror the same pattern with little that is distinctive. To mention James Beattie and James Oswald would be to suggest the element of Common Sense which appeared with Reid and which developed into a psychology less general in scope than the older moral philosophy, and which, at the same time that it popularized, brought the Common Sense position eventually into some disrepute. Of our group, all, save Dugald Stewart who was the last to die, knew Francis Hutcheson, and all, including Stewart, were of his tradition. All of them knew and were friends of David Hume, however much they might seek to refute his sceptical philosophy now and again. All of them were friends of Adam Smith. Man, with his institutions, was the object of their study, and, within their "comprehensive view," they made valiant effort to be empirical in their approach. Social scientists of the twentieth century may properly regard them as forerunners in the effort in which we too are engaged.

The writers of the century amaze us with the range of their knowledge, but to them it was only the logical implication of their being alive in the century of the Enlightenment. Voltaire, Diderot, Condorcet, Hume, Adam Smith,

Herder, Kant—all, whether they called themselves moral philosophers or not, were encyclopedic, chiefly, perhaps, because they were all devoted to the study of man. Lord Kames put upon the title page of his *Sketches of the History of Man* a quotation from Terence, to the sentiment of which every eighteenth-century scholar subscribed: "Homo sum, humani nihil a me alienum puto." Before taking fuller account of the range of the Scottish discussions, it may be well to review briefly a few of their controlling conceptions, the typical modes of thought in which their approaches were cast. At almost every point the writers exhibit an intellectual kinship, a similarity of views which, as Professor Chinard suggests, was one of the characteristics of the century.[25]

In one of his most recent writings, Professor Carl Becker speaks of the key words which may be said to unlock the doors of understanding to several different centuries. For the thirteenth those words are God, sin, grace, salvation, heaven; for the nineteenth they are matter, fact, matter-of-fact, evolution, progress; for the twentieth, relativity, process, adjustments, function, complex. For the eighteenth century the magic words are nature, natural law, first cause (and he might have added final cause), reason, sentiment, perfectibility. Now one of the things that Professor Becker is most interested to point out is that while these words seem, at first glance, far removed in meaning from those of the thirteenth, actually the philosophy expressed by them was not entirely emancipated from older bonds, and the ideal of the Heavenly City, so warmly espoused by the thirteenth century thinkers, had merely shifted to earthly foundations. He quotes the words of Diderot: "La posterité pour le philosophe, c'est l'autre monde de l'homme religieux."[26] Certainly the group of Scots, as well as the French group analyzed by Professor Becker, had their dreams of posterity and its glorious future.

Professor Arthur Lovejoy has at various times offered interpretations and reinterpretations of eighteenth-century modes of thought, and always illuminatingly. In a recent paper he has discussed what he calls the characteristic idea-complex constituting the rationalism of the Enlightenment, a particularly valuable discussion since, as he says, this complex is composed of "a coherent body of underlying assumptions, widely accepted as too self-evident to need, on the whole, formal exposition or defense."[27] We shall follow closely his analysis of the elements of the complex:

1. Uniformitarianism. This first and fundamental element stands for ideas like this: Reason is identical in all men, therefore the life of reason must admit of no diversity; the object of the effort of the religious, moral or social reformer, as of the literary critic, is, therefore, to standardize men and their beliefs, their likings, their activities and their institutions; "nature" means, beyond and through every meaning that was attached to it, uniformity, and because of this particular meaning it was the sacred word of the Enlightenment.

2. Rationalistic individualism. Every individual is so equipped as to be able to attain truth for himself.

3. Appeal to the *consensus gentium*. This appeal had been made long before the age of Deism. Hooker, in his *Ecclesiastical Polity* (1594) had written: "The general and perpetual voice of men is as the sentence of God himself. For that which all men have at all times learned, Nature herself must needs have taught; and God being the author of Nature, her voice is but his instrument. . . ." The eighteenth century changed this just enough to read "*Only* that which is uttered by the general and perpetual voice of men can be taken as the voice of God." In other words, the content of true religion is that common residuum of all historic religions. On such a presupposition as that of uniformitarianism, the Christian creed, as interpreted by the churches, seemed to be but a sort of local custom of the European peoples and therefore, on that ground, suspect; a truly catholic and universal creed was possible only if items 2 and 3 were the basis of it.

4. Cosmopolitanism. *"Natura"* and *"Natio"* were words of profoundly antithetic connotations; and Deism, being, when full blown, not merely cosmopolitan but cosmical in its outlook and temper, could admit the claim of no people and no planet to an exceptional or even distinctive role in religious history.

5. Antipathy to "enthusiasm" and originality.

6. Intellectual equalitarianism—a democratic temper in matters of religion, morals and taste, even in persons not democratic in their political views. Deism, for example, professed to be a religion "level with every man's mother-wit."

7. Rationalistic anti-intellectualism. This paradoxical-sounding term expresses a very real truth of the attitude of the century. The presumption of the universal accessibility and verifiability of all that is really needful for men to know implied that all subtle, elaborate, intricate reasonings about abstruse questions beyond the grasp of the majority are certainly unimportant, and probably untrue.

8. Rationalistic primitivism. Since truths of nature are universal, they must have been as well known to the earliest, least sophisticated men as to any other members of the race; what is more, early men were really in a better position to apprehend such truths than men of later periods, "ere wit oblique had broke the steady light." Voltaire could say: "un déiste est de la religion d'Adam, de Seth, de Noé."

9. For some, a negative philosophy of history followed from all this: a uniform standard must obviously be an immutable standard; and all the changes in beliefs, cultures and institutions which have occurred in the course of the ages must have been changes for the worse. Yet, as Professor Lovejoy himself has pointed out more recently, it was in the eighteenth century that primitivism and its resulting philosophy of history were so widely opposed with the conception of progress that, by the early part of the next century, the former conceptions had become almost obsolescent.[28] We shall see that, with the Scots, the

conception of progress was the more favored, though they were not always logically consistent in their judgment, and were frequently regretful that progress seemed to bring in its train some very undesirable concomitants.

This analysis of Professor Lovejoy's tells much of the story of the century's modes of thought. He shows how Deism, that "mixed whirl of earnest inquiry and flippant scepticism,"[29] may be seen as a specific application of the same set of ideas, and so 'may the neoclassicism of poetry and the other arts. It is apparent, even in this abbreviated report, how large a place is held by the concept of nature. As Professor Becker neatly puts it, having "denatured God, they deified Nature," and to nature, then, they turned for standards in literature and the arts, for standards in right thought and conduct. For that which was according to nature must thereby be true and beautiful and good.[30]

What other modes of thought may be taken as characteristic of the century, and where, in general, do the Scots stand with respect to such positions? Let us first look at ideas of science and scientific method.

It should be remembered that the century really preferred to speak of philosophy instead of science, and approved a procedure by using the word "philosophical" rather than the word "scientific." It would neither have surprised nor amused the men of that era to be told that philosophical principles could be applied to navigation or to farming. Dr. Johnson in 1778 declared: "I could write a better book of cookery than has ever yet been written; it should be a book upon philosophical principles."[31] Such a statement merely meant that there were available connected bodies of facts sufficiently tested and classified to be usable by the average farmer, navigator or cook, and that certain general rules governed these facts. In other words, philosophy, or science, was in their conception made up of bodies of knowledge, each body comprehended within as few general principles as possible;

or, in their phraseology, particulars were to be sunk in
the general.

Adam Smith has a few cogent comments to make on the
nature and function of philosophy:

> Philosophy is the science of the connecting principles of na-
> ture. Nature, after the largest experience that common observa-
> tion can acquire, seems to abound with events which appear
> solitary and incoherent with all that go before them, which
> therefore disturb the easy movement of the imagination; which
> makes its ideas succeed each other, if one may say so, by irregu-
> lar starts and sallies; and which thus tend, in some measure to
> introduce . . . confusions and distractions. . . . Philosophy, by
> representing the invisible chains which bind together all those
> disjointed objects, endeavours to introduce order into this chaos
> of jarring and discordant appearances. . . .[32]

He wants it understood that philosophy has a natural
order of its own; though actually it is built up from individual experiences, by way of natural philosophy or
physics, once collected it should be communicated by way
of metaphysics and logic, since all effects are results of
some character shared universally by the phenomena under observation.[33] But even in the building-up of the knowledge care must be exercised to discriminate permanent,
dependable things from others which are transient and in-
secure. Smith's discussion here recalls the much more
elaborate reconstruction of the processes of acquiring
knowledge and communicating it, as presented by D'Alembert in his *Discours préliminaire de l'Encyclopédie*.[34]

One of the aims of science is prediction. Dugald Stewart writes in this fashion:

> The ultimate object of philosophical inquiry is the same which
> every man of plain understanding proposes to himself, when he
> remarks the events which fall under his observation, with a view
> to the future regulation of his conduct. The more knowledge of
> this kind we acquire, the better can we accommodate our plans
> to the established order of things, and avail ourselves of natural
> powers and agents for accomplishing our purposes.[35]

Observation, leading to a knowledge of the established
order of things, and, in turn, some control of situations—

such, for Stewart, would seem to be the steps in a complete scientific process. In other words, empiricism and induction were the lauded methods which would lead to usable knowledge.

In investigations dealing with man and his social relations they did not practice experiment, though they spoke much of their experimental methods. Their base line, rather, was experience; thus, a kind of rough, common-sense empiricism was their position. They took what they found, but they did not manipulate and control. "Hunches" they had of the kind known to scientific investigators of all times, but they refused to call them hypotheses since that word was forever corrupted by its association with the "fantastic vortices" of Descartes. Verification was, therefore, a relatively simple step for them, as it meant only a widening of the field of observation. Theory they excelled in, since it meant, in Ferguson's words, "referring particular operations to the principles or general laws, under which they are comprehended; or in referring particular effects to the causes from which they proceed." But, if we read them correctly, the conclusion is inescapable that they thought of science as made up of systematic bodies of knowledge, characterized particularly by the lucidity and simplicity of the organizing principles. Attention was not so much directed to finding out how things actually work as it was to classifying observations under some already accepted principle of explanation. Even yet, at this date in time, we ourselves have to be reminded that science is not certain prescribed subject matter which lends itself to being systematized neatly, while other subject matter is by its nature unscientific. We have to be reminded that science exists in the degree to which we are interested in solving the problems of how things work. Systematic schemes which describe for us actually observed processes are the desired results of scientific pursuit, but organizing principles used for the sake of system itself are likely to lead us far afield, as they led these philosophers of the eighteenth century.[36]

Now all of this procedure was Newtonian, they thought, but they gave credit for the inspiration, before Newton, to Bacon. Bacon and Newton over and over were named as the masters whom they would follow—named by all save Monboddo, who expressed unremittingly his contempt for the "manual philosophers," as he called the empiricists, and for those who would "physiologize" the mind; for him no one this side of Plato would serve as master. But Locke was the philosopher of mind and morals who, to their way of thinking, embodied this procedure most perfectly. They never tired of lauding him for abandoning metaphysical and fruitless "hypotheses," and for pointing the way to an empirical study of mind, on the general principles of Bacon and Newton. To them, as to Locke, introspection of their own minds seemed an empirical beginning: what he said of ideas they could say of ideas, and sentiments and passions, "Every one is conscious of them in himself; and men's words and actions will satisfy him that they are in others."[37] What more indubitable objects of observation could empiricism demand? Here, it seemed to them, was the rock-bottom start for the study of man. As they looked into their own minds and found there ideas of benevolence, fear, vanity, justice, love, as well as ideas conveying information about the physical world; when they saw other people behaving as if they, too, experienced these same ideas and inclinations, it seemed to them that they had discovered not only an observable basis for the science of man, but one so universal that it embraced all the laws of nature at work in and for man. Hence, the organizing principles for making a science of man became for them human nature itself.[38]

We need not here go into the discussion as to how a succeeding generation came to feel that introspection as a form of observation was a most inadequate method. What we need to note is that it seemed to offer a scientific technique to these men of the eighteenth century. By means of it they came to judge that human affairs were timeless, after a fashion, and uniform, and that they could be charted and predicted. With human nature as a general principle, conduct and achievement could be deduced as probable or typical or, at least, plausible; and such generalizations served the purposes of science to them just as well as though they were strictly true at every point in the line.

Francis Hutcheson writes thus: "We must . . . search accurately into the constitution of our nature, to see what sort of creatures we are. . . ."[39] When David Hume published his *Treatise* in 1739, the title page read as follows: *A Treatise of Human Nature*: Being an Attempt to introduce the experimental Method of Reasoning into Moral Subjects. As Laird reminds us, Hume "meant . . . to become the Newton of the Human Mind."[40] Lord Kames would make the basis of science "facts sufficiently vouched, or conclusions drawn from them by a fair and chaste interpretation of nature," and would allow no "hypotheses" nor theories which the imagination creates.[41] And like the majority of his fellow-Scots, one of the sources of fact for him is intuition, which, more than reasoning, gives us first principles, certainties. Almost every page of the work of Thomas Reid bears witness to his belief that empiricism must be the beginning of science. Nor is he sure that we can or need ever arrive at that all-embracing synthesis called metaphysics. Cousin reminds us that Reid has really the Baconian contempt for metaphysics. As for the realm of moral philosophy, it offers a fruitful field for the application of the same empirical principles, he thinks, based as it is for him on the compassable facts of the human mind. The powers and principles of mind can be discovered in just the same way that we have discovered all that we know of the body, that is, by anatomical dissection and observation. Reid thinks of himself, then, as an anatomist of mind,[42] in the Baconian tradition. Newton, too, had given him courage to believe that moral philosophy could profit from the use of those methods. Newton had written, "If natural philosophy, in all its parts by pursuing the inductive method, shall at length be per-

fected, the bounds of moral philosophy will also be enlarged."[43]

Now it is clear that Adam Smith thinks of his own possible contribution to thought in somewhat these same
terms. He is eager to bring some order into the chaotic
field of social phenomena; philosophy gives evidence that
the mind of man possesses principles, abilities, which enable man to deal even with strange, wonderful and hitherto unknown phenomena; why cannot these same principles be drawn on for systematizing our knowledge of the
world of men as they have been utilized in forming more
and more valid systems of physics, and of astronomy?[44]
Human nature, then, will be Smith's starting point for all
discussions of social phenomena, both because it is the
origin of social phenomena and because it can interpret
social phenomena. Whether writing of discoveries in science, of the theory of morals, of the growth of language,
or of the increase of wealth, Smith's starting point was
human nature. Some power within us, whether reason or
feeling or a combination of both, recommends virtue to us;
the division of labor which makes for increase of wealth
flows from a direct propensity in human nature for one
man to barter with another in order to better himself.[45]
And here we come upon an idea basic to all of Smith's
work: this human nature of ours is only a part of the
whole order of nature which surrounds us and means well
for us. Glimpses of its beneficent purposes for us we have
by means of the promptings of our human frame. The
moral is clear: as a general principle, man should not be
hampered by any "adventitious" institution such as the
state, but should be left free to live in natural liberty. The
dictum is applicable not only to economic processes, but
to all of man's relationships, for the adjustment of which
he has within him a natural indicator as to what is right
and advantageous.[46]

For Dugald Stewart there is an organic unity of the
sciences which forbids that any one of them should always be examined alone. What he wants is a view of the

whole, a conspectus, even a synthesis. This presents itself
as a possibility to him because he, too, regards all knowledge, all human phenomena, as rooted in human nature.
"General psychology is thus the centre whence the thinker
goes outward to the circumference of human knowledge."[47]

But what aspects of human nature will these men take
as most fundamental, most universal, most truly human?
The terms of their replies may vary but there is substantial unanimity in their meaning: they do not regard
"Reason" as the great means of revelation to man; and
certainly they do not think that man is motivated by it,
but by those influences brought him by his senses. In other
words, they have swung away from subordination to
that cardinal principle of the Cartesians, and one ground
for the divergence is that reason seems not to be uniformly
possessed by all persons. As Hutcheson puts it, "Unhappy
would it be for mankind, if a sense of virtue was of as narrow an extent, as a capacity for such metaphysics."[48]
Rather, they will take as their empirical base line the
sensations and sentiments, which seem to operate with
more universality and more predictability than does reason. Their effort, then, is to give a naturalistic account of
the springs of human action[49]; and final judgment of action lies in the moral sense, or common sense, or sympathy, or that capacity which Hume thought the Cartesians had neglected so badly, namely, belief.

The Scottish writers shared another predilection of
the century: a passion for mathematics and mathematical
tools usable in the pursuit of science. There lay behind
them the results of what have come to be known as the
Copernican and Cartesian revolutions, results which led
to descriptions in exalted terms of the mathematical sim-
plicities of nature, the geometrical harmonies of the world-
machine. These effusions would not have influenced men
of science so much had it not been that, more immediately,
they were conscious of the work of Newton (1642-1727),
not only logical and mathematical, but empirical and experimental. They were convinced, with Newton, that ex-

periment, and not reason alone, demonstrated the correctness of the mathematical formulae, and that mathematics could, therefore, be taken as the key to the universe. "Newton's name became a symbol which called up the picture of the scientific machine-universe . . . Newton *was* science, and science was the eighteenth-century ideal."[50] Mathematics, thus, seemed to offer the tools, par excellence, of scientific method in a universe which in itself was essentially a mathematical system.

The realm of man and his institutions was not beyond the reach of this wonderful tool. Said Fontenelle, general interpreter of the century and popularizer of Cartesian thought:

> The geometric spirit is not so bound up with geometry that it cannot be disentangled and carried into other fields. A work of morals, of politics, of criticism, perhaps even of eloquence, will be the finer, other things being equal, if it is written by the hand of a geometer.[51]

It is no inexplicable thing, then, that in the preceding century, which was even more full of praise for mathematics than the eighteenth, Spinoza (1632-1677) should have written his *Ethics Demonstrated in the Geometrical Manner*, and that Thomas Hobbes (1588-1679) should have applied the deductive, mechanical and mathematical method to his analyses of man and social institutions. Grotius (1583-1645) and Pufendorf (1632-1694), likewise, were good geometricians in morals and jurisprudence, and so was Richard Cumberland (1631-1718). All of these works were familiar to Francis Hutcheson who, in his discussion of public and private good, improved on their example by using up six pages in algebraic equations. This particular effort of Hutcheson's provoked serious criticism, from Thomas Reid among others, who was, however, strongly inclined to mathematics himself[52]; and it brought ridicule from Sterne, who wrote, "None but an expert mathematician can ever be able to settle his account with S. Peter—and perhaps S. Matthew, who had been an officer in the customs, must be called in to audit them.''[53]

Allied to these concepts of mathematics, really basic to them, were the concepts of mechanism and motion. Hume has Cleanthes say, in the *Dialogues Concerning Natural Religion*, that the author of Nature must be something of an engineer, since Nature is a machine.[54] To Adam Smith, the universe seems to be under the immediate care of a benevolent and all-wise Being, who directs and administers it, superintends it as if it were a great machine in his care, and keeps it under the guidance of his invisible hand.[55] Toward the end of the century, with men like Helvetius and d'Holbach, the notion of mechanism was used in order to allow the idea of God, even as First Cause, to be completely dropped from explanations of phenomena.

Motion, of course, had from the days of the Greeks offered a fascinating set of concepts and analogies. In a succinct paragraph pointedly devoted to Hobbes, Professor George Boas gathers up some of the psychological and social applications frequently made:

> In ethics and politics motion is equivalent to human egoism. Hobbes . . . does to society what Galileo and his predecessors had done to matter, and to the individual what Machiavelli had done to his Prince. He anatomizes humanity into particles, all of which obey what will be the first law of motion: they keep moving in their own course until another particle bumps into them. Phrased ethically, man in a state of nature (that is, the social atom in free space) will obey only his own desires and, as human desires do not follow parallel lines, collision is bound to result. The state is like the solar system in that in it the paths of the individual atoms are kept fairly harmonious.[56]

For their science of man, as well as for physics or astronomy, the writers of the century sought to weld together their observations with what they called general principles.[57] The effort was to systematize, to order, to present in methodical form the diverse phenomena, to sink the particular in the general. These general principles they called laws of nature, and they said the laws were inferences drawn from experience. They were to be dis-

covered by observing the nature of things; in the science
of man they were to be discovered by observing the nature
of man and his achievements.[58] Reflecting on several of
the qualities frequently ascribed to laws of nature—
eternal, universal, immutable, readily discernible—we have
some reason for judging that they were not always discovered by experience but by the "Reason" of the Cartesians which the later eighteenth century wanted to
eschew. It must be admitted, moreover, that there would
not have been so much concern with natural laws had it
not been for Descartes, who had retaken for the modern
world the position that there is order and uniformity in
the universe on which men can count. For many that reliability was definitely linked with the idea that the Ruler
of the Universe, in promulgating these laws, had thus
expressed his will for man.[59] Thus, there was constant
interplay between the concepts of law as a generalized
description of what takes place normally, and law as an
expression of will and command. But so it goes in any age,
the transitional character of which is as marked as is this
of the eighteenth century. Conflicts, conscious and uncon-
scious, are bound to occur, and the thought must come in
"mixed modes."

And so we could go on enumerating the interrelated
concepts and procedures common to the century. We shall
note in later discussions inquiries not only into the nature
of a First Cause but of a final cause as well. Indeed, it
was often the supposed discovery of a final cause which
gave the clue to the First. We shall note the dependence
on analogical thinking. We shall find an absorbing interest
in change—change in species, change in culture, change
in political forms, change in personal fortune. Throughout all the discussions appears an unswerving attention
to the concerns of the race of men on this small planet.
The planet may be small and men may be puny, but their
efforts matter and their posterity, with time to help, may
have more advantages. Over the discussions there lingers
a note of optimism, of which too much has been made by

commentators; for not only have too many of the commentators said too much, but the optimism itself they have exaggerated.[60] Still, there is little doubt that there was considerable "relish" attached to being alive in a century when, for the first time, men really came to believe that they could guarantee a future which would be full of happiness for the human race.

The various social relations and institutions treated by the Scots were regarded as so many fields in which natural laws were to be seen at work and in which moral laws should be made operative. When they talked of domestic relations, they did not introduce matters of political organization; when they talked of contracts and inheritance of property, they did not debate the being and nature of God. In other words, they made their abstractions at will, but always they were bound by two controlling ideas: all relations and customs were to be shown as rooted in the nature of man—this was their empirical starting point; and all were to be shown as depending for their continued existence, ultimately, on ethical judgments. Ethics, thus, was the final arbiter in matters of social organization and behavior; the authors were, after all, moral philosophers, and values had to be emphasized. We may simply note here, in passing, that in our modern formulations each of those abstractions has now become a separate field of specialization and that, for the most part, we try to present our discussions freed from value judgments.

But what brand of ethics did they write? And what place did the ethical discussions hold in their systematic writings? The second question can be answered very briefly.[61] In any methodical arrangement, discussion of the principles of ethics followed the evidence offered as to the constitution of human nature—was thought of, indeed, as a logical consequent of that discussion. The effort was to discover the most satisfactory general rule of conduct possible to human beings whose nature had been just previously delineated. It was the pivotal discussion of the writer's system, and was followed by discourses on the applicability of that general rule to the various human relationships such as the domestic, the political, the religious and the economic. The fact that delineation of a set of norms and values was a prime objective did not prevent the introduction of much historical and descriptive material which was not at all subjective and evaluative, nor of many generalizations made completely independently of ethical criteria.

As for the kind of ethical theory they promulgated, several things need to be mentioned at this point, but left to later discussion for elaboration. Whether or not a particular individual held to the doctrine of the moral sense— the term introduced by Shaftesbury—whether primarily belonging to the Sentimentalist school or to the Utilitarian, all of them, with the exception of Monboddo, were determined to be empirical in their theory of morals as in other aspects of their theory. Their norms of conduct were to be determined not by innate ideas or transcendental reality, but by asking what experience declares to be good. The issue throughout concerns the authority whence ethical judgment and action are derived, and the methods by which that authority makes known its dictates—an issue ever present in ethical considerations, as a matter of fact. Now it is very interesting that, in their opposition to the "selfish" theory of Hobbes and Mandeville, which also was held to have been arrived at empirically, these eighteenth-century philosophers did not let themselves be drawn back into the camp of the Rationalists. As they fought what later came to be called naturalism, it seems to us at this distance that it might have been easy for them to arm themselves with weapons drawn from the writings of such men as Clarke and Wollaston. But as the day was already past for arming oneself confidently out of the armory of the Bible and the church, the day was now passing for trusting to reason as an infallible weapon and as a motive force in human life. What impressed these protestants against rationalism as universally effective in action was the equipment of senses, affections, passions, with which all men are endowed. On this ground they took their stand as empiricists. Looking into their inner promptings and reactions they found themselves a mixture of selfish and unselfish propensities; but since they argued from the evidence for final causes (as was the wont of the century to do and from which they, with the exception of Hume, did not depart), this kind of empiricism, this kind of naturalism gave them nothing about which to be disturbed. Behind the seeming welter of the motives of men there is always the all-wise Governor of the Universe who dictates and sanctions the scheme. Relics of rationalism remained here and there, as in the elaborate use of mathematics made by Hutcheson in his earlier formulations, and in the attribution of the quality of judgment to the moral sense as exemplified in Reid and Stewart, and somewhat in Ferguson. With the exception of Monboddo, Reid and Stewart, it was almost altogether an ethics of feeling on which they took their stand. Emotions were not to them, as to the Stoics, diseases of the mind.

At one point they were in conscious agreement with the Rationalists: both wanted to be free of external authority, especially religious authority, when it came to making moral choices; both were very sure that man has within himself an infallible guide. But reason would not serve the Scots as that guide, for reason, though it aims at intuitive truth, becomes complicated and involved in its operations. To some, also, the doctrine of innate ideas had become utterly anathema. But chiefly reason would not serve because it does not start with experience, and if Locke and Newton were to be followed, as they said over and over, experience must be the base line. We find many men of the later Enlightenment, then, and not only the Scottish group, turning from reason to feelings as being at once simpler to explain, surer as items of experience, and more effective as agents in human activity. The descriptions and analyses then shift to those organs by which feelings

are experienced and interpreted—the senses, the affections, the passions. It is not surprising, then, that we find
in a number of the writers discussions of a moral sense,
even. We find them producing an "enlarged" morality, a
system which does not keep the field of morals bounded
only by rule-deducing reason. We have analogies drawn
between beauty and virtue, and the implication is clear
that virtue, like beauty, is to be sensed rather than reasoned about.

In addition to being an ethics which was intended to be
empirical and secularized, it was for the most part an
ethics of hedonism. This characteristic almost inevitably
accompanies a trend to secularization. When the world is
viewed as man's world, to be appropriated by him, all the
values are very likely to be gathered about human happiness. But happiness is not to be interpreted narrowly as
"low pleasures," nor as transitory satisfactions, nor as
ruthless selfishness. Self-interest is justified, yes, by more
writers than Adam Smith the economist, but always it is
thought of as "enlightened." It is the kind of self-interest
which will take account of the scheme of things and see
that it is a scheme in which the best interests of all will be
achieved and happiness will result by each man's looking
out for himself.

The self-interest must be "enlightened." On that point
are agreed all the writers of the period, as they indig-
nantly attack Hobbes and Mandeville. That precious pair
had committed an outrage on human nature by painting
it so extremely selfish, whereas man is really a decently
disposed creature, even when he follows his own interests.
The essential thing is that a man should not be ruthless
in pursuit of his own ends, and that he should understand
the motives of others and the probable outcome of all their
activities. Nature seems to have formed man so that he
must pay attention to his own interests; and, if nature
thus formed him, is not that adequate assurance that the
scheme is, after all, a right one, designed for the good of
the whole, as well as of the individual? Men appear to be

fairly equally endowed with these promptings to go about their own concerns; why not believe, therefore, that the whole equipment is an effective mechanism devised by the Ruler of the Universe to keep in motion the activities of men? Thus, in their enlightened optimism, they argued.

II

ADAM FERGUSON'S SYSTEM OF MORAL PHILOSOPHY: A TYPICAL SCHEME

BEFORE turning to a discussion of the major topics presented by the Scottish philosophers in their objectives of establishing an empirical science of man and an ethic which could be empirically grounded on that science, it may be well to follow through the systematic thought of one of the spokesmen of the group. If he is really representative, we shall then have a more adequate picture of the way in which a system holds together—what its starting point is, what this assumption lends, what that inference is drawn from and to what end the whole argument is directed. When those things are laid bare we shall have a far more reliable clue to the thought of a period or group than if we began with isolated topics and made no effort to see them in their relations to a general frame of reference or conceptual scheme.

We shall in this chapter use Adam Ferguson (1723-1816) as representative of the Scottish group. His language is not so well known as is that of David Hume and Adam Smith in some of their often quoted passages, but the scope of his discussions and theirs is almost identical, and he is very clear and less verbose. He was a central figure in the Scottish group of "enlightened," a leader in the club life of Edinburgh, successor to his friend David Hume as head of the Advocates' Library, and from 1764 until 1785 professor of pneumatics and moral philosophy in the University of Edinburgh. On one of his two brief leaves of absence, in 1778, he was a member of the unsuccessful Conciliation Commission which came to America in the hope of negotiating an early peace with the colonies. Not only did he occupy a place of recognition and prestige in Scottish university life and public affairs, but he was widely read and followed abroad. His works almost on their first appearance were demanded in America and, too, were translated into French, German and Russian. Recently quite a bit of attention has been given to his importance for the beginnings of sociology.[1] Our objective at this point is not to uphold that judgment, nor to analyze and criticize his position, but simply to gain an understanding of the framework of his thought. Thereby we shall have a picture of the usual procedures in a system of moral philosophy of the period.

Ferguson was not one of those lecturers who wrote out in full what he had to say. Instead, he talked from notes, chiefly topic headings, and filled them in as the occasion and his mood of the day warranted. Incidentally it may be remarked that he acquired the reputation of lecturing with energy and fire, and of provoking real interest in his pupils. In 1766, two years after he assumed the professorship of pneumatics and moral philosophy at the University of Edinburgh, he wrote for the use of his classes a handbook called *Analysis of Pneumatics and Moral Philosophy*. This was refurbished and published in 1769 as *Institutes of Moral Philosophy*. It was really a syllabus, stripped of elaboration and designed to embrace what a teacher would regard as the essentials of his subject matter and method. When Ferguson retired after twenty years of teaching, he spent some of his leisure time in writing the *Principles of Moral and Political Science*. This work set forth no new system; extensive elaboration, such as he doubtless supplied in his lectures, and a slight rearrangement of a few topics are the only things which distinguish it from the *Institutes*. It is, as the subtitle indicates, "chiefly A Retrospect of Lectures delivered in the College of Edinburgh." We shall in the following discussion use the outline and phraseology of the *Institutes*, referring at the same time to parallel passages in the *Principles*.[2]

His first discussion in the *Institutes* is designed to place moral philosophy on an empirical basis in the field of knowledge. To be a science and not merely a description or narration of discrete facts, a body of knowledge must deal with general rules, and not with particular facts.

General rules, and their applications, to regulate or to explain particulars, constitute science. Any general rule, expressing what is fact, or what is right, is termed a law of nature.

Science, thus, by a substitution of terms, is a study of the laws of nature. These laws of nature are either physical or moral. "A physical law is any general expression of a natural operation, as exemplified in a number of particular cases." Such operations appear to involve an operating power or cause. Hence we may expect to find science dealing with relations of cause and effect. As for a moral law, it "is any general expression of what is good," and whereas a physical law "exists so far only as it is a fact," a moral law "exists in being obligatory." Together, the two kinds of law, on the basis of their generality and of their having causes and effects in human activity, make moral philosophy a parallel to physical science in the field of knowledge.[3]

In Ferguson's judgment, Sir Isaac Newton perfectly exemplified the true scientist, since he accounted for the planetary revolutions by showing that they are comprehended in the laws of motion and gravitation; Descartes, on the other hand, failed to explain anything when he resorted to the supposition of a vortex, which is only a metaphor and an hypothesis.[4]

But not all facts can be explained by rules previously known or by facts better known than themselves. Such inexplicable and unresolvable facts are ultimate, and on them finally rest all theories and principles. Such a basis of ultimate fact is provided for moral philosophy in human nature itself. In Ferguson's words,

Before we can ascertain the rules of morality for mankind, the history[5] of man's nature, his dispositions, his specific enjoyments and sufferings, his condition and future prospects, should be known.

The term which Ferguson uses for this foundation of moral philosophy is "pneumatics," and clearly it represents an eighteenth century equivalent of "psychology."

In his earlier *Analysis of Pneumatics and Moral Philosophy* the meaning is made quite clear. After saying that human nature is both animal and intellectual he goes on:

> The animal nature of man is the subject of anatomy and physiology. The intellectual nature is the proper subject of pneumatics: but being joined, many of their functions are mixed, and pertain equally to pneumatics and physiology.[6]

Man is not alone in the possession of mind or spirit, however unique he may appear when compared with the other animals on this point. It is a character which he shares with God. We are prepared, then, to find moral philosophy dealing somewhat with God as well as with man, particularly with God's purposes for the world of man.[7]

What we glean from Ferguson's approach thus far is simply his effort to orient himself and his readers for their further investigation together. He wants to make perfectly clear that he is going to be scientific, by which he meant that he is to be concerned with systems of universal laws rather than with particular, unrelated facts. Discrete facts can be scientifically envisaged only as they are explainable by something more comprehensive, by a principle so wide in its application that it is itself an ultimate, though not a particular, fact. For Ferguson this basic explanation for the achievement and activities of mankind is to be found in the nature of man; and since man's nature, dominated by mind and spirit, is of like character with God's, it will be proper in giving account of man to give account also of God's outstanding purposes and dispensations for man. Practically every philosopher of Ferguson's period thus set himself to his task by basing his work upon what he thought of as ultimate fact, that is, the constitution of man. No scholar of the eighteenth century would have thought of questioning the scientific adequacy of such a foundation. Their science was thus, in Hume's phrase, very really the science of man.

Following this introduction, Ferguson's syllabus opens up as follows: Part I, The Natural History of Man; Part

II, Theory of Mind; Part III, Of the Knowledge of God. In other words, these three sections deal with the nature of man, considered first as the species Homo, and second as an individual within the species; while the predominant characteristic stressed is mind, that feature which man shares with God.

Treatment of Man, the species, requires information on the following considerations: the form and aspect of man; his residence and manner of subsistence; the varieties of the human race; the period of human life; the disposition of man to society[8]; the principles of population growth[9]; man's freedom of choice and pursuit; arts and commercial arrangements developed by man; the phenomena of disparity among men and the results in ranks and social divisions[10]; political institutions; and language and literature. These items are those which Ferguson thinks any orderly description of the species Man would need to take into account.[11] They serve to identify man as Man, among the various other kinds of animals. They make up, in the phrase of the century, the natural history of man.

Ferguson passes next to a consideration of the characteristics of any man as an individual within the species. First he deals with man's powers of understanding: consciousness, sense and perception, observation, memory, imagination, abstraction, reasoning and foresight—all, intellectual powers. But if discussion of man's abilities stopped here, we should not be taking into account those activating traits so pronounced in him, those characteristics which are related to man's will, rather than to his intellectual understanding.[12] Ferguson indicates, then, the discussion required on the topics of propensities, both animal and rational—and it is worth noting that in the *Principles* he uses the word "instincts" instead of "propensities"; the four classes of sentiments; desire and aversion; and volition.

These twelve traits of man, effective within his nature as an understanding and an active being, represent a set of facts which any individual "recollecting what passes in his own mind," knows to be true of himself and his capabilities. They are the basic *facts* of man's mental-spiritual character. These now are to be further elaborated as pneumatics or the theory of mind, that is, as the knowledge of physical laws which have been collected from fact and which are applicable to explain appearances.[13]

First, however, the concept of law must be clarified. Most natural philosophers, says Ferguson, employ the term to mean the uniformity of a fact in nature. This usage will hold for the intellectual system, since in the operations of the mind, as well as in the material world, there are uniformities. Therefore, as freely as if he were writing of biology, he will use the term "physical laws" to represent certain uniformities of man's intellectual-spiritual nature. In doing this he hopes to avoid the ambiguities of those who write as if there were nothing in the operations of mind analogous to the observable regularities of nature. The term "moral law" has, however, a slightly different meaning: it does not refer to the universality of certain kinds of conduct; the law to which it has reference is law "which we desire to have uniformly observed," it is law "in consequence of its rectitude, or of the authority from which it proceeds," and "not in consequence of its being the fact." That there are deviations from it need not disturb us, since deviations occur even in the vegetable and animal kingdoms where physical, and not moral, law prevails: "there are deformities, distortions, and diseases; as there are in the intellectual kingdom follies, absurdities, and crimes." But,

> To avoid, as much as possible, these ambiguities, laws of the first sort, whether relating to mind or matter, have been termed *physical laws*; and laws of the second sort, *moral laws*.[14]

Referring now to the previous enumeration of traits in man's understanding, Ferguson draws from that list of *facts* three general rules, or physical *laws*: (1) the law of self-consciousness; (2) the law of perception of things not-self; (3) the law of comprehension. Referring next to the traits related to man's will, he draws likewise three laws: (1) the law of self-preservation; (2) the law of society; (3) the law of estimation, or progression.[15]

The law of society and the law of progress, we may note in passing, become the cornerstones of Ferguson's system. The beginning and the end of the whole matter seem to be as follows[16]:

Man is by nature a member of society; his safety, and his enjoyment, require that he should be preserved what he is by nature; his perfection consists in the excellency or measure of his natural ability and dispositions or, in other words, it consists in his being an excellent part of the system to which he belongs. So that the effect of mankind should be the same, whether the individual means to preserve himself, or to preserve his community; with either intention he must cherish the love of mankind, as the most valuable part of his character.

And, as to progress and man's progressive nature:

Perfection is nowhere to be found short of the infinite mind, but progression is the gift of God to all his intelligent creatures, and is within the competence of the lowest of mankind.

But this description does not exhaust the nature of man. There is the traditional question of the soul and its future prospects. After discussing the possibility of immortality from the angle of the indivisibility and activity of mind, and judging, therefore, that there must be continuation of life since annihilation is unknown in nature, Ferguson turns to another argument for surety. Wherever our knowledge extends, he says, nature speaks to us of final causes; they are the language in which the existence of God is revealed to man, and the attributes of God shown to be goodness and justice, as well as unity, power and wisdom. If we consider only the requirements of justice, we should be convinced that it demands of God that He lend another scene in which to right the wrongs incident to this.

The important consideration here for students of methodology is not that Ferguson satisfies himself as to the soul's immortality, but that he introduces into the discussion of social phenomena the concept of final causes and the purposes of God for man's life on this planet.[17]

This question now arises: on such a basis as he has laid in his discussion of the object and method of science, the nature of man and the fitness of man to be the object of scientific study, what can be said of the moral laws and their operation? The answer runs somewhat as follows:

Moral philosophy deals with moral laws, that is, with expressions of what ought to be, of what is not yet universally a fact of a kind a physical law can express. Nevertheless, it has its basis, as we have seen, in physical fact, in the constitution of man which impels him not only to preserve himself, but to be a benevolently minded member of society, and to seek always to improve himself and the common life. On that basis the moral law consciously builds the dictum that the most desirable thing for man is that he should cultivate the love of his fellows, and act always for their happiness and betterment. This injunction may find itself written in the hearts of men, in which case it is original or natural; but it may have an adventitious or conventional origin, finding itself expressed from time to time in actual law codes or established customs, which call attention to this high demand and seek to hasten its general observance. Ferguson goes on to say that to the extent to which a people possess benevolent purposes and perform benevolent actions, they will not only be virtuous but happy. They cannot achieve perfection: "men conceive perfection, but are capable only of improvement." However, the fact that they can even conceive perfection affords them a light to direct their progress, and it is the business of moral philosophy to determine the kinds of perfection toward which men should work.[18]

Discussion of law in relation to human beings is never long carried on without introduction of the term "sanction," whether pleasant or harsh, that inducement which leads to observance of the law. For Ferguson the general sanction of the moral law is the happiness which results from observance, and the misery which results from neglect of it. But in the case of overt acts, this general sanction is modified by the introduction of forcible means, for maintenance of which we have a system of compulsory law; or it is modified by considerations of propriety, in which case we say that duty, not force, nor happiness alone, is the sanction. The actions of individuals, then, may be treated in at least two ways: if they are affected by compulsory law, they become the subject of *jurisprudence*; if they are simply the concerns of duty, they become the subject of *casuistry*.[19] When, however, men are organized in communities, those actions of theirs which affect the condition and the form of the community become the subject matter of *politics*. An exception is made to the latter statement in the case of communities set as wholes in relation to one another, when, since there is no supercommunity, they become liable to the dictates of casuistry and jurisprudence as if they were individuals. The various social relations in which men find themselves are to be regarded, then, as so many fields for the application of the moral law, which may operate without sanctions of force or with the compulsions afforded by law and politics.

Jurisprudence treats of two allied subjects: the rights of men and the defences permitted them for the maintenance of those rights. It is thus prohibitory in its nature, expressing the regulative side of the law of morality which seeks to establish the greatest good for mankind. But though a person may on every occasion defend his right, there may at times be a more excellent way. He may, for example, be "more concerned to maintain and to exercise the affections of a benevolent mind" than to preserve his rights untouched. He may on such occasions yield to considerations of conscience and duty rather than defend his equal rights to the limit. His actions then fall within the field of casuistry. Whereas jurisprudence is prohibitory, casuistry is positive in its application of the moral law, requiring every possible act of good will. No compulsion enters here other than the kind which is afforded by religion, by public repute, and by conscience.[20] Nor must we be misled into thinking that morality is a matter of external actions. Virtue is really a quality of the mind. Casuistry, by laying down rules or by setting external observances, cannot make a virtuous heart, but it can by its sanctions and by its judgments of merit and demerit, procure to society more useful actions than might otherwise be the case.[21]

The realm of politics offers, for Ferguson, the third field for the application of moral law. In the first general view of the situation he seems to identify political institutions with all forms of common co-operative enterprises: "It appears from the history of mankind," he says,

that men have always acted in troops and companies; that they have apprehended a good of the community, as well as of the individual; that while they practice arts, each for his own preservation, they institute political forms and unite their forces for common safety.

It may be proved, that most of the opinions, habits, and pursuits of men, result from the state of their society [that is, from the state of their being in society]; that men are happy in proportion as they love mankind; that their rights and their duties are relative to each other; and, therefore, that their most important concerns are to be found in their mutual relations, and in the state of their communities [that is, the state of their being in communities].[22]

We should note here that Ferguson combats as vigorously as Hume had done earlier in his *Essays* the popular theory of the origin of society and government in a contract. Man was born in and for society, he insists; as for political institutions, they often originated in force, but when people for long periods availed themselves of the benefits thereof and complied with the general requirements, they consented to the government:

Here is a compact ratified by the least ambiguous of all signs, the whole practice, or continued observance of an ordinary life. The conditions here are ratified, in every age, and by every individual for himself; not merely stipulated, in any remote age, and for a posterity over which the contracting part had not any control.[23]

He quickly proceeds, however, to the discussion of the concerns of the state, especially its public economy—such resources as the number and character of the people, their wealth, and the procuring of revenue for the use of the state—and its political law.[24]

But the main discussion centers not upon the institutions themselves but upon the benefits which they bring, upon what is desirable for men under the organization of the state. This is the political realm of the moral law. Ferguson chooses to continue his treatment by using the term "political laws of nature." Among such laws are these:

1. That political institutions are beneficial, in proportion as they contribute to the safety and happiness of the people.

2. That political institutions procure the safety of the people in proportion as they are adapted to the circumstances and character of the people.

3. That the distribution of office is beneficial, in proportion as it is adapted to the constitution.

4. That political establishments are the most important articles in the external conditions of men.[25]

These pronouncements have the ring of Montesquieu's *L'esprit des lois*, as, indeed, have many statements of Ferguson's[26]; here appear especially the ideas of the interrelations and relativity of social phenomena.

This, in some detail, is the framework of the analytical portion of Ferguson's system, as represented in the *Institutes* and in the *Principles of Moral and Political Science*. Briefly put, we find that the system follows this pattern: first, a general methodological discussion pointing out the advantages of empirical procedure; second, a description of man's nature, which is portrayed as being so open to discovery by observation of others and introspection of self that man becomes an excellent object for scientific

study; third, a positing of a general comprehensive moral
law by which man should order his life—in Ferguson's
presentation, the dictum that the greatest good competent to man's nature is the love of mankind; fourth, an
outline of the several types of relations and situations in
which men find themselves confronted with alternatives of
conduct, and in which they should seek to apply either
the juridical, casuistical, or the political version of the
general moral law.[27]

The work of Ferguson's which is better known and to
which laudatory comment is frequently given is his *Essay
on the History of Civil Society,* which before its publication was called by its author *A Treatise on Refinement.* It
was consciously done in the manner of Montesquieu, whom
Ferguson admired extravagantly; and Drummond, the
Archbishop of York, judged that Ferguson had outdone
his master.[28]

We may well ask at the outset what meaning the word
"history" has for Ferguson. The Greeks, the Romans, the
Swedes, the early English and the North Americans are
mentioned often enough to lead us to a hasty judgment
that this is orthodox political history, though in abbreviated form. But the achievements discussed are other
than political: they include the arts and literature, property and law, manners and learning—an array which
would lead us to judge this a good forerunner of the twentieth century's social and cultural history. Moreover,
dates and actual time-sequences seem to be of little importance; instead, there is talk of the childhood of the
race, of its nursery days as contrasted with its manhood—
a generalized, analogical scheme. But in considerable sections of the book to which the word "history" is applied,
the discussion is of the type we noted in the *Institutes*—
"history" seems to mean simply a collection of facts in
description or narration, an orderly discussion of the phenomena under review. Pervading the whole, however, is
the definite feeling that time has seen the progress of civil

societies from an original "rudeness" to varying degrees of "polish," and that this progress was an essentially natural and predictable process, given the nature and capacity of man.

Ferguson apparently intended to use the terms "civilization" and "civil society," as equivalent expressions. We find the word "civilization" used to denote the maturity-achievement of the species whose infancy was characterized by rudeness. We hear that the aim of civil society is the securing of happiness for individuals. Whereas a rude people recognizes no bonds of connection other than those of kinship and neighborhood (the "instinctive" bonds) and its form of subordination is voluntary, under civil society there are introduced the bonds of magistrate-subject, and citizen-citizen, relationships not instinctive but inaugurated by convention and determined by law. Thus, civil society is not improperly termed a state of convention. This convention was necessitated because of the previous beginning of the holding of property which, for its maintenance, requires an ordered and secure society. Such a period of order and stability and security we call civilization. It has several valuable by-products: it offers a variety of pursuits, in contrast to the uniformity and lack of differentiation in rude societies; it calls out men's best energies and affections; it employs force only for the obtaining of justice and for the preservation of national rights; its polish extends not only to matters of citizenship but to arts, literature, commerce; finally, it is the guarantee of true liberty.[29]

A glance at the table of contents reveals the same range of interests already noted in his other works. Part I deals with the "General Characteristics of Human Nature"; Part II with the "History of Rude Nations"; Part III with the "History of Policy and the Arts" ("policy" signifying essentially political government rather than group control by kinship and custom); Part IV with "Consequences That Result from the Advancement of Civil and Commercial Arts"; Part V with the "Decline of Nations";

Part VI with "Corruption and Political Slavery," with emphasis on misused luxury as a contributing cause—a favorite theme of the century.[30] No new general considerations appear here, though we shall see that Ferguson does occasionally make his own interpretations, which depart from some, and yet are in line with other, intellectual positions that were favored by his contemporaries. Detailed discussion of these interests today would find itself parceled out among the fields of psychology, ethics, politics, economics, anthropology, geography, history, aesthetics. Not even sociologists, who are sometimes thought to be possessed of a temerity equal to Ferguson's, would attempt to deal with such a table of contents, and within the covers of one volume.

We shall quote several statements[31] which give us his cast of thought and the general tenor of his discussion:

Natural productions are generally formed by degrees. Vegetables grow from a tender shoot, and animals from an infant state. The latter being destined to act, extend their operations as their powers increase: they exhibit a progress in what they perform, as well as in the faculties they acquire. This progress in the case of man is continued to a greater extent than in that of any other animal. Not only the individual advances from infancy to manhood, but the species itself from rudeness to civilization.

Man, then, as an animal, exhibits the animal capacity of growth; but this growth, in man, is to be seen in his cultural achievement, as well as in his individual life-cycle.

Men continue their works in progression through many ages together: they build on foundations laid by their ancestors; and in a succession of years, tend to a perfection in the application of their faculties, to which the aid of long experience is required, and to which many generations must have combined their endeavours.

The fact that man's habit of life is now so different from what it must have been in primordial time has led to many wrong speculations as to

the supposed departure of mankind from the state of their nature. . . . The poet, the historian, and the moralist, frequently allude to this ancient time; and under the emblems of gold, or of iron, represent a condition, and a manner of life, from which mankind have either degenerated, or on which they have greatly improved. On either supposition, the first state of our nature must have borne no resemblance to what men have exhibited in any subsequent period. . . .

But Ferguson will have none of such speculation as to an original state of nature, though we shall see that he does firmly believe in progress. He will not, however, be beguiled into the type of "subtility" which looks for a primordial man vastly different from man as he now is. The best traditions of natural history require that it proceed in every case upon observation of and experiment with what is usual, common, normal; in the case of man we want to know the ordinary, everyday situation in which he finds himself, and not the unusual or forced situation. For that reason, a wild man alone in the woods is decidedly an uncommon man in an uncommon situation, and therefore not to be taken as typical of the species; on the other hand, "both the earliest and the latest accounts collected from every quarter of the earth, represent mankind as assembled in troops and companies." This fact of society, then, should be taken as the foundation of all our reasoning relative to man; it is senseless to look for a time when man was without social bonds. Society is the mode of existence which nature has given him:

With him the society appears to be as old as the individual, and the use of the tongue as universal as that of the hand or foot. If there was a time in which he had his acquaintance with his own species to make, and his faculties to acquire, it is a time of which we have no record, and in relations to which our opinions can serve no purpose, and are supported by no evidence.

Our unit of investigation, then, becomes not single men but groups of men, societies.

Mankind are to be taken in groupes [sic], as they have always subsisted. The history of the individual is but a detail of the sentiments and the thoughts he has entertained in the view of his species: and every experiment relative to this subject should be made with entire societies and not with single men.

Men as individuals are born now with the same physical and mental characteristics as in the beginning of man's life on the planet. These traits belong to man as the wing belongs to the eagle and the paw to the lion, always the same. But each individual man has still to grow up from infancy to maturity. In that growth, however, he does not change his essential nature; he simply lives it out to its full capacity. Now the life of man in societies is analogous to the life-span of the individual; man in his original condition of society is comparable to a baby, and the progression in the forms of society that man has gone through has no more made him a different creature than does adolescence change a child into a creature of different species. There has in both cases simply been growth and progress of a natural kind.

On this basis we are not warranted in thinking that any invention or contrivance which appears relatively late in the history of man is an artificial, or, to use a word favored by Ferguson, an "adventitious" product. Instead, we should regard it, with all other activities of man, as natural, a product of his original nature just now developed to function in this particular way; "for all the actions of men are equally the result of their nature." But one of the most outstanding of man's traits is this ability to invent and contrive, particularly with a view to modifying and improving his present situation. The state of nature, therefore, is not to be sought in some far-off time or place, but here and now, anywhere where human beings are functioning normally.

If we are asked therefore, where the state of nature is to be found? We may answer, It is here; and it matters not whether we are understood to speak in the island of Great Britain, at the Cape of Good Hope, or the Straits of Magellan. While this active being is in the train of employing his talents, and of operating on the subjects around him, all situations are equally natural. . . . If the palace be unnatural, the cottage is so no less; and the highest refinements of political and moral apprehension, are not more artificial in their kind, than the first operations of sentiment and reason.

Man, then, has never "quitted the state of his nature"; he "only follows the disposition, and employs the powers that nature has given"; and

The latest efforts of human invention are but a continuation of certain devices which were practiced in the earliest ages of the world, and in the rudest state of mankind. What the savage projects, or observes, in the forest, are the steps which led nations, more advanced, from the architecture of the cottage to that of the palace, and conducted the human mind from the perceptions of sense, to the general conclusions of science.

Yet another idea is introduced in definition of the phrase "state of nature." If we grant that in one sense all actions of man are the result of his nature, this opens the way to accepting too easily mistakes and misapplications of his industry. Man needs a standard, therefore, "by which to judge of his own proceedings, and arrive at the best state of his nature. . . ." And he will find, asserts Ferguson, that "the proper state of his nature, taken in this sense, is not a condition from which mankind are forever removed, but one to which they may now attain; not prior to the exercise of their faculties, but procured by their just application." The subject for inquiry becomes, then, not a question as to what is natural or unnatural, but "What is just, or unjust? What is happy or wretched, in the manners of men? What in their various situations, is favourable or adverse to their amiable qualities?" To such questions we may hope to find answers, and, Ferguson is sure, we shall be conducting an inquiry of more importance for our future achievements than if we contented ourselves with delineating the supposed condition from which we sprang.

This decision, obviously, is in line with the point of view of the *Institutes*: we should find the most complete basis of fact concerning man, and on that build our ideas as to what man can and ought to do. In this way we shall be proceeding scientifically, and at the same time with some hope of achieving a social order more in keeping with man's ultimate possibilities. There are proper lessons

to be taken from history, and a right reading of the past
is in order.

Man's life on this planet has seen many changes: "the
generations that *were* and *are*, hasten to make way for
those which are to come. . . . While the things that were
are passing away, things that were not are brought into
being." All nations "have been derived from a feeble original, and still preserve in their story the indications of a
slow and gradual progress"[32] by which they have come to
the civilized state. He cites the people of sacred history,
the early Greeks and Romans, the Gauls and the Germans,
as evidence of what man was like and what he did in the
youth of the world. But, interestingly enough, when examples of uncivilized peoples are made much of, those chosen
in almost every instance refer to the North American Indians. His justification is a statement perfectly acceptable
to those who still, unfortunately, cling to the comparative
method as elaborated by Comte:

Thucydides, notwithstanding the prejudice of his country
against the name of *Barbarian*, understood that it was in the
customs of barbarous nations he was to study the more ancient
manners in Greece. . . .

It is in their [the Indians'] present condition that we are to
behold, as in a mirror, the features of our own progenitors, and
from thence we are to draw our conclusions with respect to the
influence of situations, in which we have reason to believe that
our fathers were placed.

What should distinguish a German or a Briton, in the habits
of his mind or his body, in his manners or apprehensions, from
an American, who, like him, with his bow and his dart, is left to
traverse the forest; and in a like severe or variable climate, is
obliged to subsist by the chase?

If, in advanced years, we would form a just notion of our
progress from the cradle, we must have recourse to the nursery;
and from the example of those who are still in the period of life
we mean to describe, take our representation of past manners,
that cannot, in any other way, be recalled.[33]

Among the peoples of the world who have been or are
still without the advantages of political organization, or
who, to use his phrase, are not "in civil society," there are

to be distinguished two degrees of rudeness. There are both savages and barbarians, and the history of man, in formula, has thus been a progress from savagery, through barbarism to civilization. We cannot, in this brief résumé, take much notice of Ferguson's account of the first two conditions, except to comment on his wide reading of travels and voyages, the usual reliance on classical authors and the freshness of his presentation. It was the era of civil society on which he wished to focus his discussion and on which he lavished his praises.

Civil society represents, essentially, a concerted plan based on political force. But in speaking of a concerted plan, Ferguson is very emphatic that he has no reference to any specific concerted act, such as was at the heart of the several theories by Hobbes, Locke, Rousseau and others regarding the supposed contract which ushered in political rule. Human affairs have simply continued their progress:

> What was in one generation a propensity to herd with the species, becomes in the ages which follow, a principle of natural union. What was originally an alliance for common defence, becomes a concerted plan of political force; the care of subsistence becomes an anxiety for accumulating wealth, and the foundation of commercial arts. . . . He who first said "I will appropriate this field; I will leave it to my heirs"; did not perceive, that he was laying the foundation of civil laws and political establishments. He who first ranged himself under a leader, did not perceive, that he was setting the example of a permanent subordination, under the pretence of which, the rapacious were to seize his possessions, and the arrogant to lay claim to his service.

And driving his meaning home more firmly, he adds:

> No constitution is formed by concert, no government is copied from a plan. . . . The seeds of every form [of government] are lodged in human nature; they spring up and ripen with the season.[34]

As the establishing of political government is not deliberate, neither are some of its results. Liberty, for example, and the public welfare are often by-products rather than avowed objectives; casual relationships may result in conditions which appear to have been planned. The tone and character of a nation are determined quite as much by the casual subordination connected with the unequal distribution of property and influence as they are by the particular kind of subordination required by the constitution itself. Once established, however, certain ideals and achievements may be deliberately maintained, sometimes even by the energy and idealism of one man or one party in the state. One must not expect much rationality and conscious planning in the affairs of this creature, man:

Mankind, in following the present sense of their minds, in striving to remove inconveniences, or to gain apparent and contiguous advantages, arrive at ends which even their imagination could not anticipate; and pass on, like other animals, in the track of their nature, without perceiving its end. . . . Every step and every movement of the multitude, even in what are termed enlightened ages, are made with equal blindness to the future; and nations stumble upon establishments, which are indeed the result of human action, but not the execution of any human design.[35]

Whatever the circumstances under which a nation comes into being, and however casual some of its activities, every government must be consciously concerned with three objectives: it must defend its population, it must distribute justice, it must preserve and guarantee the internal prosperity of the state. To the discussion of these objectives the rest of the book is devoted, with much attention given to the by-products of political organization. He considers, for example, the division of labor with its concomitant conditions of subordination and dominance in certain groups of the population, the increase of wealth, the growth of learning, the improvement of the arts and literature.

In connection with his discussion of national defense Ferguson takes another of those positions which was original with him and set him off from the conventional position of his century. While admitting the difficulty of deciphering whether a particular war is one of defense or conquest, and lamenting that war should ever be made a subject of traffic, with human blood bought and sold for bills of exchange, he realizes that war remains, in civil societies as well as in rude ones, one of the major activities; indeed, it finds itself perfected in civil societies. But—and this is where he makes his own standing-ground—it is vain to hope for peace. Conflict is in the nature of men and their affairs. "Mankind . . . appear to have in their minds the seeds of animosity, and to embrace the occasions of mutual opposition, with alacrity and pleasure. In the most pacific situation, there are few who have not their enemies, as well as their friends." Yet these manifestations are "consistent with the most amiable qualities of our nature, and often furnish a scene for the exercise of our greatest abilities." And civil society itself would probably not have come into being but for rivalries of peoples and the consequent resort to war.[36] Many examples are offered of national conflicts, some of which were waged for defense, some for conquest; but when all has been explained, it remains true that "rivalship of separate communities, and the agitations of a free people, are the principles of political life, and the school of men"; mankind is possessed of a restless spirit and conflict in its extreme form, war, furnishes it with one of its principal occupations.[37]

With all of the benefits brought by political organization, what is the hope for the permanence of states? Ferguson's answer runs somewhat as follows: Human affairs are characterized by vicissitudes of fortune. Great nations before now have fallen when they were unwilling to confess their defects and work effectively to correct them. Moreover, some states have been conquered by enemies from abroad before they gave any signs of interior decay. History is full of such instances and apparently no moral reasons can be assigned: they appear to be simply meaningless reverses of fortune. Other states have seemed to manifest "a kind of spontaneous return to obscurity and weakness." All such cases lead to "a general apprehension, that the progress of societies to what we call national greatness, is not more natural than their return to weakness and obscurity is necessary and unavoidable. The images of youth, and of old age, are applied to nations. . . ." But this sort of explanation is not adequate, though the image is familiar and, he thinks, apposite. We must look for other causes of cessation of national eminence. In general, there are two such causes: first, the general fickleness of mankind, which lets them grow weary of even successful achievement; second, some change of situation which removes or alters the objectives which had once called out the spirit of the citizens but which now, instead, crushes and debases it. In the commercial arts, for example, the need to perfect the mechanisms, of which every one is conscious, may in time turn into absorption in concern for the profits for individuals; a sense of common interest is, therefore, lost, and the condition of the nation becomes precarious.[38]

It is not so simple a reckoning as a calculation in merchandising, nor is it all a matter of administrative arrangement. A nation's strength, first and last, rests in its men, and when citizens become corrupted in any way by lawlessness, luxury or laziness, there is danger ahead.[39] The lesson is clear, then, for individuals who make up a state: as citizens they must be discriminating as to the moral values involved in political institutions, alert to detect any falling away of idealism and integrity in themselves and their fellow citizens, and willing to bear the actual burdens of government.

Thus Ferguson ends his natural history of civil society, avowedly in the manner of Montesquieu, who was to his mind a "profound politician and amiable moralist."[40] In it he has endeavored to show that "all the actions of men are equally the result of their nature"; but, quite as much, he has considered such questions as: "What is just, or unjust? What is happy or wretched in the affairs of men? What in their various situations, is favorable or adverse to their amiable qualities?" His conviction is that "it is of far more importance to know the condition to which we ourselves should aspire, than that which our ancestors may be supposed to have left."[41]

It can with truth be said that the set of ideas dealt with by Ferguson was representative of his Scottish contemporaries. They were all, with the exception of Monboddo, concerned to make clear their methods of investigation which they called Newtonian, Baconian, experimental, observational; they were all concerned with the nature of man, with his social institutions and his total culture; they were all concerned with human history, though to us some of their efforts in that field seem strangely unhistorical; and while, first and last, they were all concerned to discover what is right, what is better in the life of man with his fellows, the basis for that rightness and that betterment was sought in what is fact.

III

MAN'S PLACE IN NATURE

ONE set of problems which agitated the century so devoted to human interests concerned the accurate conception of man. Was he only a tiny unnoticed speck in the
great universe, as the Copernican theory implied? Was he
a mechanism, as Hobbes had made out, a bit of matter
irritated by motions, as La Mettrie, too, insisted? Was
he a composite result of his sensations, and could you make
a man, in Condillac's bold way, by adding now one and
now another set of capacities?

Let us see the general answers with which the Scottish
philosophers met these questions. Man, for them, was
never reduced to nothingness, in however large terms they
comprehended the universe, because one of their main
tasks was to urge man to act significantly and worthily.
For the same reason they could not make him out a mere
mechanism, for they thought they saw in him evidences of
his participation in the character of the contriver of the
whole machine. With more conviction, they tried to see
him as a peak in the scale of nature, much lower than God
and the angels, of course, but standing higher than the
other animals by reason of his intelligence and his speech—
though here Monboddo again left the company of the
rest of the school, holding that speech was not a necessary
trait of man's. They followed closely the publications of
Linnaeus and Buffon and Maupertuis, and they read ea-
gerly the accounts of travelers who had wandered among
strange peoples. They were struck with the vast differences in culture, as well as with accounts of men of different physical features, but, on the basis of their major
presupposition that human nature is fundamentally the
same, they solved the problem of differences in achievement by judging the different peoples to be at different
stages of maturity. Here again Monboddo provided as a

countertheory the diffusion of all culture from Egypt, instead of the belief that each group must usually go through the same stages in a sort of developmental pattern. Often there was a hint that peculiar circumstances of history might have been responsible for certain physical traits, as well as for certain customs and institutions, but to these writers the peculiarities of history did not belong in a scientific account, so their effort was to find general, universal principles of explanation.

Inevitably, with so much talk of law and system as characterized the century, the question arose concerning the freedom of man. Were the Scots, with their revised and more moderate theology, escaping from the determinism of Calvinism only to fall into a mechanistic determinism with the same degree of lack of freedom? Across the channel La Mettrie, d'Holbach, Morelly and, to some extent, Condillac were expressing in extreme terms their belief in man the machine, a cog in the great mechanistic system of the universe. Lord Kames posed the question in this form: can man possibly be a free agent, any more than can a planet circling in its orbit? And if he is not free, what becomes of his vaunted morality, which presupposes liberty of choice? To these questions Kames devotes many pages. His general answer is that in so far as man is governed by the law of nature, which is the law of his own nature, his actions are as strictly caused as any motions on the part of planets. But one of the necessary items in our equipment is our *feeling* that we are free to decide and to initiate. And indeed we *are* free, only whatever motives incline us to certain choices are enchained with other choices and motives of the past and have become a part of our nature; hence we are not really free at each moment of decision.[1]

Thomas Reid and Adam Smith give their answers in slightly different terms. Man, Reid says, is a being whose powers are worthy of the Author of them; all materialistic, egoistic interpretations which depreciate man are, then, to be deplored. We may properly think of the nat-

ural world as a grand machine, held in a system of necessity; but man has been given a dominion of his own, a
realm of moral freedom.² Smith describes the universe as
a great machine, under the watchful care of a benevolent
overseer. The superintendence of it belongs to God; man
is thus left free to secure his own happiness and that of
his friends and his country. The rest man leaves to the
guidance of the invisible hand.³

For Francis Hutcheson the problem of law and freedom
was solved in terms of the older philosophy of the microcosm and the macrocosm. It was another of those Stoic
modes of thought mediated to him by the man he so much
admired and chose to follow, Lord Shaftesbury. Hutcheson speaks of the universe as a symmetrical, beautiful and
kindly system; benevolent affections and virtuous acts are
also beautiful and symmetrical. The exercise of the moral
sense within each of us, approving and commending us to
a life of grace, keeps us in mesh, as it were, with the larger
system of the universe. It is a graduated universe, from
the lowest order of life to God, and the parts receive their
character from the symmetrical design of the whole. Man
in no sense, then, can be an isolated atom, for he is indis-
solubly a part of the cosmic scheme of things.⁴

Monboddo, too, reverts to the terminology of the microcosm and macrocosm, influenced directly as he was by the
Greek philosophers. Man is a microcosm, a system by himself, within the system of systems which is the universe.
But he is a mixture of other systems even within himself,
a composite of elemental, vegetable and animal life, all of
which he governs and orders by his intellect. He is, indeed,
a most various animal and a wonderful composition.⁵

Though there was much repetition of these old and new
philosophical ideas about man's freedom and his place in
the universe, one thing was becoming indubitable: man is
a member of the animal kingdom, and any description of
him must include terms appropriate to that classification.
By native equipment he is a unique animal, but still an
animal; in many ways he is a defective animal, in that, for

example, he must offset by his own devices the effects of
harsh climate in which he cannot live unless he takes
measures of his own invention to deal with it. Hutcheson
calls him the chief animal of the earth; Stewart, a rational
and social animal, whose reason has set him apart from
the brutes and has been the agent in his progress to the
present degree of civilization. Smith says man is an animal
in almost constant need of the help of his fellows, and
multitudes of them, at that. One of the interesting features
in Smith's account is that he is much less concerned to
emphasize man's intellectual uniqueness; he takes for
granted what Hume set out to prove, that man's life is
lived much more on the instinctive basis than on the rational. The division of labor, for example, is not the effect
of human wisdom; its advantages and its results in opulence are ours just because men have the propensity to
barter, a trait common to the race. Food, clothing, lodg-
ing are wants of all kinds of animals; for man, some improvement has to be added to everything before he can
use it to eat, wear or live in. This means the development
of the arts in all their variety to cater to needs-plus-taste,
and the resulting involvements of society thus root in
these original, simple, animal requirements. The time had
passed when one could assent to the dictum of Thomas
Aquinas that the significant character of man was "his
desire to know the truth about God and to live in communities." Man had to be seen as one of the animals,
whatever else might be said of him.

The seventeenth century had left a good legacy of scientific findings. Harvey's experiments on the circulation
of the blood had instigated further investigations into the
workings of the human mechanism. Then came, in the
course of the century, the work of the microscopists,
Hooke, Leeuwenhoek, Swammerdam and Malpighi, with
all that that meant for increased knowledge of cell-struc-
ture and the minute functionings of living bodies. The
time was ripe for comparative studies in anatomy and
physiology, and for efforts at better classifications. The

last year of the century saw the publication of Dr. Edward Tyson's *Orang-Outang, sive Homo Sylvestris: or The Anatomy of a Pygmie*, a discussion popular enough to have the book reprinted in 1751. What interests us is not that Tyson proved, to his own satisfaction, that "pygmies" are apes or monkeys and not men—his specimen was really an infant chimpanzee—or even that Buffon supported him, but that he resorted to dissection to prove his case, and to careful description of morphological traits.[6]

The French mathematician and astronomer, Maupertuis, almost equally interested in hybrids and monstrosities, published in 1746 his *Vénus Physique*. In the essays of this volume he discussed the origin of men and of animals, and ventured the suggestion that the white race was the original race since white is the color tending to reappear in variations. Maupertuis, before Diderot, also suggested that present living forms have been derived from a small number, perhaps even a single pair, of ancestors. John Hunter (1728-1793), comparative anatomist, surgeon and collector of a great museum, had observations like these to record:

The monkey in general may be said to be half beast and half man; it may be said to be the middle stage.[7]

And:

Is not the human being a congeries of every animal? Has he not the instinctive principles of every animal, with this difference, that he chooses or varies the mode of putting those principles into action?[8]

In 1779, Dr. Peter Camper's *An Account of the Organs of Speech of the Orang-Outang* refuted Tyson's claims by proving that his apes could never learn to speak because of the formations of their vocal organs. Camper further distinguished himself by his method of measuring skulls of brutes and man with his "Facial Line"—one of the very first efforts to deal with actual dimensions. This was the stimulus for the development of the "vertical scale" for measuring skulls, a device of Johann Friedrich

Blumenbach, who had earlier taken his stand on the specific unity of the human race.[9]

When there was so much interest and so much activity, why was more attention not given to the emergence of new species, to the problems of evolution? One answer is to be found in the popularity of a view which we now call the Great Chain of Being, "next to the word 'Nature' . . . the sacred phrase of the eighteenth century."[10] This world-view was so satisfying that it did not push investigation into the right channels for a discovery of evolution. But let us take account of that complex of ideas in the words of Professor Lovejoy, who has set forth the concept in its history and consequences. He speaks of

the conception of the universe as a "Great Chain of Being," composed of an immense, or—by the strict but seldom rigorously applied logic of the principle of continuity—of an infinite number of links ranging in hierarchical order from the meagerest kind of existents, which barely escape non-existence, through "every possible" grade up to the *ens perfectissimum*—or, in a somewhat more orthodox version, to the highest possible kind of creature, between which and the Absolute Being the disparity was assumed to be infinite—every one of them differing from that immediately above and that immediately below it by the "least possible" degree of difference.[11]

We cannot here follow Professor Lovejoy's exposition further than to note that such a concept when applied to biology had, for centuries, directed thought toward the fixity of species rather than toward transformation, and that classifications were in the nature of inventories rather than representations of "the program of nature, which is being carried out gradually and exceedingly slowly in the cosmic history." Much effort in the eighteenth century was spent in finding organisms near the bottom of the scale and in the intervals between man and the great apes. "Missing links"—flying fish, reptile fish, mermen and mermaids, wild woods-men—were sought with avidity, in the hope that a demonstration of the continuity of this great fixed chain of life might be given. Then, after the middle of the century, there began to be interpretation to

the effect that the chain was, after all, a ladder, and that
new forms might emerge from older ones. The principle
of plenitude, one of the basic ideas in the complex making up the idea of the Chain, would still be operative;
some forms of life simply would be later in actually taking their place, though potentially they were always in
the scheme of things. Thus occurred, in Professor Lovejoy's phrase, the temporalizing of the Chain of Being,
and thus evolutionary conceptions of several kinds become tenable to those whose minds hitherto had been
closed to any interpretation of the universe other than a
static one.[12] It was a long time before any one theory with
clarity of outline appeared, and really not until Charles
Darwin's *Origin of Species* was a mechanism of evolutionary change convincingly set forth. Much fumbling was to
go on in the fields of biology, philosophy and theology.
Not even the two greatest taxonomists of the century,
Linnaeus and Buffon, were free enough of the older formulation to break into completely fresh ways of thought. Let
us look at the problems as Linnaeus (1707-1778) left
them.

Linnaeus, in his *Systema Naturae*, identified two species
of the genus Homo, Sapiens and Monstrosus,[13] the latter
affording evidence that he, as well as Maupertuis, was
puzzled by deformities and monstrosities. He spends very
little time identifying his Homo monstrosus, however,
saying only, in general, that the variations seem to be due
to climate or art, and listing the half-dozen places in the
world where may be found beardless men, men with conic
or flattened heads, or men who are unusually indolent or
timid or infertile. What of his Homo sapiens? After noting the general characteristic that he is a diurnal animal
and varies according to education and situation, Linnaeus
turns to classifying the varieties: the copper-colored, the
fair, the sooty, the black. One of the Linnaean procedures
which amazes twentieth century readers is the mixing of
zoological terms with judgments of character and disposition, with notations as to clothing, and with statements

concerning the institution of government associated with each zoological variety. There is, for example, "the black, phlegmatic, relaxed African. His hair is black and frizzled, his skin silky, his nose flat, his lips tumid; he is indolent and negligent; he anoints himself with grease; and he is governed by caprice."

But our amazement grows when we discover among Linnaeus' varieties of Homo sapiens, the first to be listed in fact, this description: "Four-footed, mute, hairy . . . wild man." Even Linnaeus had been puzzled, then, by Wild Peter, the dumb boy who could not walk, who was found in the Hanover woods in 1724 and taken to the English court for the edification of a Hanoverian king. Linnaeus was, as one of his English admirers suspects, probably misled by accounts of credulous travelers, for in an earlier edition of the *Systema Naturae* he had even made one of the two species troglodytes or orang-outangs.[14] At any rate he remained a puzzled naturalist. As he wrote to a friend in 1747, "Show me a generic character . . . by which to distinguish Man and Ape. I myself most assuredly know of none. . . . But if I had called Man an Ape or vice versa, I should have fallen under the ban of all the ecclesiastics. It may be that as a naturalist I ought to have done so."[15] Blumenbach quoted him as writing in the *System*: "it is wonderful how little the most foolish ape differs from the wisest man, so that we have still to seek for that measurer of nature who is to define their boundaries."[16]

Now in this conception of the smallness of the differences which exist between forms, these men of the eighteenth century were voicing a principle inherited from Aristotle and rationalism, one which underlies, with others related to it, the conception of the Chain of Being:

Nature proceeds little by little from things lifeless to animal life in such a way that it is impossible to determine the exact line of demarcation, nor on which side thereof an intermediate form should lie. . . . Indeed, there is observed in plants a continuous scale of ascent towards the animal. So, in the sea, there are certain objects concerning which one would be at a loss to determine whether they be animal or vegetable.

Nature passes from lifeless objects to animals in such unbroken sequence, interposing between them beings which live and yet are not animal, that scarcely any difference seems to exist between two neighboring groups owing to their close proximity.[17]

Buffon thought that every possible link in the chain of life actually exists. Linnaeus wrote: "All species are certain diversities of form which the Infinite Being created so in the beginning; which forms, according to immutable laws of generation, produce always their like." And again, "Every genus is natural and was in the beginning of things created such." Bonnet in 1745 attempted to fill in all the niches with so much more precision and rigor that his system became an absurdity.[18] Blumenbach, acknowledging the usefulness of the concept, offered the following criticism: "They have attributed it to the Creator in the plan of his creation, and have made its completeness and connexion to be sought for in the fact that nature, as the saying goes, *makes no leap*, *because* creatures with respect to their outward habits can be arranged so closely in gradation one with another."[19]

Alexander Pope, who failed to express no doctrine that was current in the century, however much he might blur the outlines of it, in the *Essay on Man* (1733-1734) gave voice to this complex of ideas in this fashion:

> See, through this air, this ocean, and this earth,
> All matter quick, and bursting into birth.
> Above, how high, progressive life may go!
> Around, how wide, how deep extend below!
> Vast chain of being! which from God began,
> Natures aethereal, human, angel, man,
> Beast, bird, fish, insect, what no eye can see,
> No glass can reach; from Infinite to thee,
> From thee to Nothing.—On superior powers
> Were we to press, inferior might on ours:
> Or in the full creation leave a void,
> Where, one step broken, the great scale's destroy'd:

> From Nature's chain whatever link you strike,
> Tenth, or ten thousandth, breaks the chain alike.
>
> .   .   .   .
>
> All are but parts of one stupendous Whole,
> Whose body Nature is, and God the soul.[20]

For most Scots the thing was put satisfactorily by William Smellie (1740-1795), naturalist, antiquarian and printer to the University of Edinburgh. Kames suggested to him that he write a book on *The Philosophy of Natural History*, and it proved to be very popular, going through six American editions and being translated into German. In the chapter entitled "Of the Progressive Scale or Chain of Beings in the Universe" he has these things to say:

> There is a graduated scale or chain of existence, not a link of which, however seemingly insignificant, could be broken without affecting the whole.
> In the chain of animals, man is unquestionably the chief or capital link, and from him all the other links descend by almost imperceptible gradations.
> Every creature is perfect, according to its destination.
> Man, even by his external qualities, stands at the head of this world.
> In descending the scale of animation, the next step, it is humiliating to remark, is very short.
> Man, in his lowest condition, is evidently linked, both in the form of his body and the capacity of his mind, to the large and small orang-outangs.
> These again, by another slight gradation, are connected to the apes, who like the former, have no tails.

And he concludes his discussion with this homily:

> Were there no other argument in favour of the Unity of Deity, this uniformity of design, this graduated concatenation of beings . . . seems to be perfectly irrefragable.
> Let man . . . be contented. His station in the universal Scale of Nature is fixed by wisdom. Let him contemplate and admire the works of his Creator; let him fill up his rank with dignity, and consider every partial evil as a cause or an effect of general good. This is the whole duty of man.[21]

To the Scottish philosophers, even those relatively unversed in the lore of natural history, the discussions of the naturalists could not fail to be of interest. Moral philosophy had long discussed the degrees of civilization, the causes of stagnant cultures, and the causes that bring advancement. They were sure that individuals make progress in the course of living out their life cycles; they were fairly sure that most societies, unless retarded by some accident of situation or history, would tread the path from rudeness to civility so glowingly described, as we have seen, by Ferguson.[22] But when they considered the forms of life, their judgment was that these had been created and were unchanging, but so delicate were the differences in forms when arranged in a series that the series itself represented a kind of progression, even though the process of differentiation was not a progress or evolution in the true sense.

As for man's place in that series, most of them would have agreed with Alexander Pope:

> . . . in the scale of reas'ning life, 'tis plain,
> There must be, somewhere, such a rank as Man;
> And all the question (wrangle e'er so long)
> Is only this, if God has placed him wrong?
>
> .   .   .   .
>
> Then say not Man's imperfect, Heav'n in fault;
> Say rather, Man's as perfect as he ought:
> His knowledge measur'd to his state and place;
> His time a moment, and a point his space.[23]

Lord Kames puts the matter in this fashion:

It certainly will not be thought, in any degree, inconsistent with the pure benevolence of the Deity, that the world is filled with an endless variety of creatures, gradually ascending in the scale of being, from the most groveling, to the most glorious. . . . If, at first view, it shall be thought that infinite power and goodness cannot stop short of absolute perfection in their operations, and that the work of creation must be confined to the highest order of beings in the highest perfection; this thought will soon be corrected, by considering, that, by this supposition a great void is left, which, according to the present system of things, is filled with beings, and with life and motion. And, supposing the world to be replenished with the highest order of beings, created in the highest degree of perfection, it is certainly an act of more extensive benevolence, to complete the work of creation, by the addition of an infinity of creatures less perfect, than to leave a great blank, betwixt beings of the highest order, and nothing.[24]

Kames discusses another phase of the problem because of its bearing on the "history" of man and undertakes in the first of his *Sketches* to contribute his mite, as he says, to the discussion of whether there be different races of men or only one race. He begins his attack by directing witty jibes at his opponents. How strangely imperfect the human race would be if it were impossible to distinguish a man from a monkey, or a hare from a hedgehog till it were known whether they can procreate together! Yet that is what Buffon's rule, taken over from the first botanical taxonomist, John Ray, demands. Linnaeus, too, has wandered wonderfully far from nature in making his classifications; his purpose must have been, Kames says, to enable us from the nipples and teeth of any particular animal to know where it lies in his books. The Linnaean scheme resembles the cataloguing of a library according to size or binding, but with disregard to content. How whimsical, he says, to class a man with a bat and to deny that a whale is a fish simply because Linnaeus chose the distinguishing marks which he did! Animals are no less distinguishable by their tails, long, short, or no tails, or by hands. What virtue is there in Linnaeus' preference for breasts and teeth as taxonomic aids?

Coming now to man, analogy would lead us, Kames thinks, to judge that, as there are different races of animals and plants in different climates, so there must be different races of man. Buffon's theory cannot be maintained that man is one race, found in several varieties because of the long action of the food and climate of a particular locality; for in the same kind of climate live Laplanders and Finlanders, but they are very different people. In almost the same climate Negroes and Abyssinians live quite separately and are unmistakably different; while, conversely, over a wide range of climatic variations all American natives are copper-colored. Nor can environmentalists give too much credit to the sun, for its effects certainly do not carry over to babies of sun-tanned parents. The conclusion would seem to be, rather, that there are different races of man fitted for the different climates, not by chance, but by design and creation.

When it comes to Kames' substantiation, we must admit that it is weak, and we are not surprised that his biographer and most of his friends regretted that he had attempted this discussion, since its quality would not lead a reader to judge correctly of Kames' knowledge and power. Among the evidences he offers for his position are the following: the distinguishable degrees of kindness and hospitality which some tribes show toward strangers; the differences in courage and cowardice, which cannot be ascribed to climate in spite of the claims of several notable theorists, including Montesquieu himself; the color of Negroes; some striking, unnatural customs; the frame of man, which certainly does not appear to be equally at home in every climate. Such as the evidence is, it would logically lead him, he says, to the conclusion that the present diversities in human beings are the result of an original creation by God of pairs of male and female, each pair differing from every other pair and suited to the locality where God placed them to propagate their kind and to develop their languages and cultures on different patterns. But this cannot be the judgment, for on the unquestionable authority of Moses we have it that God created only one pair of the human species. Moreover, that pair did not partake of savage characteristics, but were exceedingly well-informed. "Whence then the degeneracy of all men unto the savage state? To account for that dismal catastrophe, mankind must have suffered some terrible convulsion . . . ," and then follows his account of the confusion of Babel, which is "the only known fact that can reconcile sacred and profane history." That deplorable event reversed all nature: by scattering men over the face of all the earth, it deprived them of society, and rendered them savages. From that state of degeneracy, they have been emerging gradually. Some nations, stimulated by their own nature, or by their climate, have made a rapid progress; some have proceeded more slowly, and some continue savages.[25]

Thus, by insisting on racial distinctness which originated at Babel and has persisted ever since, Kames became the first of the "racialists" in the interpretation of human society.[26] Confused his reasoning was, and unscientific his sources were, but, at that, he was not greatly out of line with much of the thought of the century.[27]

We shall deal in detail with only one other of the Scots, James Burnet, more frequently called Lord Monboddo. He was, as we have noted, reputed to be the most learned man in all of Scotland, with the exception of Sir William Hamilton. No one exceeded him in the number of his eccentricities and crotchets. He was the rival of Lord Kames on the bench and in literary achievement, and, as Henry Graham says, the only thing the two men had in common was longevity. They "ridiculed each other's books, jeered at each other's speculations, scorned each other's law, and laughed at each other's hobbies."[28] It seemed as though they were doomed always to be in each other's way. Frequently their volumes would be published at about the same date, and reviews would appear in the same issue of the journals of the day. Usually those reviews were far more favorable to Kames, it must be said, but later readers have, for the most part, found Monboddo the more interesting figure. The reason for this is doubtless the fact that a superficial examination of his writings leads one to think that here is a pre-Darwinian evolutionist. We shall see in how far this judgment has been wrong.

One of the fundamental problems for Monboddo is the distinction between man and the other animals, a distinction which lays the basis for any philosophy of man. With his contempt for his contemporaries and their "manual" philosophy, and his admiration of the ancients, he does not surprise us when he repeats many of the Greek, especially the Aristotelian, positions. He does not depart far from the conventional line when he announces that man is distinguished from the brutes by the possession of intellect, and that intellect in a man is very different from sense in a brute. But he means to attack particularly the philosophy of "Mr. Locke" and "Mr. David Hume," both of whom seem to confound sensations and ideas, Hume indeed calling an idea only a weaker sensation. "Now," says Monboddo, "if there be no distinctions betwixt sensations and ideas, there is certainly none betwixt sense and intellect." What things do we see man doing that testify to his being possessed of intellect? Man pursues the beautiful, says Monboddo, rather than the merely useful; he follows dictates of his own will and is not at the mercy of immediate and temporary impulse; he can work for ends and not confuse them with their means.

. . . we are capable of intellectual pleasure; and therefore are by nature an animal of a higher order, and destined for greater happiness, though, for want of cultivation of our intellect, and by prevalence of our animal nature over it, (not an animal nature governed by infinite wisdom, like the animal nature of the brute, but by our imperfect intellect), we are often degraded to brutes, and made more miserable even than they, at least for a certain time.[29]

Often, as we follow his long arguments, we come upon a paragraph of the kind which has helped to lead interpreters of Monboddo astray, for, on first reading, it sounds like an evolutionary reconstruction of the species Man. What it represents is one of many statements by Monboddo of his understanding and use of the conception of the Scale of Nature, or the Chain of Being. For example:

This is the scale of being, rising by proper gradations from mere matter and sense to intellect, through the medium of memory, imagination, and opinion. Some animals appear to have only sense, such as muscles, [sic] and other shell-fish. There are others that never attain even to sense in any degree of perfection, but fill up the interval betwixt the vegetable and animal, participating something of the nature of each, from which they have the name of zoophytes. Other animals, besides sense have memory and imagination; and some perhaps only one of these two; but man, being a little world, as the antients [sic] called him, has in his frame a portion of every thing to be found in nature. He has in his body all the elements of which the inanimate world is composed; he has the growth and nutrition of the vegetable; and he has sense, memory, and imagination, belonging to the animal life; and, last of all, he acquires reason and intellect. Thus is man formed, not however at once, but by degrees, and in succession: for he appears at first to be little more than a vegetable, hardly deserving of the name of a zoophyte; then he gets sense, but sense only, so that he is yet little better than a muscle; then he becomes an animal of a more complete kind; then a rational creature, and finally a man of intellect and science, which is the summit and completion of our nature.[30]

One of the main concerns of Monboddo here would seem to be to prove that, just as in the universe there must be every possible gradation of links in the Chain of Being in order for the universe to be full and perfect,[31] so in man there must be contained every quality which enters anywhere into the composition of animals. Man is an animal, the most perfect animal; therefore he must encompass within himself all animal properties. But, as in the universe there is gradation, so in man, who mirrors the universe, there is also gradation. Some men are more perfect than others; that is, some individuals come nearer realization of the full potentialities of the species. But most men in the course of their lives achieve something of manlike abilities. In still other ways man is a mixture:

. . . he is rational and irrational; he has intellect, and he has not intellect; he is a biped, and he is not a biped; he is a land-animal, and he is a water-animal; and among other varieties, he is social, and he is not social. In short, he appears to be placed on the confines betwixt different kinds of beings; and ás the zoophyte is in the middle betwixt the vegetable and animal, so man appears to occupy the space betwixt the several classes of animals.

Further:

. . . man participates so much of the gregarious animal as to have no aversion to the society of his fellow-creatures, far less to be the natural enemy of his own species, as certain species are of others; and . . . he also has so much of the nature of the solitary wild beast, that he has no natural propensity to enter society, but was urged to it by motives to be afterwards explained. What, among other things induces me to think he is of this mixt kind, is the formation of his teeth and intestines.[32]

And he goes on to explain that man has teeth both for tearing and grinding, whereas animals usually have only the one or the other; and as for man's intestines, they are not so short as those of animals of prey nor so long as those of animals which live on the fruits of the earth.

Man has had quite a career. Originally an innocuous animal, feeding upon the fruits of the earth, he became in time a hunter, and the wild beast became so predominant in him that in some places he even came to eating his vanquished enemies. With all his faults, however, man is still the most excellent animal form, since he is governed by intellect, rather than by instinct. It is this intellect which forms what is properly called man and which constitutes him a social and political animal; and we may truthfully say that by means of it man has made himself; he is his own product.[33]

Man's career had, however, started long before the era in which he was known as a "frugivorous" animal. He had been, once upon a time, a much more godlike creature. He had had what the Greeks called a golden age, from which he had afterward fallen, as penance for the sin of intellectual pride. His second beginning was on the level of a creature; he was solitary and unsocial, and had only the capacity for, but not the achievements of, intellect and science. This time he had to struggle to win for himself what had been originally the gift of God, and this long hard effort makes up a large part of the history of the species Man.[34] In such allegorical fashion, Monboddo insists, the Mosaic account of the fall of man should be interpreted. One of his reasons for so insisting was that it allowed him to follow Plato in holding that all knowledge which we acquire in this life is an imperfect recollection of what we knew in a former life. This interpretation of Monboddo's of the fall, with its emphasis on the superiority of life-conditions before the penance was imposed, gave him the comfort, unusual for him, of agreeing with one of his contemporaries, and on Rousseau he bestows frequent approval for his accounts of the desirableness of man's earlier condition.

The struggle in which man has had to engage since the fall has brought man-made results in cultural achievements—that has to be granted. But Monboddo is pretty clear that the creature, as a physical being, has continued to degenerate from his godlike nature. This is shown in his decreased vitality, shortened stature and his dependence on conveniences and luxuries. Moreover, by his wars and commercial enterprises man destroys other creatures and lays waste lands, so that sometimes he seems the most mischievous of animals and very far from happy. He is at once the noblest and most degenerate animal of the earth.[35]

Animal creature as man now is, he exhibits a most wonderful variety; there are more kinds of man than of any other animal God has made. As to color, there are white, black, brown, red and yellow men; there are large and small men; there are all shapes of face and figure: there are men with tails, men with one eye in the breast or perhaps in the forehead, men with one leg much longer than the other, and there are mermen and mermaids. To those sceptics who question the veracity of reporters who have seen such men and maidens Monboddo replies gravely that he prefers to follow Aristotle in maintaining that everything exists which is possible to exist; otherwise, something would be wanting in the System of Nature.[36]

It is the men with tails who claimed his attention most consistently. As Professor Chauncey Tinker says, "His perpetual emphasis on the caudal appendage put all his readers in hysterics." Samuel Johnson said of Monboddo: "Other people have strange notions, but they conceal them. If they have tails, they hide them; but Monboddo is as jealous of his tail as a squirrel." He was known to interrupt court proceedings, at which he was presiding, long enough to send a note to a newcomer just returned from a far journey to inquire if by chance he had found

in his wandering a race of men with tails.[37] He was charmed
with the story of a seventeenth-century Swedish traveler
who saw on an island in the Gulf of Bengal men with tails,
waving them as cats do; Borneo was supposed to shelter
a whole race thus equipped; and he, Monboddo, could produce legal evidence that there had been a mathematics
teacher in Inverness, Scotland, who had a tail half a foot
long. Other "wild" people fascinate him: he had seen and
talked with Wild Peter, found in the woods of Hanover in
1724 and brought to England for observation by Dr.
Arbuthnot and for presentation to King George.[38] He had
talked with Memmie LeBlanc, *la fille sauvage de Champagne*, and had caused to be translated and published the
account of her life. We have seen that Wild Peter put
even Linnaeus to some confusion, and that it was not
definitely established for some time that Peter was only
a poor dumb boy, who could not walk erect and who had
been lost from human society and did not, therefore, de-
serve a separate niche in the System of Nature as an independent creation. As for Memmie, it was true that she
ate much raw meat, that she killed rabbits and ate them,
that she had prodigious strength, and that, even though
her friends had her baptized, she remained rather wild.
Some persons were sure she was an Eskimo, out of her
native habitat, but behaving like a pretty good Eskimo
even in Champagne. For Monboddo, however, these specimens all represented various points along a scale, at one
end of which was Man-not-fully-man, at the other end,
Man-fully-man. The differences between the end terms were
due to differences in the achievement of intellect, and that
could be told, roughly, by the achievement of language.[39]
He was sure "that there was a progress in the species such
as we are sure there is in the individual."[40] No wonder he
has sometimes been taken as a precursor of Charles Darwin. What Monboddo really intended will appear as we
proceed.

In almost every chapter of his two voluminous works
appear the orang-outangs, the natural men, the wild men

of the woods. To quote Professor Tinker again, "This in itself was sufficient to draw upon him the ridicule of his contemporaries; for though they were eager to assert the essential nobility of the savage, they had no disposition to extend their admiration to the animal kingdom and dwell on the simple dignity of orang-outangs."[41] It is true that many of his contemporaries ridiculed him, Blumenbach, for example, calling him "the renowned philosopher and downright caprice monger."[42] Lord Kames, according to Ramsay of Ochtertyre, said he wondered that Monboddo "had not more pride than to swallow a Frenchman's spittle."[43] Ramsay goes on to imply that the Frenchman referred to was Maillet, Consul in Egypt for the French king, who, after writing a really good book about Egypt amused himself by putting forth a book called *Telliam* (his name spelled backward). This book was translated into English in 1750. In it Maillet maintains that man was originally a fish, that his skin under a microscope even now looks like scales, and that physicians even now cure many diseases by using sea-water, resorting to man's natural medium to restore him to health. In the course of his history man dropped first his fins, then his tail, but there are still many men with tails, even a race of them, says Maillet; and the common expression, *homines caudati*, "men with tails," is by no means a metaphorical usage only, but is founded on truth.[44] Now Monboddo did know the book of Maillet, and he cites it, but only once or twice. His authorities were, rather, Pliny, Pausanias, Marco Polo, Herodotus, Diodorus Siculus, Sir Francis Drake, Sir John Marburgh, the Swedish Keoping, Rousseau and many travelers among the islands of the seas. So, if any Frenchman's spittle was swallowed, it was probably that of Jean-Jacques.[45]

However open to suggestion Monboddo was, we must remember the experiments of Tyson and Camper and the classification of Linnaeus, all of which testified to considerable concern with the problem of man's nearness to this same orang-outang. Monboddo himself tells us that the

Royal Society of London became so excited over the orang-
outang that it planned to send out a special investigator
to Africa.[46] James Dunbar, in his *Essays on the History
of Mankind in Rude and Cultivated Ages*, reminds his
readers that "Upon the discovery of America, doubts were
entertained whether the natives of that country ought not
to be accounted a race of orang-outangs. But the infallible edict of a Roman pontiff [1537] soon established
their doubtful pedigree."[47] Many amusing paragraphs
could be quoted which would afford us a good laugh over
this reading and thinking of the impassioned Monboddo,
but let us choose one of his sober statements in which he
sums up his evidence for judging orang-outangs to be a
"barbarous nation" of humanity:

. . . the Orang-Outang is an animal of human form, inside as
well as outside: . . . he has the human intelligence, as much
as can be expected in an animal living without civility or arts:
. . . he has a disposition of mind, mild, docile, and humane:
. . . he has the sentiments and affections peculiar to our species,
such as the sense of modesty, of honour, and of justice, and
likewise an attachment of love and friendship to one individual,
so strong in some instances that one friend will not survive the
other: . . . they live in society, and have some arts of life; for
they build huts, and use an artificial weapon for attack and defense, *viz.* a stick; which no animal, merely brute, is known to
do. They shew also counsel and design, by carrying off creatures
of our species, for certain purposes, and keeping them for years
together without doing them any harm; which no brute creature
was ever known to do. They appear likewise to have some kind
of civility among them, and to practice certain rites, such as
that of burying the dead.[48]

But Monboddo has more fundamental problems than
simply the finding of humane orangs and men with tails.
He is deeply concerned with the graded Scale of Nature
and he wants to fit all his specimens into their proper
niches. He cannot approve Linnaeus' system—one other
single point of agreement with Kames—for mammae and
teeth seem "artificial" criteria to him and not true "philosophical" standards for distinguishing genera and species.
A true standard, he says, should be more in keeping with

the original classifications of logic, and should consider the degree of intelligence manifested by different groups of animals. Because he did not use this measurement of intelligence, but a physical measurement, Linnaeus did not include the orang-outang in the species *Homo sapiens*, the diurnal man; rather, he made him a separate species, *Homo nocturnus*, the man with the *membrana nictitans* which we do not happen to have. What sophistry, says Monboddo, when so many travelers are impressed with the intelligence displayed by orangs! Why not use a truly philosophical standard, that of intelligence, a standard guaranteed since the days of the Peripatetic philosophers? By any such standard we should have to judge the orang-outang as being in the first stage of human progression, in the "infantine" state of the species, whose maturity is characterized by the achievements of intellect and science.[49]

As usual he falls back for support on Aristotle. Aristotle, he says, has defined man to be "a creature of intellect and science *only in capacity*; marking in this way the progress of man, as well as of everything else on this earth, from capacity to actuality; for everything here has first the capacity of becoming something, before it is actually that thing." And again,

Aristotle . . . has told us, that man is more fitted by nature to be a biped than any other animal. But from thence I infer, that he did not think that he was by nature a biped: For if he had thought so, he would not have said that man was fitted by nature to be a biped more than any other animal . . . but he would have said plainly and shortly that he was by nature a biped. But if he had said so, he would have been mistaken; for it now appears certain, that man is by nature a quadruped.[50]

And then he lists sundry instances of savages caught in different parts of Europe who were going on all fours when found. Because they were not walking erect, they should not be put beyond the pale of man any more than is the orang-outang, who does not speak. Both groups represent man-in-capacity, not yet come to man-in-actuality, but just as surely man as is a human baby. Indeed, the progress *within* the species can be no better seen than when compared to the growth processes of a single individual.[51]

It is interesting to see the use which Monboddo makes of the accounts of orangs and wild peoples in building up the steps of "the wonderful progression of man." Peter, the Wild Boy, really represents a more "infantine state" than does the orang-outang because, while Peter could make a few strange sounds, he could not walk erect. The orang-outang had become a biped and could walk erect. True, he sometimes walked on all his feet, just as some savages, Monboddo avers, will drop down on to four, as if they were not far from a more primitive way and slipped back into it. But the orang in mind, as well as body, had acquired the traits of man: he had a sense of decency, and justice and honor; he had some arts, as seen in his ability to strike a fire and in his concern to bury his dead. Memmie LeBlanc, *la fille sauvage de Champagne*, represented a third stage. For not only could Memmie speak, but she could sing like a bird, and she could swim, which is an ability not natural to man as to most animals. In the country from which she had been brought before her shipwreck, children were accustomed to the water from birth, but her nation lived without the art of fire. Memmie, moreover, could leap from limb to limb like a squirrel, and when she was found in the river, after the shipwreck, she had a fish in her hand.

In other words, as Monboddo goes on to interpret his series, the natural or first state of man was that before he learned to walk erect. The second was entered when man mastered his first art, the ability to use his own body, and when he began to live in groups as the orang-outangs do. What prompted this association Monboddo does not say, other than that some convenience or necessity was served. Man is both solitary and gregarious, even political it would seem, and the best answer is that God intended him to be the animal who could live in civil society. The third stage was entered when more food, and food of greater variety, was called for by an increasing population, by the size and longevity of men and by their procreative abilities. Having learned to use their bodies well by now, to extend them by the use of tools, men could turn to hunting and fishing to meet these maintenance needs. This required co-operative effort and the development of language, that foundation of all the arts and sciences which now bless man's life. Only after men could speak together could they develop the arts of agriculture and polity and all other arts.[52]

That last sentence brings us, when all the rest has been said, to what was the most fundamental concern of Monboddo. His main purpose was to prove that language was not natural nor necessary to man.[53] By finding a group of beings, manlike but nonspeaking, he thought he proved his contention that language, as delightful and useful an ability as it was, was an achievement which came in the course of man's history as man. His species Man, then, included at one end of the scale men who do not talk, the crang-outangs and all the other wild men; and at the other, the men who do talk. But both groups are men, the one as truly as the other. The changes that come, come *within* the species, and not from one species to another. One of his diatribes against Linnaeus may well be quoted here:

. . . for the capacity of intellect and science . . . supposes that an animal may be a man, without being actually intelligent or scientific. . . . Being ignorant, therefore, of his progression of the species, which I hold to be a fundamental principle of the history and philosophy of Man, Linnaeus has supposed that men, in the first stages of this progression, were of a species different from other men; when he might as well have supposed that an infant among us was of a species different from a full grown man.[54]

So, we have to say of Monboddo, if we are to speak correctly, that he was no precursor of Charles Darwin, since he was not concerned with the origin of new species.[55] Erasmus Darwin was probably the nearest precursor in the eighteenth century of his own grandson. Species were as fixed for Monboddo as for Linnaeus or any other believer in the Scale of Nature. He would have agreed with Charles Darwin on the general Aristotelian statement that nature does not make leaps, but beyond that they would have had little else in common.

And yet that statement is not quite the truth. For to Monboddo, as for the other Scots, there has come the belief that whatever else may be said of man, the characterization must start with the fact that he is an animal.[56] That man has wrought out his culture—many cultures, indeed—witnesses to a certain uniqueness in his equipment. But not one would have disagreed with the author of the article "Homme" in the *Encyclopédie*: "If one wishes to understand him [man] in respect to his natural qualities, one must class him as an animal."

IV

MAN'S PAST

WITH all its other concerns, the eighteenth century was tremendously interested in history. Commenting on the popularity enjoyed by writings on historical subjects, Professor Black of Sheffield remarks:

> It would be no exaggeration to say that the vogue of historical books between 1750 and the outbreak of the French Revolution was as great as the vogue of political literature in the age of Shakespeare or of the novel in the age of Scott. Everyone read it and talked about it.[1]

The authors of history themselves were fairly complacent about this favorable disposition of readers everywhere. Voltaire wrote, "L'histoire est la partie des belles-lettres qui a le plus de partisans dans tous les pays"; Gibbon, "History is the most popular species of writing"; and Hume, "I believe this to be the historical age and this the historical nation." Hume, again with that satisfaction he was always to feel over his conquest of the French, wrote of the response there to his *History of England*, "They will drive me out of France à coup de compliments et de louanges."[2]

Just as everyone read history and talked about it, so it can be said with an equal amount of truth that almost everyone who had literary aspirations wrote it at some time or other in his life. As Professor Black points out, history was considered a branch of literature, and a branch in which "elegance," so loved of the century, could express itself with considerable freedom. So conceived, history lent itself excellently to apostrophe, to eulogy, to scornful condemnations, to elaborated and figurative speech. Persons of a literary turn of mind, then, found it an appropriate field in which to exercise their talents. And Professor Black adds, as another explanation of the vogue, that its very association with philosophy brought it into popu-

larity. The result of this association was not history for
history's sake, but history for philosophy's sake.[3]

Though ethics was the section of philosophy which they
hoped would be greatly illuminated by the appeal to history—Bolingbroke's phrase, "history is philosophy teaching by examples," comes to mind—ethical considerations
were not the only philosophical ones at work by a good
deal. History, besides showing the outcomes of good and
bad choices, would show those principles of repetition and
uniformity, those sequences of behavior, which philosophical, i.e., scientific, requirements demanded. Though
these principles were rooted, they thought, in the uniformity of human nature, a concept not so tenable with us
today, we must acknowledge that here was an approximation to what we should call scientific method. The concern
of later historians with accuracy in detail and with those
very particulars which the eighteenth century feared because they could be dealt with only as particulars, is one
of the reasons that history still is usually not classified as
a science. Science, though it starts with particulars, does
not rest in them, but searches for repetitive factors and
processes.[4]

Undoubtedly one of the motives for the writing of history was pride in the achievements of the age, and the
desire to set them off favorably against the comparative
lack of achievement in the past. It was a "polite" and
"polished" generation, whose accomplishments could be
portrayed advantageously by the side of those of "rude"
and "barbarous" periods of the past or of some other
section of the world. True, one of the conventional topics
was the warning of the degeneration and catastrophe that
awaited any people giving themselves up to luxury and
soft living. True, too, there was a nostalgia (also probably conventional) for the simpler, more wholesome, more
"natural" life of earlier epochs.[5] And, especially for
French writers, there was the desire for changing the
present order into a better one for posterity. But when
all those items are noted, the fact remains that most liter-

ary men were extremely complacent about their century, glad to be alive in it, and more than glad to portray its accomplishments and the degrees or steps by which, in general and for the most part, these had probably come into being. Though the end product was what held their attention, and the delineation of the processes leading to it was frequently highly generalized, there was very decidedly the feeling that any present is rooted in its past and some account must be taken, therefore, of that past.

There is no escaping the fact that there was everywhere in western Europe a new regard for the past; history could reveal what had happened to man in former days and what man had caused to happen. Here was something other than speculation; here was an empirical basis; here were actualities. Sir Leslie Stephen goes so far as to say that in the last half of the century "what is permanently valuable may be regarded as a feeling after the historical method. . . ." Speaking of Hume's turning to historical investigation, Sir Leslie remarks:

> Thus the moral which Hume naturally drew from his philosophy was the necessity of turning entirely to experience. Experience, and experience alone, could decide questions of morality and politics; and Hume put his theory in practice when he abandoned speculation to turn himself to history. Whether because they shared Hume's doubts, or because, without much speculation, they recognized the failure of previous philosophers to reach any fruitful conclusions and saw no more promising road to success, Hume's ablest contemporaries followed his example.[6]

Those very ablest contemporaries were, of course, Gibbon, Voltaire and William Robertson, Principal of the University of Edinburgh. A host of writers whose works have not stood the test of time were, however, widely popular in their day.

There was Antoine Yves Goguet, whose *De l'origine des lois, des arts, et des sciences; et de leurs progrès chez les anciens peuples* (Paris, 1758) was translated and published in Edinburgh three years later and frequently quoted by British authors.[7] There was James Dunbar, a

regent at King's College, Aberdeen, for thirty years and
teacher of moral philosophy. The book which concerns us
here is his *Essays on the History of Mankind and Cultivated Ages*. This book came out in London in 1780 and
went into a new edition the next year. Among the essays
were the following: "On the Primeval Form of Society,"
"On Language as an Universal Accomplishment," "Of
the Rank of Nations, and the Revolutions of Fortune,"
"Of the General Influence of Climate on National Objects," "Of Fashions That Predominate among Various
Tribes of Mankind," "Of the Hereditary Genius of Nations." Dunbar is not, as could be guessed from the titles
of the essays cited, interested primarily in chronology.
He is concerned with "the order of improvement," and he
notes that degeneracy, as well as improvement, is incident
to man. Like any orthodox social scientist of today, he is
much more interested in the achievements of a group or a
folk than he is in identifying and lauding superior individuals; he does not interpret history by the light of the
"Great Man Theory." There was Gilbert Stuart's *View
of Society in Europe, in Its Progress from Rudeness to
Refinement*, published in Edinburgh in 1778, more limited
in scope than Dunbar's work, centered on a period more
modern than was Goguet's.

Three French historians of the popular and even superficial sort who were read throughout the century were
Rollin, Raynal and Charlevoix. Their anecdotes and moral-
izings were repeated by many authors, both French and
British. A seventeenth-century writer, of more deeply
philosophic cast, continued to have an undoubted influence on conceptions of the past and of history writing.
Bishop Bossuet (1627-1704), tutor to the dauphin at the
court of Louis XIV, was concerned to make an intelligent
and a Christian prince out of his charge, and to that end
he prepared several books which found greater appreciation in the world beyond the palace bounds than in the
responses of that unprincely young boy. Among these
were the *Discours sur l'histoire universelle* (1681) and the

Histoire des variations des églises protestantes (1688). The latter was the work which converted the young Gibbon to an acceptance of Catholicism, brief though the conversion proved to be. The *Universal History* is noteworthy because it represented an effort to bring up to date St. Augustine's *City of God*, a Catholic philosophy of history in which the active agent, the great cause of all events, is Providence. That theme could hardly be accepted by the eighteenth century, but Bossuet continued to provide a scheme for the classifying of historical materials and periods. When Turgot and Condorcet turned to write of the progress of intellect and of the resulting progress in arts, science and social organization, Bossuet's scheme was adopted, with its succession of ages, its almost complete neglect of peoples beyond Europe, its assumption of the unitary character of history. The change rung in by Turgot and Condorcet was the substitution of progress for Providence as the agent and effective cause of the changes from age to age, but Bossuet's general scheme continued to be seen in the works of many authors.[8]

And, of course, no listing of French historians could omit the great commentator Montesquieu and the effects of his *Considérations sur les causes de la grandeur des Romains et de leur décadence* (1734) and *L'Esprit des lois* (1748). A modern critic writes of him: "He no longer proposes to solve the 'Why?' and 'Wherefore?'—the justification or the end of existence—but only its 'How?'—its rules and conditions."[9]

Here, then, were a few of the century's many attempts to describe and explain man's past. They present us with an array of topics treated with varying degrees of historical perspective and accuracy—particular peoples, particular institutions, a series of peoples seen as succeeding one another as the instruments of God, particular ideas, ideas in general, the development of intellectual ability, customs both trivial and important. The treatments represent a mixture of politics, of aesthetics, of ethics, of

anthropology, and always to the fore is some assumption
as to the working of human nature in history.

By seeming lack of attention to the type of history we
know best, namely, political and national history, we do
not mean to imply that it was not being written. There
had, indeed, been a good deal of it written since the Ren-
aissance. In the fifteenth, sixteenth and seventeenth centuries there had appeared the works of Aeneas Sylvius,
Machiavelli, Johannes Turmair, Polydore Vergil, Sir
Thomas More, George Buchanan, Sir Francis Bacon,
William Camden, Lord Clarendon, Bishop Burnet, Hugo
Grotius and Samuel Pufendorf.[10] These writings were,
many of them, definitely concerned with the experiences of
a particular people, or of a particular period, but they
were more than political annals. Much description of personages and of common people and their manners was
afforded, many comparisons were made with neighboring
nations or with peoples on the other side of the globe,
many side-excursions were entered on in the effort to explain or speculate on a given situation.

It was not then, by any means, an untrodden road which
eighteenth-century writers set upon when they turned
themselves to history. What was new was the self-consciousness with which authors went about their task. History could not, by philosophers, be written in annalistic
form; nor could it overstress uniqueness, discreteness, particularity, though it should deal with fact. If history was
to become the preoccupation of the philosophic mind, it
had to be viewed philosophically, that is, it had to be seen
in a system which possessed some degree of coherence,
some few ultimate principles of explanation to which events
could be referred. What could make a coherent system,
acceptable to the philosophic mind, from all of the facts
of history, all of the epochs, all of the personages? What
principle or principles of explanation could cover such a
vast collection of facts? The answer, for the philosophers,
was in terms of the basic facts of human nature, which
were thought to be ultimate in that they were everywhere

and in all ages the same. The authors did not overlook diversity, but they considered that the basic element, human nature, was always present, whether in France under Louis XIV, in England under the Stuarts, in India under the Brahmans, or in America under the leadership successively of aborigines and Spanish conquerors.

When we turn to the group of Scottish writers of the century, we find that one of them, Thomas Reid, interested himself not at all in the problems of man's past. He did not concern himself with the physical aspects of man's life; he did not write of domestic or political economy, of jurisprudence, of religion or of government. His range was limited to psychology and theoretical ethics, with a little attention given to aesthetics. This was an unusual limitation for an eighteenth-century philosopher to put upon himself and it disappointed one of his interpreters considerably. The Reverend James McCosh, who was for so long the Scottish president of Princeton University and throughout his life an exponent of the Scottish philosophy, was especially eager to extol Reid as the bulwark against Hume's scepticism; he had to admit, however, that unless Reid taught his classes more than he put into print his system of moral philosophy would appear very defective, as judged by the scope accepted by most of the philosophers toward the end of the century.

Now it may be simply that Reid did not find time and energy to write out his thoughts on these subjects. Or perhaps he felt that such discussions required another kind of preparation and information which he did not have and that he had better eschew them altogether. It may be that the clue lies in the dictum of his teacher, George Turnbull, who had said that the application of the moral law could proceed solidly only on historical example, and that no one could be prepared for such application unless he had read carefully the histories of different nations and was well versed in public affairs generally.[11] Reid certainly was less conversant with the affairs of his time and with history than any of his Scottish contemporaries, so it may have seemed to him the part of wisdom to heed Turnbull's warning.

Francis Hutcheson had a particular interest in history which was characteristic of him—and of many others. His efforts were rather consistently directed toward establishing an aesthetic and metaphysical basis for a morality of naturalism, and for this history is useful. "History derives its chief excellence," he says, "from the representing the manners and characters; the contemplation of which in Nature being very affecting, they must necessarily give pleasure when well related."[12] From time to time he indulges in that species of history which delighted the century and which Dugald Stewart named "ideal," "hypothetical," "theoretical." At another time he admits that such a story is more truly a logical justification of an existing institution than a record of its history. Occasionally, in the manner of Hume, he draws on history to explode some dogma which he does not like, but which either has a foothold or is trying to secure one.[13] Certain topics, favorites with all seventeenth- and eighteenth-century philosophers, are dealt with by Hutcheson: nature, the state of nature, laws of nature, contract, comparison of cultures, culture origins—sometimes historically, sometimes not. His chief concern is not, after all, to inquire into points of history about facts, but to show what wise and just motives enter into the making and maintaining of states.[14]

Hutcheson apparently had his reservations about the literature of travel and adventure which provided much grist for the mills of eighteenth-century writers on customs and manners. He could not escape at least one of their discoveries, however, namely, that men do not have the same forms of institutions the world over. The phase that interested him chiefly was, of course, the diversity of moral principles. He continued to hold that men are possessed, universally, of a moral sense; and that it is innate, and not due to custom, education or example; the content of its judgments changes, however; its objects of approval vary, according to certain sets of ideas which obtain among each particular people. Different people have different ideas as to what constitutes happiness; they vary in the limits they set to the group within which they wish to make certain moral attitudes dominant; different religions make different demands in order to satisfy their deities. But, however strange these different views appear to an outsider, within the group holding them they hang together by a law of association and make themselves a sort of system which distinguishes the culture of that system from every other.[15]

It is frequently said that Adam Smith made much use of history throughout his works. And indeed there are many little historical narratives tucked away in his pages. In the *Wealth of Nations*, for example, are to be found short accounts of the beginnings of navigation and civilization in the countries around the Mediterranean; of systems of coinage; of China's social organization, in contrast to European, and what its results are for class differentiation, wage levels and standards of living; of the trend of Europe after the fall of Rome toward a town economy instead of a rural economy; of some developments in the relations of banking and commerce in England and Scotland; of the educational policies of Great Britain. But for the most part these historical accounts, accurate and informative though they may be, are used by Smith not as data from which to draw generalizations, but as examples of a theory already advanced. What he is interested to trace, primarily, is the natural progress of opulence, and these little episodes either illustrate the ways in which a particular society has proceeded according to the natural order of things, or, by some arbitrary policy, has entirely inverted the natural order and has not operated on the principle of natural liberty. To quote an able economist on the point of Smith's use of history: "The germs of a genetic treatment are there, but they are tributary and subordinate to the system of natural liberty."[16]

Another use Smith makes of history is to assume that

certain historical facts are legitimate propositions from
which may be deduced a long series of consequences. For
instance, mercantilism seemed to him inherently unfair
and harmful to all classes of the population except the
commercialists who were profiting under the system of
subsidies and monopolies. He, therefore, on the basis of
fact that he knew, i.e., the evils of governmental interference of the kind which sustained mercantilism, argued for
the removal of government from business, for freedom of
trade. But it was not enough for him that the simple facts
had to be combatted—they must be seen as belonging to
a system, to a theory. So Smith analyzed the evils of mercantilism as contravening the system of freedom of initiative which a natural order of society provided everywhere,
and which, when not interfered with, works beneficently for
all. He was not arguing for capitalism on a large scale—
machine production was still extremely limited in 1776—
and one wonders, remembering his concern for farmers
and laborers as well as for entrepreneurs, what his position
would have been could he have lived on into the nineteenth
century to hear his theory distorted to the advantage of
one group.[17]

For one of his most characteristic approaches to the
problem connected with man's past record, we shall let
Dugald Stewart, his younger friend, present the claims
for Smith's achievement. Stewart wrote the first account
of the life and writings of Smith, and in the course of his
paper he discussed, very favorably, Smith's *Dissertation
on the Origin of Languages*. In the judgment of Stewart
this essay is "a specimen of a particular sort of enquiry,"
entirely of modern origin and of a kind "which seems, in
a peculiar degree, to have interested Mr. Smith's curiosity. Something very like it may be traced in all his different works, whether moral, political, or literary." Since
there is, Stewart continues, a marked difference in the
institutions, ideas, manners, arts which we enjoy and those
enjoyed by rude peoples, "it cannot fail to occur to us as
an interesting question, by what gradual steps the transi-

tion has been made from the first simple efforts of uncultivated nature, to a state of things so wonderfully artificial
and complicated." But history offers us little information
on the subject, and the answers are to be had by resorting
to another source:

> In this want of direct evidence, we are under a necessity of
> supplying the place of fact by conjecture; and when we are
> unable to ascertain how men have actually conducted themselves
> upon particular occasions, of considering in what manner they
> are likely to have proceeded, from the principles of their nature,
> and the circumstances of their external situation. In such en-
> quiries, the detached facts which travels and voyages afford us,
> may frequently serve as land-marks to our speculations; and
> sometimes our conclusions *a priori,* may tend to confirm the credi-
> bility of facts, which, on a superficial view, appeared to be
> doubtful or incredible.

Stewart would not have us think that such accounts
serve only to gratify curiosity. They have, he thinks, their
scientific value:

> In examining the history of mankind, as well as in examining
> the phenomena of the material world, when we cannot trace the
> process by which an event *has been* produced, it is often of im-
> portance to be able to show how it *may have been* produced by
> natural causes.

Then he christens the procedure:

> To this species of philosophical investigations, which has no
> appropriated name in our language, I shall take the liberty of
> giving the title of *Theoretical* or *Conjectural History*; an ex-
> pression which coincides pretty nearly in its meaning with that
> of *Natural History,* as employed by Mr. Hume, and with what
> some French writers have called *Histoire Raisonnée.*

But interpretations may vary as to how things may
have come about. That, however, is no deterrent. Stewart
defends the method in this fashion:

> But whether they have been realized or no, is often a question
> of little consequence. In most cases, it is of more importance to
> ascertain the progress that is most simple, than the progress
> that is most agreeable to fact; for, paradoxical as it may appear,
> it is certainly true that the real progress is not always the most
> natural. It may have been determined by particular accidents,

which are not likely again to occur, and which cannot be considered as forming any part of that general provision which nature has made for the improvement of the race.[18]

In this little interpretation we have the key not only to Adam Smith's discussion of the natural progress of opulence and how that has sometimes been inverted, but to much of our later literature concerning the history of institutions and culture. Bagehot said of Smith that he wanted to show "how from being a savage, man rose to be a Scotchman"[19]; for Smith, or anyone else, to try to answer such a large question involves a high degree of abstraction and simplification and even speculation unless he resorts to history of a very different sort. We have been slow to recognize the fictional nature of many such answers, and Adam Smith's influence is still to be seen in methods, as well as in some doctrines, of economics and of the more general relations of men.

For Stewart himself the history which most concerns him is the history of ideas. To him we owe much for the accounts he gives us of the changes rung on ideas not only by his contemporaries, but by his predecessors in philosophy. His *Dissertation Exhibiting the Progress of Metaphysical, Ethical, and Political Philosophy since the Revival of Letters in Europe* was comparable, for English readers, to D'Alembert's *Discours* which introduced the *Encyclopédie*. Not only in this essay but throughout his discussions and notes he deals in cool-headed fashion with systems of thought which have gone irregularly, now this way and now that, in the course of years. But when he comes to generalize, his judgment is that there has been a progress of reason in the race, as natural a process as the growth of reason in a single human being or as improvement in a bee's technique of cell-building. Behind all such progresses and in all stages, even the rudest, is the guidance of an invisible hand.[20]

The history of man's past is seen, by him, simply as the progress of intelligence. Details, facts, localities, influences drop from his mind, and he does not think that much information could be had which would enlighten us. Lacking full materials of history concerning steps, whether gradual or otherwise, Stewart supplies the place of evidence with conjectures as to what might naturally have happened, given man as he is constituted. Thus, as we have already seen, he works out from a psychological center, along what he regards as the normal lines of development for rational creatures. The result is that he, too, gives us what he calls theoretical or conjectural history. When he recognizes occasionally that here and there a development has occurred which might not have been expected, which was not the most natural, he passes it by with little notice other than to say that the actual is not of much importance for the delineator of the past who is interested in simplicity of outline and in seeing the relations between institutional development and the general state of development of peoples.

Since the influence of Montesquieu is usually interpreted as having made for a more factual history, let us see Stewart's word on that matter. Discussing the merits of Smith's several theoretical histories—those dealing with mathematics, language, astronomy, opulence—he goes on to say:

> Montesquieu considered laws as originating chiefly from the circumstances of society, and attempted to account, from the changes in the condition of mankind, which take place in the different stages of their progress, for the corresponding alterations which their institutions undergo. It is thus, that in his historical elucidations of the Roman jurisprudence, instead of bewildering himself among the erudition of scholiasts and of antiquaries, we frequently find him borrowing his lights from the most remote and unconnected quarters of the globe, and combining the casual observations of illiterate travellers and navigators, into a philosophical commentary on the history of law and of manners.[21]

This paragraph is interesting for a number of reasons, written as it is in a spirit of praise by a man whose reputation was so high. There is suggested here one very valid clue to the reasons for the popularity of this theoretical history—the Lord President Montesquieu had written it.

And he had written it, not on any theory of the primacy of facts for history, but on his theory that all knowledge is knowledge of relations. On this basic presupposition, he saw any institution or custom in a particular time and place as an expression of all the related influences playing upon it, external as well as spiritual. Fluctuations in institutions, then, may be correlated with fluctuations in the operative influences, especially those influences that are intellectual and moral. A disciple of Montesquieu's, then, might think that when he correlated certain phases of institutional development with certain phases of intellectual development he was following in the footsteps of his master. This, at any rate, would seem to be implied in Stewart's remark, and is worth remembering in connection with the popularity of this "natural" history.

One other comment in the paragraph is significant, and it is connected with the first. Stewart speaks of Montesquieu's practice of "borrowing his lights from the most remote and unconnected quarters of the globe, and combining [such] into a philosophical commentary on the history of law and of manners." Now, since Auguste Comte, we have been calling this procedure "the comparative method." It may bring into comparison a culture trait of one historical epoch with that of another, preferably living, people. It may bring into comparison, very roughly to be sure, the state of an art, the slight variations in a commonly held idea, the similarity of customs of peoples. The purpose of the comparison is to supply in the series of forms of one of the peoples or items compared, a series which has missing links or lack of information, information from the other series which is believed to run so nearly parallel to the first that a valid substitution can be made. But what lies at the root of this procedure of comparison is a set of assumptions:

First, the successive modifications which constitute the forward march of humanity are always slow, gradual and continuous. Second, these modifications follow invariably an order which is fixed and determined. Third, the differences between groups are due to the inequality in the speed (*vitesse*) with which they pass through the consecutive stages.[22]

For the clearest and most cogent analysis of the fallacies involved in this method and for an exposition of the damage which its use has done to history and the social sciences, we have the work of Professor Teggart, just cited, which is invaluable. We cannot here repeat his arguments nor even indicate the several threads of ideas which are woven into this method of thought he criticizes. We can note only that in their preoccupation with their conception of the universe as orderly, and their notion that any realm of "the natural" was a realm for scientific investigation, these men of the eighteenth century saw only justification for this method of comparison which could result so easily in devising pseudo-historical pictures of the past. Not that they would have called them "pseudo"-historical—that is our word; they called them natural, hypothetical, conjectural, theoretical. Whatever the adjective favored by the particular author, his product represented, as Professor Teggart says, "not some curious aberration of thought, but a most serious effort to lay the foundations for a strictly scientific approach to the study of man."[23] We have seen several examples of it already in our account, and more will follow. When it was such a popular form one wonders why historians have not taken the trouble to analyze its objectives and its fallacies, beyond calling it "curious."

Turning our attention now to Lord Kames, it is evident that he had a considerable amount of the historical spirit, if by that we mean, rather simply, an interest in putting a bit of the time dimension into his analyses. But aside from his records of the decisions of the Court of Session and a few other concrete studies, his historical accounts resolve themselves into a succession of "progresses." The different parts of his *Sketches of the History of Man*, for example, concern the progress of men as individuals independent of society and of men in society, and the progress of the sciences—all the subdivisions are entitled in the

same fashion. The object of the work is to trace the progress toward maturity which different nations have made
since the post-Babel degeneracy. Of that "terrible convulsion" we took some account in Chapter III, when we
discussed Kames' speculations as to the unity or diversity
of the species Man. It was a convenient catastrophe for
Kames himself: it not only allowed him to enunciate his
racialist theory on the diversity of man, but it allowed him
to reconcile a rather pale primitivism with an ardent belief in progress.[24]

Though after Babel the races were different, they all
shared a common human nature. Even the peoples who
have developed most slowly give evidence of being possessed of a moral sense and a sense of taste, though both
are faint and obscure. By the law of our being, these
various abilities "refine" and "polish" gradually in individuals and in races. The human reason, in general, has
its nonage, just as any individual goes through such a
depressing stage. Morality, too, has made a gradual progress, being found in a state of infancy among savages and
a state of maturity among polished nations. And government has had its very simple forms fitting for the infancy
of societies. In his discussion of the arts, he gives an interesting variation of his scheme of slow and gradual change.
It seldom fails, he says, that arts make rapid progress
"when a people happen to be roused from a torpid state
by some fortunate change of circumstance. . . ." The
"prosperity contrasted with former abasement, gives to
the mind a spring, which is vigorously exerted in every
new pursuit." Another cause of activity is engagement in
some important action whose outcome is doubtful, such as
a struggle for liberty, or resistance to an invader; emula-
tion, too, is a spur, but it is a disadvantage, rather than
an advantage, when some extraordinary genius kills the
hope in his compatriots of equaling him.[25]

For the most part the various "progresses" are marked
off into stages which sound very much like those of early
anthropology. Hunting, fishing and agriculture, for ex-

ample, represent the familiar generalized story of the
forms of man's maintenance; religion has its many stages,
from rudest polytheism until the true theology of one
benevolent God is achieved by the "gradual openings of
the human mind with respect to Deity." In all his accounts
he relies on a procedure, the use of the comparative
method, which he describes explicitly in his *Historical
Law Tracts* and which merits quotation here, since it is
a procedure until recently used by some historians of social institutions:

> We must be satisfied with collecting the facts and circum-
> stances as they may be gathered from the laws of different
> countries: and if these put together make a regular chain of
> causes and effects, we may rationally conclude, that the progress
> has been the same among all nations, in the capital circumstances
> at least; for accidents, or the singular nature of a people, or of
> a government, will always produce some peculiarities.[26]

It was this work of Kames, just cited, which sought to
follow Bolingbroke's dictum that, while one of the vantage
grounds to which scholars in the law must climb is historical knowledge, the other is metaphysics—metaphysics
here defined as the knowledge of the secret recesses of the
heart and the abstract reason of all laws. This attempted
combination brought from Hume a very caustic comment.
In a letter to Adam Smith, dated April 12, 1759, he said:
"I am afraid of Kames' *Law Tracts*. The man might as
well think of making a fine sauce by a mixture of worm-
wood and aloes as an agreeable combination by joining
metaphysics and Scottish law."[27] As for the history here
introduced, it delves into the introduction of feudalism
into Scotland, the beginnings of Parliament, the laws of
succession, the laws of property and customs of honors
and ranks. Much of it is theoretical, much of it actual
record, but all of it Kames wants to connect with manners
and politics in order to be more "rational." And yet, as a
lawyer, Kames was well aware that legislation has occasionally made drastic changes in the life of a people; and
he knew, too, that wars and commerce and migrations

have resulted in a blend of cultures. It is difficult, then, to trace out original culture patterns from the blends with which we are confronted; difficult, too, to trace out a generalized "progress," but, where it can be approximated, that is the ideal of a "rational" history.

In spite of a religious orthodoxy greater than most of his friends', and in spite of his being pretty completely conformist with respect to many eighteenth-century modes of thought, Kames has a most amazing way of striking now and again a very modern note. For example, one of his most interesting discussions of this character concerns a possible substitute for a standing army. In great detail, he outlines a system which embraces features of the R.O.T.C. and C.M.T.C. And he even provides for the execution of public works under military organization in a way that suggests the depression's C.C.C.![28]

Monboddo would fearfully resent being classed with Kames as a compromiser on the issue of primitivism or progress, but so he is judged by Professor Whitney.[29] Perhaps he would be somewhat mollified to know that he is thought to have compromised to a far greater degree than had his hated rival! The religious scruple which dictated Kames' necessity to reckon with the fall of man was operative to a greater extent in Monboddo, compelling him to reckon not only with the fall, but with the end of the world as it is foretold in the Christian Scriptures and as interpreted philosophically. It is no wonder, therefore, that he found himself hard put to it to make sense of his several convictions drawn from religion, to say nothing of those other convictions drawn from Plato and Aristotle and the men with tails. Just as his absorption in orangoutangs of all sorts led to his being judged an early exponent of biological evolution, so the large place given to criticisms of civilization and praise of the natural life has led to false judgments as to his view of man's history. Many have supposed him to be utterly pessimistic about the life of man in society, always looking back in nostalgic mood to the days of simplicity and bliss; but, as Professor

Whitney remarks, "his final word is not primitivism but progress." Let us turn to his account of the history of man.

Man was made the only intelligent animal on the earth, and was made in the image of God; but at that he was the lowest species of intellectual being in the universe. The Supreme Being, of perfect intelligence, has below him other ranks of intelligent species: "archangels, angels, cherubims, seraphims, and, in order to make the system of nature compleat, there must be many species of intellectual beings below them, till we come down to man, the lowest species of intellectual beings that we know."[30] But as the most intelligent being on the earth, man was to be governor of it, and as such, he should have been the happiest of creatures, whereas he is very miserable. What accounts for his condition?

In answering that question Monboddo gives us his interpretation of the fall of man. He rejoices that the Christian religion supplies an explanation which was lacking in Plato, though Plato recognized that man had fallen. But the explanation as given by Moses and accepted by Christians must be treated always as a parable, as an allegory:

I think, it would be impious (for it would be a ridicule of Religion), to suppose that the Trees of Life and of the knowledge of Good and Evil really existed. . . . This allegory, when explained in the manner I have done, gives a very probable account of the fall of man; for it was very natural, that being so much superior to all the other animals on this earth, by his being the only intelligent animal, he should fancy himself still more superior, and believe himself to be nothing less than a god.

So, then, by his sin of intellectual pride man fell into a state where he lost the use of his full intellectual powers, and was left only with the capacity to reacquire them over a long period of time. In plain words, he "became a creature, such as Aristotle has described him, only capable of intellect and science," but not actually possessing them. In this state he was a quadruped, a solitary and unsocial animal, such as Wild Peter of the Hanover woods, without

intelligence and science. But not all men stayed in this
state forever; some became herding animals, thus advancing to some degree of social organization, though not
achieving intelligence. And here Monboddo produces his
orang-outangs again, as examples of beings in the herding stage. But admirable as the orang-outangs are, they
do not represent that achievement which should belong to
man, and it could hardly be expected that man should remain in that niche.

The faculty of intellect, which only remained with him after
his fall, is a latent quality in him, which can only be produced
by degrees; and it is only civil society, and the close intercourse
of men with one another in that society, that bring forth this
latent quality by giving him occasion to exercise it, in the same
manner as other latent faculties in our natures are produced,
such as the use of speech, of music, and, I may add, of every
other art and science, which all belong to our nature, but are
only exerted by use and practice in civil society.[31]

Civil society, then, was to be the medium and the agent
for the rehabilitation of man, for the restoration to him
of all his faculties in actuality, so that he would be somewhat as he was before his fall. But as, throughout nature,
things are formed by degrees, so with civil society. It was
not agreed upon all in one day by a great group of herd-
ers; rather, it came about here and there by way of family
cohesion and co-operation, as may be judged from the
fact that North American Indians are organized into
small nations which consisted originally of not more than
three families. But wherever it came into being, it produced the improvement of the intellect, or, to use a stronger
word, the acquisition of intellect. Such gains were possible
because of the close intercourse of men in civil society, and
that, in turn, was possible only because of the wonderful
invention of language. "Language, therefore, is the foundation of all the improvement we can make of our mind
in this life: And it must have been invented before any
other art." It must have been invented in the very first
age of civil society, and there must have been some supernatural aid offered man to enable him to create such a

marvelous tool. Only after the invention of language, the parent art, could men learn to form ideas, really to think, and still later to invent the arts and sciences.[32]

And then Monboddo takes a position which should endear him to the hearts of the diffusionists of the G. Elliot Smith school in anthropology, for he sees Egypt as the parent country of all the arts and sciences. There men first became men again. From there culture spread, by conquest and by migrations of people, to the Near East, to India, to Europe. It would have been unnecessary and superfluous for every country to have invented its own culture. He continues to hope that the orang-outangs may still learn speech, and from that progress to other arts, particularly if a people possessed of culture should settle near them.[33]

Thus, it is due to civil society that man has the arts and sciences, has such happiness as he has or will have in another life, and that he comes to any idea of God. But, at that, man's estate is not an ecstatically happy one. For his intellect is still weak, "very much weaker than he had before his fall," and he cannot but fall into errors that are moral evils, that arise from wrong judgments as to what is good or ill. He indulges the pleasures of sense, and this indulgence leads him to depart from that natural way of eating and drinking which the animals observe. Consequently his physical body is weakened by unnatural strains put upon it, and his mind is diverted to the furnishing of devices and luxuries instead of being held to nobler pursuits. Another false judgment man makes, which is not sensual but proceeds from the intellect itself: man loves the beautiful, the admirable, but his taste in that may become as perverted as his taste in food, and vanity and ambition may, then, become the ruling motives of men. All men are likely to be so swayed at times, but vanity is a very noticeable failing with rulers in civil governments and leads to many miseries for their subjects.[34]

So strongly does Monboddo stress the misery of man that it rather startles the reader to come upon his equally emphatic praise of civil society and its advantages. It is, perhaps, his own way of expressing the optimism of the century, not the unqualified and blatant optimism frequently attributed to it, but that philosophical variety which viewed the universe as the best that, under the circumstances and limitations, could be created. So civil society seems to Monboddo: it would have been preferable, conceivably, had man never fallen; but since, in the exercise of his God-given intellect, he had, the only way of restoration for him was in a kind of life which would call out and develop those very faculties he had lost by his sin. This stimulus civil society affords him; indeed, he is required in it to use his mind; so, imperfect though it is, civil society represents the best life man can possibly have.

But though this is true, its imperfections will bring civil society to an end. The deterioration of the animal body is evident not only from the many diseases of mankind, but from the great decrease in population everywhere observable. The race is, literally, dying. It is "in such a state of decline in mind, body, and in numbers, that it would be irreconcilable with the wisdom and goodness of God, that man should continue in the wretched state he is in for any very much longer time." History, philosophy and Christian revelation agree that the end of this world is near. Some great convulsion of nature will change the whole scene, though Monboddo thinks the change may be in different countries at different times. But a new Heaven and another Earth, inhabited by a new race of men called Saints, will take the place of this scheme of things, as foretold in Christian Scriptures, and man's apprenticeship in civil society will have had its reward. Thus will come to an end on this planet the history of man, "that most curious and most wonderful animal upon this earth."[35]

This is Monboddo's strange account drawn from religion, from history, from ancient philosophy and from his own speculation on the morals of man. A primitivistic philosophy it is, if we choose to emphasize the perfect state of man at his original creation; primitivistic, still, if we choose to accent only his praise for the instinctive life and economy of the animals and of natural men, and civilized man's subsequent physical degeneration. But, involved in contradictions though it is, as Professor Whitney so clearly shows, Monboddo's "final word is not primitivism but progress."[36]

Referring again to Ferguson's approach to history, after noting other historical writings of the century, we can see that in this field, too, his procedure was fairly typical of that of his contemporaries, and that he made no radical departures in method. He, too, wrote what would still be called a genuine history—his *History of the Progress and Termination of the Roman Republic* (1783) —and he wrote also that generalized, psychogenetic, analogical, "natural" history—his *Essay on the History of Civil Society* (1767). Both books were exceedingly popular, the former continuing to be reprinted for use in schools and colleges, even in the United States, until the middle of the nineteenth century, and the latter just now being highly spoken of by sociologists as a forerunner of their discipline.

For his Roman history, as he tells us in the "Advertisement," he drew on Dionysius of Halicarnassus, Plutarch, Florus, Polybius, Appian, Dion Cassius, Nepos, Caesar, Cicero, Tacitus, and, where matters of natural history were involved, he sought the authority of Pliny and, where geography, Strabo. The work is written with considerable liveliness, and with noticeable emphasis on the military exploits of various Roman generals. Perhaps this emphasis is to be explained by the term of military service Ferguson himself had done, when as a young man he was with the Black Watch in Flanders. Personalities loom large, also, with Ferguson's judgments as to their character and achievements. It is amusing to read his characterization of Julius Caesar as a "successful adventurer," in itemized terms that would, to many persons, be equally applicable to the most recent pretender to Caesar's position in the Italian peninsula.

Several points of view are expressed which are typical of the assumptions of most of the historians and moralists of the century. For example, there is the biological analogy applied to human history. Rome, he says, "came by degrees to its greatness . . . so much we may safely admit on the general analogy of human affairs." And, at the conclusion, writing of the termination of the republican period, he gives this judgment:

The military and political virtues, which had been exerted in forming this empire, having finished their course, a general relaxation ensued, under which, the very forms that were necessary for its preservation were in process of time neglected. As the spirit which gave rise to those forms was gradually spent, human nature fell into a retrograde motion, which the virtues of individuals could not suspend; and men, in the application of their faculties even to the most ordinary purposes of life, suffered a slow and insensible, but almost continual, decline.

The concerns of the moralist emerge frequently; a good example occurs in his discussion of the merit of party leaders in the later period of the republic—the Gracchi, Marius and Cinna, Caesar and Pompey, and Cato are discussed and judged as to their motives and performance. Combined with the discussion of virtues and vices is considerable political theory and knowledge of practical politics, and no doubt his readers felt that history did qualify as philosophy teaching by examples.[37]

Of the *Essay on the History of Civil Society* we shall say nothing further here except to recall several major themes: his contrast of "rudeness" and civilization; his cogent criticisms of the prevalent conceptions of the state of nature, both of man and of society; his insistence on the fact of society as primordial; his use of the comparative method; his ethical weighing of the advantages and hazards of civilization; above all, his confidence that there is a principle at work in the affairs of men which brings progress, a confidence resting not only on his generalizations from history, but on his belief that man has, even within himself, such a principle which leads him to work toward perfecting himself and his institutions.

In any consideration of eighteenth-century history, David Hume's name would, without question, be well toward the top of the list of authors. As a living historian has recently said, his *History of England* for three-quarters of a century held the field against all others.[38] Not until Mill and Macaulay was he superseded, and his popularity was not really eclipsed until the appearance of Green's *Short History of the English People* in 1874.

Let us, then, see what kinds of questions Hume thought worth investigating historically when he had turned from speculative philosophy. What kind of history did Hume write? What, in his opinion, constituted experience-data for the historian? What prepossessions did he have, if any, in the way of values ascribed to one period or another as offering subject matter for the historian?

The physical aspects of man's life concern Hume less than they do most historians. Habitation, climate, food, tools, are scarcely mentioned. One of his longest and most learned essays is devoted to the study of population, a definitely sociological topic, but the object is to criticize and discredit the claims made by ancient historians for vast populations.[39] The stabilizing of property by the consent of social groups and the resulting binding ideals of justice he discusses more than once.[40] He speculates, with many historical references, on the conditions which stimulate progress in the arts and sciences, and attempts to fix the limits beyond which refinement becomes dangerous luxury[41]—the latter, a perennial subject for moralists. A glance through his *Essays* discloses his political interests, treated nearly always by appeal to history. He discusses parties and their coalitions, civil liberty in relation to different forms of government, the justification of government, the causes of the phenomenon known as national character, the making of a science of politics on the basis of psychology and history, the elements of the perfect commonwealth. The most significant of these interests, perhaps, is his concern that writers be more accurately historical when discussing the origin of government. His arguments on this point should have put an end to what Coleridge called the "metapolitical school."[42] Even though on some very remote day in man's past there may have been a voluntary reception of command from an acknowledged superior, it is foolish, he insists, to cite that incident as the origin of government; it is political, not personal, force that is to be accounted for, and practically every state has begun in usurpation and conquest. A glance around the globe, too, will disclose how untrue it is that the citizens of a state are free to enter into contract with the rulers, and how unlikely it is that rulers will admit that their subjects are not their subjects but co-parties to a contract with them. Continuance of political power is due to habit and education on the part of the people and to the fact that the race of man never passes off the stage entirely at one time as silkworms and butterflies pass, and so never has the chance to make arrangements *de novo*. Every fact of history and of contemporary politics refutes, thus, the favorite doctrine of the Whigs; and then, in true Tory fashion, he points out the duty of passive obedience.[43]

With others of the eighteenth century Hume was much interested in the position of women in various societies, past and present. He notes that while men in barbarous cultures enslave the women and thus demonstrate their own superior status, the same demonstration of superiority is made among polished people by the show of gallantry which men make to women. As if anticipating his experience in Parisian salons, he points out that a company of women is a very school for manners, embellishing, enlivening and polishing society. He discusses the wide differences which obtain regarding marriage laws and freedom of divorce; he pronounces categorically in favor of inseparable ties, but with as much realism as any modern protagonist who desires the greatest freedom for both man and woman, though without overworking the claims of romantic love.[44]

What, in general, can be said of the historical method pursued by Hume in these various brief discussions?

First, we have to admit that he is not entirely free of the practice of describing analogically a change in institutions and even in whole nations. For example, he says that death is as unavoidable for the political as for the animal body; that the mortality of the fabric of the world is evident, that it has an infancy, youth, manhood and old age as really as any individual organism in it, though we are unable to say in which period it now is; that there is a natural course of things for industry and arts and trade; that there is a natural tendency to rise from idolatry to theism and sink again to idolatry, evidence of a kind of flux and reflux in the human mind; that there is an ultimate point of depression as well as exaltation, from which human affairs return in a contrary progress and beyond which they never pass in their advancement or decline. This represents a typical interpretation of social change, current since the time of the Pre-Socratic philosophers. The question they phrased thus: "What is change like?", and the answer, as indicated, was given in terms of an analogy, usually biological.[45]

Since the Quarrel of the Ancients and Moderns, however, the opinion had spread that there need be no decadence for the culture of men, and no repetition of immaturity; instead, there lay ahead infinite progress. Times already past had witnessed the youthful ignorance of the race; the race now was mature, and while individuals would grow old and die as hitherto, the race would continue to accumulate learning and conveniences without end. In other words, the old cyclical interpretation shifted to that of a progress: we have grown and are continuing to grow toward wiser and happier ages. The analogy of growth is still the basic idea, but all suggestion of failing powers and cessation has been dropped. To this popular philosophy of history, too, David Hume often gives his tacit consent. Man makes a progress from being simply a family-organized creature into being a politically or-

ganized creature; there is a rise and progress of the arts
and sciences to be delineated; there is a natural progress
of human thought; the mind gradually rises from inferior
to superior thought as it abstracts from that which is imperfect, and forms nobler ideas of perfection.[46]

On this line of reasoning, Hume shares another contemporary failing: since civilization is the last term of the
progressive series, it is the only profitable period for the
historian's full treatment. The "adventures of barbarous
nations, even if they were recorded could afford little or no
entertainment to men born in a more cultivated age. . . .
The only certain means by which nations can indulge their
curiosity in researches concerning their remote origin is
to consider the languages, manners and customs of their
ancestors, and to compare them with those of neighboring
nations." But such a resort to the records of the past has
its dangers, he thinks:

> Above all, a civilized nation, like the English, who have hap-
> pily established the most perfect and most accurate system of
> liberty, that ever was found compatible with government, ought
> to be cautious of appealing to the practice of their ancestors, or
> regarding the maxims of uncultivated ages as certain rules for
> their present conduct. An acquaintance with the history of the
> remote periods of their government is chiefly *useful* by instruct-
> ing them to cherish their present constitution from a comparison
> or contrast with the condition of those distant times. And it is
> also *curious,* by showing that the remote, and commonly faint
> and disfigured originals of the most finished and most noble in-
> stitutions, and by instructing them in the great mixture of acci-
> dent which commonly occurs with a small ingredient of wisdom
> and foresight, in erecting the complicated fabric of the most
> perfect government.[47]

He is free of one of the common errors of the eighteenth
century in that he is impatient of quick correlation of
culture and climate. In discussing the question of national
character he says "nor do I think, that men owe anything
of their temper or genius to the air, food or climate . . .
physical causes have no discernible operation on the human
mind." He leans rather to what he calls moral causes, such
things as revolutions, the plenty or penury in which people

live, the nature of their government, and their situation with regard to neighbors—causes which "work on the mind as motives or reasons," all of which call for explanation themselves at other times, of course. He admits freely that there is something accidental in the first rise and progress of the arts in any nation; and yet the admission does not lead him to weight his explanations with chance. To do that would at once cut short all further inquiry concerning the situation under investigation. The items enumerated above as moral causes are obviously conditions which can be historically identified for given people at given times; they are conditions which affect groups of people, not single individuals alone, and, in turn, they are products of the interrelated life of groups. By this recognition which he constantly gives to groups and to the welter of social relations, Hume is partially freed from the false logic of individualism, and is that much nearer achieving a truly historical perspective,[48] and one which must belong to the social sciences.

Hume's essays and speculative discussions are full of accounts which would now be called "the new history." Kings, battles and dates are passed over for discussions of manners, customs, ideas, institutions. And yet, when we turn to the *History of England*, we find that the content of chapter after chapter deals with dynasties, decrees and campaigns, in straight chronological order. All of the culture-history of the English until 1688 is relegated to four brief appendices scattered throughout the work. And yet he himself had written, at the introduction of one such section: "The chief use of history is, that it affords materials for disquisitions of this nature"[49] [manners, finances, arms, commerce, arts and sciences]. Even within the more conventional field to which he limits himself there is little that seems unique in his treatment or searching in its explication. Personage after personage is very much the same, event after event is not particularly distinguishable. He must really have believed what he once wrote, that men are so much alike that history has

little which is new to tell us, and chiefly shows up the constant and universal principles in human nature.[50]

That is not to say that there are not very telling judgments on characters and situations, judgments which in
Hume's day provoked bitter controversy. One recalls his
characterization of the Puritans and of the Catholics, of
Cromwell and of Charles I.[51] It was Hume's gentleness in
dealing with the Stuarts, especially his defense of Charles
I, which brought such a storm of controversy against his
History of England; a Whig generation was an odd time
in which to write a Tory history.

What, at root, is the reason for the dissatisfaction we
feel in Hume's history? Professor Black offers a suggestion, when he says that on Hume's theory of the sameness,
the uniformity of human nature which underlies history
as well as the other "moral" sciences, history becomes "a
repeating decimal. The great drama is transacted on a
flat and uniform level; each age or group working up into
forms that are already familiar the common stock of attributes."[52] And yet this is not to say that a vast amount
of factual material is not handled. The whole library of
the Faculty of Advocates was at his hand, the best collection of books in Scotland, and there is evidence enough
that he drew heavily on it.[53] It is his pervasive psychology
which lays the blight, and which, in spite of his recognition
of differences in culture, makes him see things as of the
same pattern after all. As Strachey puts it, "the virtues
of a metaphysician are the vices of a historian."[54]

And yet we cannot deny that here and there he seems
to shake off his psychology. For instance, he is certain
there is something accidental in the first rise and progress
of the arts in any nation. He remarks that he does not
remember a passage in any ancient writer where the growth
of a city is ascribed to the establishment of a manufacture,
as if to imply recognition of the historical importance of
such an establishment wherever it occurs. We have already
noted the pointedness with which he declares that there is
no historical warrant for talking of a state of nature, or

of the political contract. He uses the phrase "laws of nature," but to mean only those actual rules relating to property and promises which men have devised, and to which are added the laws of nations.[55]

In spite of his psychology which leads him to stress similarities, Hume is very conscious, as the whole of the century was, of the differences in culture which are to be found over the world. How to account for them puzzles him. He says in "A Dialogue" that ultimately they root in the first principles of utility and agreeableness, but along the way they are determined by fashion, vogue, custom, law. If this is to leave considerable explanation still wanting, it represents the same kind of inadequacy which is to be found in some discussions of our own recent past, for example, those of Sumner in his *Folkways*, of Ross in his *Social Control* and his *Social Psychology*, and of Tarde in his *Laws of Imitation*. When he discusses the conditions stimulating to the arts and sciences, he mentions free government as the best nursery because its laws make for security, security for the free play of curiosity, and curiosity for knowledge. He mentions next the contiguity of small states connected by commerce and policy, a contiguity which stimulates both imitation and jealousy, and breaks up authority. Transplanting and borrowing are as possible as they are because people are imitative, and rarely are known to lose useful arts. Finally, he is sure that in any state when perfection is reached, the arts and sciences begin to decline, because men become hopeless of rivaling a perfect product.[56]

It is no wonder that modern social psychologists claim Hume as an eighteenth-century progenitor. And yet, amidst all this talk of human nature, he offers, as Professor Teggart has pointed out, some very correct clues as to how we may approach the study of man, remembering that man has a past as well as a nature. There is the recognition of differences which supply matter for investigation, whereas too early a judgment of similarity closes the pursuit. These differences remain more or less fixed or stable for long periods. Next comes the recognition of the innumerable modifications which an institution or a people undergoes, minute variations which do not produce a different thing. Then there is the admission that sometimes real breaks come and that after them there is a real difference in behavior, and in culture elements as well.[57]

But Hume cannot escape his century. In spite of his feeling for history, in spite of his much writing of it, his historical method is vitiated by a fundamental assumption. This assumption, shared by all his contemporaries, is that the starting point for all humanistic study, including history, is man's nature, his psychology. Most of his historical studies, then, turn out to be that species of history which he calls "natural" and which Dugald Stewart calls "hypothetical" or "conjectural." In them, as we have seen, a simple logical or psychological element is taken as the earliest genetic element, and "natural" logical deductions thereafter are made to correspond to a time scheme.[58]

Understandable this method is for the eighteenth century. It represented the best scientific account of man's past then thought to be available: it was shorn of particularity and uniqueness, and represented instead what, to the witness, was the usual, the normal, therefore the scientific. But we cannot pass it by as an expression of method which had its day and ceased to be. We cannot regard it, using other words loved of the century, as something "curious" and "amusing," and leave it at that. For there have been consequences that have introduced serious problems into the procedures of the social sciences.

Recently Sir Grafton Elliot Smith has outlined, in a convincing way, the results of applying this kind of historical treatment to the pre-Columbian civilizations in America. He maintains that William Robertson's *History of America* (1777) and W. H. Prescott's *Conquest of Mexico* (1843) are vitiated in their historical adequacy by this same kind of psychologizing: since the powers of nature (including human nature) are uniform and unfailing, it may be taken for granted that civilizations will grow up independently and spontaneously and follow, more or less, the same general course. It is unfortunate, too, that the early English anthropologist, Sir Edward Burnett Tylor, threw the weight of his great influence away from adequate historical research toward this "lapse into the methods of Cartesian scholasticism. . . ."[59]

As well founded as this criticism is, and as useful as is his analysis of the "prejudices" displayed by the early historians of America and anthropologists in their refusal to deal fairly with the facts of diffusion (and, of course it must be remembered that "extreme" diffusionism is Sir Elliot's "prejudice"), his discussion lacks the clarity and detail in dealing with the concepts involved which characterizes an earlier discussion, that of Professor Teggart. In his *Theory of History* Professor Teggart lays bare the whole framework of thought within which such expressions as eighteenth century "natural" history were possible and, by the century, justified. His treatment includes also discussion of procedures typical of sociology and anthropology since Tylor's day, and traces the history of directing concepts further back than the Cartesian period with which Sir Grafton Elliot Smith begins.

Professor Teggart's discussion should be read in entirety by all who want to understand some of the major methodological problems faced by social scientists. What is presented most clearly is the impasse in which these sciences are involved when they undertake to deal with the past. History, as he sees it, has subordinated itself to the art of history-writing, an art which sees any given present as a situation to be explained in terms of the dramatis personae and the dramatic events leading up to it; and, as an art form, it allows a great deal of the personal bias, temperament and philosophy of the historian to enter into the abstraction he chooses to make and into his composition.[60] This, obviously, is not the kind of explication of the past which would stand comparison with the efforts to account for the past of rocks or animals, fields of investigation in which there are no dramatis personae whose histrionic abilities may be exploited by an artist. And it is not the kind of account acceptable to social scientists, who, no more than geologists and zoologists, deal with unique individuals. These scientists are interested not in a chain of events which happened once, but in processes which have repeated themselves many times, in many places, around the world.

The life sciences, and those dealing with men in their social relationships, do not recognize situations, but conditions of things which are to be investigated. This, in the case of the social sciences, directs attention to things which undergo change, things like ideas, institutions, customs, arts, which have changed in the past and which, because of those changes, are in the condition they are today. This type of change is usually thought to be slow, undramatic, and is commonly called evolutionary.[61] Thus, students of man and his past are confronted with two modes of investigation which proceed on totally different sets of assumptions and afford totally different results— the historical with its pitfalls of artistry, and the evolutionary which also has a heritage to be reckoned with.

In analyzing the foundations in thought for the concept of evolutionary change, Professor Teggart first takes account of the heritage from Aristotle, particularly the conception of the aim of scientific inquiry as being the determination of what is "natural or normal, in contradistinction to what has happened by accident or chance." In such a conception the principle of change is seen as a sort of drive in the entity under investigation toward the fulfillment of the possibilities inherent in it[62]—a definitely teleological view. Then, after the Quarrel of the Ancients and the Moderns in the late seventeenth century, when the Moderns had "won" by appeal to Cartesian principles, the opinion became prevalent that not only was knowledge a sort of natural entity which, of itself, would come to full flower, but that the whole of man's civilization was such an entity and that it, too, contained within itself an inner principle of change pushing always slowly toward fulfillment. Every element of that civilization was full of the same vital principle, so that civilization as a whole, or one institution or one idea, could be investigated from that point of view. One thing was certain: any later period would reveal improvements over an earlier. Differences in degree of civilization, differences in functioning of the institution, differences in the richness of an idea, could be accounted for by the different proportions of realization, or actualization, of the potentialities involved. In any case, these changes were natural changes, it was held, undergone because of the natural principle at work, and the outcome was desirable. To put it in other words, these changes spelled progress.

In viewing the use made by the eighteenth century of this set of ideas, Professor Teggart reminds us that the "judgment that progressive change is natural carried with it . . . a world of implication which twentieth-century thought has been too ready to overlook." Not only was the "natural" opposed to the "miraculous" and to the "artificial" as earlier, but to the "monstrous," the "accidental," the "unusual," and, later, to that which was unique rather than repetitive. This complex of ideas was based most immediately on the same Cartesian philosophy which had served well the cause of the Moderns, and which in several of its aspects was good Aristotelianism. The beliefs involved Descartes' conceptions of the laws of nature, and the purpose of those laws; the Cartesian idea of the System of Nature, which could be viewed analogically in the similitude of the normally functioning human body; and the notion of the most normal kind of change which nature knows, namely, the slow, gradual, teleological process of growth.[63]

After an analysis involving such items, together with richness of illustration, Professor Teggart writes:

We are now in a position to see that the "theoretical," "conjectural," "hypothetical" or "natural" history of the eighteenth century represents, not some curious aberration of thought, but a most serious effort to lay the foundations for a strictly scientific approach to the study of man.[64]

Yes, "a most serious effort to lay the foundations for a strictly scientific approach to the study of man." The eighteenth century was right in insisting that particular-istic history was no adequate scientific basis for a science of man; it was right in searching for a kind of history which was comparative, which would reveal repetitive proc-esses resulting from similar factors. But the timeless and eventless accounts of the past which were produced in that century did not really serve the aims of a later social science much better than accounts which emphasize per-sons and situations in the dramatic formulations of the more conventional histories, except to indicate wrongly the kind of history needed. The reader must at this point, however, be referred to Professor Teggart's own provoca-tive discussion for suggestions as to a way out of the impasse.

V

HUMAN NATURE

THE Scottish moralists were convinced that there could
be no sound science of man unless it were built on "the
facts of human nature." But there was considerable variety
in the accounts given of this section of "the laws of nature," and a great many treatises appeared on what we
might now call "the raw material of socialization." One
captious critic of Kames and Hume was distinctly an-
noyed:

> Within this half-century there have appeared so many essays
> and inquiries concerning human nature, as may possibly per-
> suade an unattentive reader, that the nature of man is changed
> from what it was a hundred years ago, or that, until of late, it
> never was rightly understood.[1]

The term "psychology"[2] did not come into use until
toward the close of the century, and if we apply that label
to the work of the Scots and their contemporaries we want
to be clear that it was not altogether the kind of psychology we know today. There were no laboratories, no tests
and measurements. Serious efforts were made to use physiological terms, as far as possible, when accounting for our
mental-emotional behavior and for our ways of coming
to know our world, but the phrase which best describes the
undertaking is "the philosophy of mind." Over and over
again we find the subject matter treated as the understanding and the passions, the understanding and the will,
the rational and the sensible powers, or the intellectual
and active powers.

Inevitably, with Descartes, Hobbes and Locke in the
immediate background, the philosophy of mind could not
but concern itself with epistemological questions: what are
the sources of our knowledge and what guarantees its
validity? Of the Scottish contributors to the answering of
these questions Hume will never be forgotten, and (in the

nineteenth century) Reid was quoted everywhere. But every other man of the group had his own answers. The earliest, Hutcheson, was not argumentative, and in the main accepted the Lockeian position throughout, with frequent references to Shaftesbury's interpretations; Ferguson, because of his extended discussion of propensities or instincts seems less philosophical and more psychological than some; Hume wished to push Lockeian psychology to its logical limits, and Reid set about refuting Hume and rescuing philosophy from the Humean scepticism; Kames and Dugald Stewart mirror fairly faithfully the position of Reid, with Stewart providing a sort of grand summary of preceding writers who were not sceptics; and Monboddo was, on most counts, a Platonist.

We shall in this chapter take some account of Hutcheson, Hume, Reid and Ferguson as those members of the group offering arguments of most significance.

Hutcheson's approach may be seen from this brief passage:

Now the intention of nature, with respect to us, is best shown by examining what these things are which our natural senses or perceptive powers recommend to us, and what are the most excellent among them? and next, what are the aims of our several natural desires, and which of them are of the greatest importance to our happiness?[3]

Here, in a sentence, are to be seen his belief in final cause, his concern with happiness as an objective and a criterion, and his determination to be empirical rather than a priori and dogmatic—for it is to "our structure and frame" he will look for "some clear evidences showing the proper business of mankind."

A complete analysis of the constituents of human nature must take into account both the body and the soul. Of these, the soul is the "nobler" part. Analysis reveals that the soul has two classes of powers: the Understanding and the Will. The Understanding "contains all the powers which aim at knowledge"; the Will, "all our desires pursuing happiness and eschewing misery." Perhaps an outline form would most quickly indicate the scope of Hutcheson's treatment:[4]

HUMAN NATURE

A. Body

B. Soul:

I. Understanding—embracing all the powers which aim at knowledge.

1. Senses—including every power of the soul by which certain feelings, ideas or perceptions are raised when certain objects are presented.

(1) Direct and antecedent senses—presupposing no previous ideas.

a. External senses—depending on certain organs of the body which raise feelings or notions in the soul when an impression is made on the body.

b. Internal senses [called, by some, Consciousness or Reflection].

(2) Reflex or subsequent senses—"by which certain new forms or perceptions are received, in consequence of others previously observed by our external or internal senses; and some of them ensuing upon observing the fortunes of others, or the events discovered by our reason, or the testimony of others."

a. Aesthetic appreciation.

b. Enjoyment in discovery of truth.

c. Sympathy or fellow-feeling.

d. Desire for action.

e. Conscience or the moral sense—"by which we discern what is graceful, becoming, beautiful and honorable in the affections of the soul, in our conduct of life, our words and actions . . . What is approved by this sense, we count right and beautiful, and call it virtue; what is condemned, we count base and deformed and vicious." This sense of moral good and evil is implanted by nature in persons of all nations and epochs.

f. Sense of honor and shame—founded upon the moral sense, or presupposing it, but yet distinct from it and all other senses. It operates as we are conscious of approval or disapproval of our fellows.

g. Sense of the ridiculous—a very important sense for the refining of the manners of mankind and correcting their faults.

II. The Will—containing "all our desires pursuing happiness and eschewing misery."

1. Selfish desires.
   (1) Calm and stable desires: of good for one's self, of aversion to evil, of joy when good is attained or evil avoided, of sorrow when good is lost or evil befalls us.
   (2) Turbulent desires or passions—vehement, blind, impetuous impulses, including desires for power, fame or wealth.

2. Disinterested desires.
   (1) Calm and stable desires.
      a. Benevolence, or good will.
      b. Aversion: in such forms as compassion, indignation.
      c. Joy: in such forms as delectation, pride, arrogance, ostentation.
      d. Sorrow: in such forms as shame, remorse, dejection, brokenness of spirit.
   (2) Turbulent and passionate desires—"nor have we names settled to distinguish always the calm from the passionate."

III. Dispositions relating equally to understanding and will.

1. Disposition to associate or conjoin ideas or affections, "however disparate or unlike, which at once have made strong impressions on our mind . . . To this association, is owing almost wholly our power of memory, or recalling of past events, and even the faculty of speech."

2. Habits. "For such is the nature both of the soul and body, that all our powers are increased and perfected by exercise."

3. Desire to obtain whatever appears as a means to an immediately desirable object, e.g., wealth and power, since they are means of gratifying other desires.

4. Powers of speech and eloquence.

Several comments may be in order here. Quite apparent is the adoption of the Lockeian position on the contribution to knowledge of the direct and antecedent senses. In the *Inquiry*, Hutcheson writes of the mind's passivity in receiving sensations; of its activity, as well, in compounding ideas, comparing objects, observing relations and proportions, abstracting and defining. "But," making a stab at the Rationalists, he ended, "if there be any simple ideas which he [a person] has not received, or if he wants any of the senses necessary for the perception of them, no definition can raise any simple idea which has not been before received by the senses."[5] Hutcheson is uncomfortable whenever he refers to the number of the external senses. Sensible perceptions depend on certain organs of the body; they certainly include tastes, smells, colors, sounds, colds, heats; but also there are hunger, thirst, weariness and sickness, which do not correlate with particular organs so easily. He thus anticipates the predicament in which many a later psychologist found himself:

All these powers exert themselves in a way too dark for any of us ever to apprehend completely: much less have the brutes any knowledge to direct them to the teats of their dams, or notion of the pressure of the air upon which sucking depends. At first indeed we all alike act by instincts wisely implanted by a superior hand.[6]

What, exactly, are sensations, or rather, what knowledge do they bring us of the external world? Hutcheson answers:

These sensations . . . are not pictures or representations of like eternal qualities in objects, nor of the impression or change made in the bodily organs. They are either *signals*, as it were, of new events happening to the body, of which experience and observation will show us the cause; or *marks*, settled by the Author of Nature, to shew us what things are salutary, innocent, or hurtful; or intimations of things not otherways discernible which may affect our state; tho' these marks or signals bear no more resemblance to the external reality, than the report of a gun or the flash of the powder, bears to the distress of a ship.[7]

Here is something very much like Locke's representative realism, and it is followed by a discussion of the primary and secondary qualities of objects, also very much in Lockeian mood. The distinction between primary and secondary qualities was not, of course, original with Locke but reached back to Democritus; Locke had revived the discussion, and, after him, every philosopher felt called upon to say something on the subject. Locke had written that the primary qualities, such as duration, number, solidity, extension, motion, belong to the object itself, while the secondary qualities, such as smell, taste, color, sound, are really subjective, belonging to our minds but not to the objects. Hutcheson agrees, but goes further by saying that the correspondence of our ideas of primary qualities with the qualities themselves can be attributed to no other cause than the operation of God Himself, through a law of nature.[8] This position is much like the Occasionalism of Malebranche or even the Pre-established Harmony of Leibniz—and how near, therefore, to the doctrine of innate ideas which Hutcheson abhorred! These primary qualities are suggested to our minds by the "concomitant sensations," as Hutcheson calls them, sensations which could not stand alone but must always accompany other sensations. And in two places, at least, he speaks of these not as sensations of duration, of solidity, et cetera, but as ideas.[9]

In 1728, three years after the publication of his *Inquiry*, Hutcheson published a volume, the aim of which was to afford the details suggested but not fully worked out in the earlier work. This second book was *An Essay on the Nature and Conduct of the Passions and Affections*. Manifestly, since the moral life was not to be allowed to rest on reason, but primarily on feeling, it was necessary to make out a good case for the adequacy of feeling in such functioning, and for the existence of a moral sense fully as sensitive as any other. So he set himself the task of inquiring into the "various natural principles or natural dispositions of mankind"—and the result is a more than fair psychology of the emotions.

In the opening section he writes, "The nature of human actions cannot be sufficiently understood without considering the affections and passions." He proceeds to the classification and descriptions of our senses and the affections and passions attending them:

1. The external senses—as described above.
2. The internal sense: "the pleasant perceptions arising from regular, harmonious, uniform objects; as also from grandeur

and novelty. These we may call, after Mr. Addison, the pleasures of the imagination; or we may call the power of receiving them, an internal sense." Then he adds, "whoever dislikes this name may substitute another."

3. The public sense—"our determination to be pleased with the happiness of others, and to be uneasy at their misery . . . This is found in some degree in all men and was sometimes called . . . *Sensus Communis* by some of the antients. This inward pain of compassion cannot be called a sensation of sight. It solely arises from an opinion of *misery felt by another*, and not immediately from a visible form."

4. The moral sense—as described above.

5. The sense of honor and shame—as described above.

We are conscious of just so many types of desire, too, corresponding to the classes of our senses:

1. Desires of sensual pleasure.
2. Desires of the pleasures of the imagination.
3. Desires of pleasures arising from public happiness, and aversion to the pains arising from the misery of others.
4. Desires of virtue and aversion to vice.
5. Desires of honor and aversion to shame.

Again, Hutcheson is sure his classifications are imperfect and incomplete and makes way to accommodate other classes, such as the secondary desires of wealth and power, the use of which is to assist in the gratification of all other desires, and desires which, by some circumstance or other, are peculiar to a given age or nation or class, such as particular forms of dress or etiquette.[10]

How does he define his terms when it comes to distinguishing sensation, affection, passion? Some states, when they are immediate perceptions of pleasure or pain from the object or event which is present, are simply sensations. Some other states are affections or passions, perceptions produced not directly by object or event, but by our "reflection upon or apprehension of their present or future existence; so that we expect or judge that the object or event will raise the direct sensations in us." He goes on to illustrate: "When a man has a fit of the gout, he has the painful *sensation*; when he is not at present pained, yet apprehends a sudden return of it, he has the *affection of*

sorrow . . ."; and then, showing his difficulty, he adds
". . . which might be called a sort of sensation: as the
physicians call many of our passions internal senses." As
for passion:

> When the word *passion* is imagined to denote anything differ-
> ent from the affections, it includes a strong brutal impulse of
> the will, sometimes without any distinct notions of good, public
> or private, attended with "a confused sensation either of pleas-
> ure or pain, occasioned or attended by some violent bodily mo-
> tions, which keeps the mind much employed upon the present
> affair, to the exclusion of everything else, and prolongs or
> strengthens the affection sometimes to such a degree, as to pre-
> vent all deliberate reasoning about our conduct."[11]

This is an interesting volume to bring side by side with
some of the psychology of our time. Some of the discussions, with the change of a few words here and there, could
be made to sound quite modern. It was an influential book
in the psychological discussions of its day, and one which
furthered the empirical, naturalistic accounts of man.

David Hume's scepticism with regard to our ability to
acquire accurate and full knowledge by way of our intellectual powers; his discussions, from this sceptical angle,
of causality, and the nature of the self as simply a heap
of perceptions; his criticisms of miracles and all revealed
religion—all of these arguments have served too often to
draw attention from the plan of work which he set himself
when he issued the famous *Treatise of Human Nature* in
1739. The title page announced that his objective was to
introduce the experimental method of reasoning into moral
subjects. Book I dealt with the understanding; Book II
with the passions, the springs of life, and Book III, published later, with morals, particularly with the social arrangements which men have effected and which preserve
a rather nice balance between self-gratification and good
will and justice. On such a groundwork all of Hume's later
writings rest: his discussions of taste and art, of government and political economy, his constant writings on religion. Laid deep are the assumptions that human nature
is everywhere the same; and that it is the active social life

which demands the concern of philosophers rather than the life of speculation. It begins to be clear how Hume could talk about human nature as constituting the whole of the science of man.

At the risk of seeming inexcusably naïve, and of disregarding the volumes of critical discussion devoted to this question, let us ask simply at what conclusions Hume arrived with regard to the understanding. It goes without saying that he could not countenance the doctrine of innate ideas, against which Locke had contended. The "*new* way of ideas" was to be his, too, with all that that meant for consideration of sensation and reflection as the twin sources of knowledge. It should be remembered that popular interpretation of Locke's contribution had it that most knowledge comes to us from without, by way of our rather passive senses, and that our minds are little more than a *tabula rasa.* This was to emphasize, relatively, the importance of the external world, which is thus able to impress itself upon our receptive senses. But after Locke, Berkeley had written, likewise in empirical vein as he understood it, but with totally different results. What his philosophy brought into prominence was not the aggressive external world and passive impressible minds, but minds so aggressive, so active, so unified, that they literally make the world which they comprehend. There may be in existence things which are not perceived by any mind but God's, but certainly, said Berkeley, the only things which we experientially know are those things we do perceive. The perceiving mind, then, is the clue to the universe, the major factor in it; in a sense it is the world, and all we can validly say as to things outside the mind we say only as those things are perceived by the mind. A startling, idealistic conclusion, manifestly, for British empiricism to come to, when it had started, even earlier than Locke, with the matter and motion of Hobbes.

So Hume thought, and set himself to clarify the situation. He would agree with Locke as to the sources and channels of knowledge—sensation and reflection. For

Hume each experience comes to us in impressions, and leaves us with ideas which are fainter than the impressions. He would agree with Berkeley that the only world we know, we know in our perceptions. "Let us chace [*sic*] our imagination to the heavens, or to the utmost limits of the universe; we never really advance a step beyond ourselves, nor can conceive any kind of existence, but those perceptions, which have appeared in that narrow compass." But his self was a very different one from that of Berkeley in which to be compassed. For, to Hume, the self is "nothing but a bundle or collection of different perceptions, which succeed each other with an inconceivable rapidity, and are in a perpetual flux and movement." Or, as he puts it in another place: "When I turn my reflection on *myself*, I never can perceive this self without some one or more perceptions; nor can I ever perceive anything but the perceptions. 'Tis the composition of these, therefore, which forms the self." In truth, "the notion of a *soul*, and *self*, and *substance*" is feigned only to help us neglect the interruptions to and intervals between our perceiving—or, in other words, to provide us with some feeling of continuity.[12]

For the century so committed to praising man and his capabilities, this was a devastating blow to pride. And, as if that were not enough, Hume went on to subject even those perceptions to indignity. Impression-perceptions come to us singly, they are complete in themselves, they never give us the least intimation of anything beyond. "In other words," as Professor Laird puts it,

his doctrine was that impressions were *non-representative* and *atomic*. Being non-representative they were insusceptible of truth or falsity, i.e. of agreement or disagreement either with fact or with other ideas. Being atomic all our perceptions are different from each other, and from everything else in the universe; they are also distinct and separable, and may be considered as separately existent, and may exist separately, and have no need of anything else to support their existence. . . .[13]

But if all ideas are derived from impressions and "no kind of reasoning can give rise to a new idea," what is it

that allows our mental life to have any sort of connected-
ness, logic, continuity? Hume's answer is that there is a
uniting principle "by which one idea naturally introduces
another," "a gentle force which commonly prevails." This
is the principle of association. It corresponds somewhat
to the principle of attraction in the physical world, and
while we see its effects everywhere, we do not know its
causes and must simply accept it as one of the original
qualities of human nature. Three situations with respect
to ideas lead to their being associated: when ideas resemble
each other in some way, when the objects behind them are
contiguous in time or space and when ideas suggest the
relation of cause and effect. In any situation in which any
of those qualities is present in ideas, the ideas are likely
to group themselves together so that we not only have a
train of simple ideas but a grouping of simple ideas into
more complex ideas.[14]

The thoughts about cause and effect we hold as frequently as we do, not because we have ever had *proof* of
any cause causing the effect that is associated with it, for
there is no *known* connection between objects that should
be so called; we hold to the idea of cause and effect because
we do have the experience of objects being or seeming to
be, in several instances, conjoined. But scrutiny of all the
known cases where causation is supposed to be involved
brings us to just this: the idea is never suggested by one
object in isolation, but only by some *relation* among objects. Further scrutiny reveals that the relation connected
with causality turns out to have a double aspect, contiguity
and succession being its two faces. But why do we infer
causality from impressions of contiguity and succession?
Simply by custom, says Hume, or a principle of association that gives us not a simple idea but a *belief* that the
two objects are in a cause-effect relation. And "belief is
somewhat more than a simple idea. 'Tis a particular manner of forming an idea," "a lively idea related to or associated with a present impression"; and though no philosopher has ever been able to explain how this liveliness, this

vivacity is produced, we do have it and as firmly as if it were an immediate impression.[15]

But liveliness and vivacity, as terms, do not seem to belong to knowledge as knowledge. And so Hume admits, saying that belief, of which they are the characteristics, is "more properly an act of the sensitive, than of the cogitative part of our natures."[16] Where are we, then, as for the part which the understanding plays in our lives?

Hume's answer is that it has a rather limited function. It does afford us, by way of the ideas left by our impressions of the external world and by reflection on them, knowledge. This knowledge has to be built up for us by the principles of association working on single, simple impressions and ideas. We can readily see why some impressions and ideas are easily associated, but some others are bound together simply by custom. And some are bound by belief, which cannot vouch for truth, but does somehow give us conviction of truth. All of which is to say, as Hume intimated in no uncertain fashion, that there is more than one kind of certainty by which men live. If the cognitive powers do not provide all that one could wish, admit it, but continue to live with gusto, for life consists in much more than intense thinking. The understanding serves us well enough for practical matters and even for a good way into philosophy; if it subverts itself entirely when pushed too far or expected to function without the aid of other capacities, that is not the fault of the understanding but of our false estimate of it. To arrive at a just estimate of its powers, but also of its limitations, was what Hume thought he had done. His scepticism was not doubt of the worth of life but "doubt based upon intellectual difficulties." As Professor Laird interprets him:

If a man reflected *hard* he became sceptical; and the reflective part of his nature might conflict with the conclusions of his sensitive beliefs, or at least unsettle them. If so, the rest of the man's nature rose up and restored the balance . . . the thesis of Hume's general philosophy was simply that reason took its place among other natural forces.[17]

Having seen all round the problems of the understanding, Hume then turns, in the fashion of the day, to consideration of the springs of action, the passions. His treatment of this topic hinges considerably upon the method and findings of the preceding investigation. Here, no less, he wishes to be Newtonian in his use of observation and in the parsimony of principles by which he explains. The principle of association, made so much of in his treatment of the understanding, stands him in good stead here, too, and helps him make his case that any object can be either loved or hated, according to the association it has. As Brett says, "The guiding principle of his discussion is the destruction of *a priori* theories which really begin with the idea of objects that *ought* to be loved or hated. This ethical point of view Hume intends to exclude from his scientific 'anatomy of feelings.' "[18] In this, he was once again taking his position against Descartes.

Just as in the working of the cognitive powers there are found ultimate facts, such as belief, which cannot be thoroughly explained, so in the operation of the passions there are ultimates. For example, why should our loving a person be connected in our minds with wanting him to be happy? Hume replies that there is no reason, abstractly considered, why there should be this connection or why love should not be attached to the desire for the unhappiness of the loved one. But the fact remains that these desires are linked in the concomitant fashion which we experience and so must be accepted as a rock-bottom finding in any study of the passions.[19]

His basic psychology of the passions is that of pain and pleasure. Pains and pleasures are regarded as "merely perceptions . . . consequently interrupted and dependent beings," but they "operate with greater violence, and are equally involuntary, as the impressions of figure and extension, colour and sound, which we suppose to be permanent beings." They lack that constancy which we think of as belonging to objects supposed to have a continued existence; and though they have "a certain coherence or regularity in their appearances, yet 'tis of somewhat a different nature, from that which we discover in bodies."

Now pain and pleasure may stand for evil and good, respectively; without the possibility of sensation and the thoughts related to it we should be largely "incapable of passion or action, of desire or volition," since it is "the chief spring or actuating principle of the human mind." If we cannot say that pain and pleasure cause vice and virtue, we can say that pain and pleasure are inseparable from vice and virtue, respectively.[20]

Arising immediately from pain or pleasure are the direct passions: desire and aversion, grief and joy, hope and fear. These direct passions are impressions of good and evil, or pleasure and pain, that arise "most naturally," "with the least preparation," as by an original instinct the mind tends to unite itself with the good. Desire, for example, "arises from good considered simply."[21] The indirect passions proceed from the same principle of pain or pleasure, "but by the conjunction of other qualities." They are pride, humility, ambition, vanity, love, hatred, envy, pity, malice, generosity and their dependents. These latter are complex passions that tend to characterize a person over a period of time and to be related to an object, whereas the direct passions are provoked and have no reference necessarily to an object. Both direct and indirect passions can express themselves in either calm or violent form, and in both forms they operate on the will:

'Tis evident passions influence not the will in proportion to their violence, or the disorder they occasion in the temper; but on the contrary, that when a passion has once become a settled principle of action, and is the predominant inclination of the soul, it commonly produces no longer any sensible agitation.

Indeed, "strength of mind implies the prevalence of the calm passions above the violent."[22]

What, in Hume's theory, is the will? It is an immediate effect of pain and pleasure, and yet it is not properly to be called a passion. He says he means by it nothing but "the internal impression we feel and are conscious of, when

we knowingly give rise to any new motion of our body, or
new perception of our mind." But it must be understood
that it is not reason which gives rise to volition or which
produces action, or to the prevention of either. It is only
some passion which can move the will, and that, in turn,
is aroused by prospect of pain or pleasure. So, Hume concludes:

> Reason, of itself is utterly impotent in this particular. . . .
> We speak not strictly and philosophically when we talk of the
> combat of passion and of reason. Reason is, and ought only to
> be the slave of the passions, and can never pretend to any other
> office than to serve and obey them.[23]

The principle of association, made so much of by Hume
in his treatment of the understanding, comes into play in
the passions, too. Affections and passions are as easily
related as are ideas or impressions of knowledge, though
association itself produces no emotion, nor does it give
rise to any new impression or passion. "An easy transition
of ideas, which, of itself, causes no emotion, can never be
necessary, or even useful to the passions, but by forward-
ing the transition betwixt some related impressions." But,
as Laird points out, there is a difference in the working of
association in the two fields of ideas which Hume did not
clarify. Ideas, according to Hume, "may be compared to
the extension and solidity of matter," while impressions,
especially the reflective ones, may be compared "to colours,
tastes, smells and other sensible qualities." On the basis of
this distinction, "ideas never admit of a total union, but
are endowed with a kind of impenetrability, by which they
exclude each other, and are capable of forming a compound by their conjunction, not by their mixture." But
impressions and passions, on the other hand, "are suscep-
tible of an entire union; and like colours, may be blended
so perfectly together, that each of them may lose itself,
and contribute only to vary that uniform impression,
which arises from the whole."[24] Thus, Hume used the term
association

in two fundamentally different senses, *viz.*, (a) the clustering of unmodified entities, and (b) a fusion where the constituents lost their former identities and became indistinguishable in the new total fact . . . and since what Hume set out to explain was the *apparent* simplicity and integrity of various *compound* passions, he necessarily relied upon fusion more than upon atomic association.[25]

In his effort to resolve his first principles into as short a list as possible, Hume overworked his principle of association.

An aid second only to association was Hume's principle of sympathy, a power of the imagination which communicates to us the inclinations and sentiments of others even when they differ from ours, and which relates us in warmth of feeling with others:

We have a lively idea of every thing related to us. All human creatures are related to us by resemblance. Their persons, therefore, their interests, their passions, their pains and pleasures must strike upon us in a lively manner, and produce an emotion similar to the original one.

We thus find in ourselves the very sentiments and passions which we see at work in the other person, but, though we are so similar, our attention is not directed to ourselves in such times, but to him in his tension.[26]

Since one of the objectives for a moralist was to lay a psychological foundation for a system of ethics, we may ask what kind of basis for ethics Hume had laid. Obviously, it is not one of reason, since reason, an inert principle, can never be a motive power to the will. His basis is a naturalistic one: trust your impulses and feelings, Hume seemed to say; use your reason to compare various impulses when they are not in agreement, but launch out as confidently on your senses—here, your moral sense—as you do when you trust your eyes.

Several close resemblances to Hutcheson should be pointed out. The two writers shared the desire to be Newtonian, that is, empirical; they agreed on the subject of disinterested desires and on the nature of sympathy; they offered very much the same discussion of "impressions of reflection"; and, above all, they were at one in their conviction that the reason is impotent as a motive to action.[27] Hutcheson had not provoked a storm of controversy because he had not disintegrated the self nor the chain of cause and effect; however liberal his New Light theology in the eyes of his critics, he had not landed himself or his readers in scepticism.

Now this was the situation in philosophy which challenged Reid to the combat. He entered the lists in 1764 with his *Inquiry into the Human Mind on the Principles of Common Sense*. This work had been begun as early as 1739, when Hume's *Treatise* appeared, and had been discussed in sections by members of the Aberdeen Philosophical Society to whom Reid read various essays. It was later incorporated into his *Essays on the Intellectual and Active Powers*.

Let us see how he begins his discussion. After noting in general the "low state" of philosophy, he comments in caustic fashion on the errors of his forerunners; Descartes, Malebranche, Locke, Berkeley, all are characterized pungently. But it was the author of the *Treatise of Human Nature* who had done the greatest damage: he had, apparently, intended to show "that there is neither human nature nor science in the world." If one applies Hume's principles one will find himself, Reid declares, in a position where he will desperately cry out:

I find I have been only in an enchanted castle, imposed upon by spectres and apparitions. I blush inwardly to think how I have been deluded; I am ashamed of my frame, and can hardly forbear expostulating with my destiny. . . . I see myself, and the whole frame of nature, shrink into fleeting ideas, which, like Epicurus' atoms, dance about in emptiness.[28]

Such scepticism was the "monster" brought forth in 1739 (the year of Hume's *Treatise*), but the monster was only the natural issue of this new way of ideas. The root of the difficulty, Reid is convinced, lies in the acceptance of the hypothesis that we do not really perceive things which are external; the examination of that hypothesis, then, becomes his task, and his hope is that, as a result, philosophical inquiry will be freed from subjectivism and scepticism. His way of doing this is to try to destroy "the foreignness of matter to mind."[29]

"It must be by an anatomy of the mind that we can discover its powers and principles." But the anatomist of mind has a much more difficult task than the anatomist of body, since it is only his own mind he can examine with any accuracy and distinctness, with no opportunity for comparing it minutely with minds of others. Moreover, the working of habits, associations, abstractions, makes it hard for us to know what the original elements were. From this point of view, the mind may "be compared to an apothecary or chemist, whose materials indeed are furnished by nature; but, for the purposes of his art, he mixes, compounds, dissolves, evaporates, and sublimes them, till they put on a quite different appearance. . . ." But Reid insists that he will proceed with caution and humility, and perhaps later a truly "just system" may be built upon his analyses; in any case, he will make no effort to display genius, for he is convinced that "genius, and not the want of it . . . adulterates philosophy, and fills it with error and false theory."[30]

The simplest beginning will be an analysis of the five senses, with the object of stating a new theory of perception to transplant the subjective theory of ideas. Sensation he defines as "a simple and original affection or feeling of the mind, altogether inexplicable and unaccountable," but one which may be trusted to give us knowledge, not just of an idea but of a real world external to our minds. One of his recent interpreters sums up his position on this point in this way:

Hard, angular, and unlovely the world may be, it is still there whether anybody thinks of it or not, a fact just as true and real as the mental world. . . . Nor did Reid agree with such utterances as Hume sometimes made, that anywhere he turned he ran into a perception; on the contrary, Reid ran into the outside world!

The position which he maintains is that "there is no fallacy in the senses. Nature always speaketh the same language, and useth the same signs in the same circumstances."[31]

But perception is a different matter. We have a perception when a sensation suggests a "notion" or "conception" of an object, along with a belief that that object exists.

> This belief is not the effect of argumentation and reasoning, it is the immediate effect of my constitution. . . . This belief . . . is none of my manufacture; it came from the mint of Nature; it bears her image and superscription; and, if it is not right, the fault is not mine: I even took it upon trust, and without suspicion.

Sensations are used as signs by perception. But while sensations themselves are never false, the person may misread the sign and thus have a false perception. His experience at some time may lead him to attach a false notion or conception or suggestion to a sensation and he may never have learned to correct the attachment. Likewise, his powers of credulity may be stretched so that he is willing to believe more than sensations warrant. But, when these things have been said, perceptions, too, appear to be fairly trustworthy, and we need not fear we are being befooled in our world.[32]

Sensation, perception and belief are not the only powers we have. There are, in addition, memory, conception, abstraction, judging, reasoning, taste, moral perception, consciousness, each of which he explains somewhat, and he implies that there are others which he will not explain. Some powers are original and natural, and may be called faculties; others are acquired by use, exercise and study, and should be called habits.

Of the list of powers just given above, we shall make brief comment on three only. (1) We should judge correctly from the inclusion of moral perception among the powers that Reid belongs with the moral-sense school of moralists. And he was just as sure as Hutcheson was that we may trust our faculties in that sphere quite as much as in other realms. (2) In criticizing so bitterly the reasoning of his predecessors Reid had no intention of saying that reason, as reason, is not a power of the mind to be trusted. What he said, in effect, was that reason should not be used to question truths that are self-evident, for which no proof can be demonstrated, truths which should be accepted intuitively.[33] (3) Consciousness, that principle never called in question, even by Mr. Hume, Reid says cannot be logically defined. "The objects of it are our present pains, our pleasures, our hopes, our fears, our desires, our doubts, our thoughts of every kind; in a word, all the passions, and all the actions and operations of our own minds, while they are present." But it is asking too much of consciousness to expect that it can afford us knowledge of the way in which our minds work; examination of consciousness, then, is not adequate as a foundation for a system of philosophy of mind.[34]

Reid's main objective was "a vindication of perception, as perception, in contradistinction to the vague sensational idealism, which had ended in the disintegration of knowledge."[35] The distinctive characteristic of perception is that it is an act of judgment or belief, the judgment-belief character being included in the very act of perceiving. Reid puts it thus:

Such original and natural judgments are, therefore, a part of that furniture which nature hath given to the human understanding. . . . They are a part of our constitution, and all the discoveries of our reason are grounded upon them. They make up what is called *the common sense* of mankind.[36]

Such a finding comes not by trying to catch a sensation while it is in the very act of turning into something else, in the manner of Mr. Hume, but by reflecting on the immediacy with which our minds act on what is presented to them. Reflection, to Reid, is no less empirical as a method of dealing with phenomena than was the method of Hume; it is far more trustworthy and sound, and will not lead into the morass of scepticism. It means that we shall be basing our philosophy on the principles of common sense.

Now what did Reid mean by common sense? We know that his emphasis gave the name of Common Sense School to such of the Scots as chose to rally to his standard. But exactly what was implied in the term and what purpose did it serve in his philosophy? The answer is a little embarrassing.

In the *Inquiry* (1764) very little definiteness is given the concept, and much misunderstanding was the result. In his later work, *Essays on the Intellectual Powers* (1785), Reid reckoned with these misunderstandings, but still was not very succinct. He had thought, he said, that "common sense" was as unambiguous a word and as well understood as "the county of York"! His most recent expositor, Dr. Olin McKendree Jones, has reduced Reid's meanings to four:

(1) Common sense is equivalent to common experience, common knowledge gained empirically.
(2) It means sometimes *principles,* considered either as (a) natural principles of the mind, such as sensation and belief, or (b) the natural laws of mind, comparable to natural laws of the physical sciences which are the discoveries made by empirical analysis.
(3) Common sense frequently means the self-evident truths of knowledge and morals. They represent intuitive, irresistible beliefs, implanted in our constitution by God.
(4) But sometimes it means opinions generally agreed upon, though not self-evident. Examples of such opinions are belief in a material world, belief in the cleavage between right and wrong, et cetera.[37]

Some of the criticisms that could be made of the concept are at once apparent from the bare statement of definitions given above. What might be guessed is the misuse to which the idea would be put by persons who were not good philosophers. Reid's friends, James Oswald and James Beattie, each appealed to Reid and to common sense, and by their voluminous and fatuous writings brought considerable discredit on Reid and the general position, as well as on themselves. Their chief contemporary critic was Joseph Priestley, who in 1774 in his *Examination of*

Reid's Inquiry, Beattie's Essay, and *Oswald's Appeal to Common Sense* had some very cogent criticisms to make. Reid's tactics did not include retaliation, nor much of further explication of his position; he simply continued to repeat his position, so that, unfortunately, what started out to be a critical tool for reaching truth, became a dogmatic defense against other tools and other interpretations of truth.

Since so much is usually made of Reid's attacks on Hume's system, two things may usefully be said here of their common endeavor: (1) Both men were loyal to empirical methods, as they thought; that Hume's empiricism led him to think that the mind knows nothing but ideas, and Reid's that it really knows the external world, is not so important as that both were working on the lines suggested by the new methods of science. (2) Hume, no less than Reid, admitted the limits of the understanding, and pleaded for the validity of the claims of practical life. Hume's admission of limits did not prevent his speculating, though the speculation led to scepticism; Reid was more content to leave the matter as unfruitful for knowledge and unwholesome for life.

Reid's *Essays on the Active Powers* (1788), while fulfilling in a formal way the second requirement of the two set by the division of the faculties into speculative and active powers, or, understanding and will, is not of the same quality as his earlier works. It was the book of his old age and for it he felt no such impulse to take a strong position as he had in his *Inquiry* and even in his *Intellectual Powers.*

He defines active power as "an attribute in a being by which he can do certain things if he wills." Analysis of this attribute requires giving an account of the passions, appetites, affections of "every motive and incitement to action."[38] His classification is as follows:

1. Mechanical principles of action: instinct and habit. These are called mechanical since they operate without

will, intention or thought. He is most impressed with all those instincts which appear in infancy:

The art is not in the child, but in him who made the organ. In like manner, when a bee makes its comb so geometrically, the geometry is not in the bee, but in that great Geometrician who made the bee, and made all things in number, weight, and measure.[39]

2. Animal principles of action: appetites, desires, affections, natural temper. Most of these are found in the brutes as well as in man, and call for exercise of intention and will, but not of judgment or reason.

3. Rational principles of action. Contrary to Hume, Reid insists that among the various ends of human actions "there are some, of which, without reason, we could not even form a conception. . . ." The ends he has in mind which require reason are those to which these two questions are addressed: What is good for us upon the whole, and what appears to be our duty?[40]

Reid's doctrine of the moral sense is that "there is a principle in man, which, when he acts according to it, gives him a consciousness of worth, and when he acts contrary to it, a sense of demerit." It is a principle found universally—and it is to be regarded as an original power of mind. Reid does not object to this principle's being called a sense if we will understand that all our senses bring us always real judgments, and not mere impressions. Every sense brings us immediately the testimony of nature, and likewise this moral sense "is the testimony of nature, and we have the same reason to rely upon it."[41] But man is a free moral agent and some persons unwisely disregard the testimony of the moral sense, as they do that of the other senses.

While Ferguson's work was not marked by an elaborate psychology, it came nearer being what we regard as psychology, and not epistemology, than did the work of Reid. He was greatly influenced by Reid, however, in the matter of emphasizing that the mind is active rather than passive, and in the attention he gave to consciousness as a source of knowledge. He writes, for example, "Perception and memory are active exertions of mind, and not a mere figure or motion impressed on body." As for consciousness, it is the first and most certain source of knowledge; it is aided by perception which also gives primary or immediate knowledge, and by testimony and inference which yield derived or secondary knowledge.

Consciousness is the first and most essential attribute of the mind. It is expressed in what grammarians term the first personal pronoun *I* or *Ego*, and is stated in every sentence of which that pronoun is the subject.

The knowledge obtained by reflection, from consciousness, is, of all others, the most intimate and sure. . . . Here the evidence of reality remains unshaken and unattended by the boldest assaults of scepticism. The very statement of doubt is a dogmatic assumption of personal existence and thought.[42]

Without attacking Hume directly and by name, he disagrees with the conclusions to which his friend's logic had been pushed. The following criticism appears to have Hume as its object:

Inquiries . . . into the cause of belief, in matters of conciousness, or evident perception, appear to be misplaced, and only insinuate a question, where nature has refused to admit of a doubt.

And, in a note, he adds: "We must not say, with the sceptic, that nature has given us ideas or impressions of things, and left us to collect the reality of an object from thence: She has given us perception; and this is at once a knowledge of its object."[43]

Even more pointedly this is meant for Hume:

Scepticism, no doubt, by restraining credulity, may guard against one species of error, but, carried to extreme, would discourage the search of truth, suspend the progress of knowledge, and become a species of palsy of all the mental powers, whether of speculation or action.

The sceptic, indeed, sometimes affects to distinguish the provinces of speculation and of action. . . . But speculations in science are surely of little account, if they have not any relation to subjects of actual choice and pursuit; and if they do not prepare the mind for the discernment of matters relating to which there is actual occasion to decide, and to act, in the conduct of human life.[44]

One aspect, at least, of Hume's argument had been accepted by Ferguson, namely, that concerning causality. He is, henceforth, willing that scientists should cease investigating causes, and supplying them from imagination when they do not actually know them, and he agrees that they should take as their goal not the relating of effects to causes, but the search for laws of nature. This shift in objective will allow them to treat of a multiplicity of diversified appearances, of a series of facts well known to exist, and of their applications and consequences, and will not lead them to advance such fictitious suppositions and explanations as Descartes was betrayed into when he was on the search for a cause.[45]

For Ferguson, as for Hobbes and most others who had succeeded him, the functions of the mind were conceived to be knowing and acting. Mental powers, then, were spoken of as the cognitive and the active, and the two aspects of mind as understanding and will. The cognitive powers were to be seen at work when any of the following operations took place: consciousness (i.e., reflection), perception, observation, memory, imagination, abstraction, and the applications of several of these operations (especially observation and abstraction) to the formulations of science. The active powers of man, on the other hand, are engaged not in pursuits of knowledge but in the business of affective response. Man feels and chooses and makes efforts, as well as receives knowledge—though it should be remembered that Ferguson regarded the mind in its cognitive functions, in its knowledge-getting, as active, and not a mere passive tablet.[46] But, falling in with the popular terminology, he outlines the activity of man's nature as consisting in propensities, sentiment, desire and volition, and he lists three laws for the will:

(1) The law of self-preservation.
(2) The law of society. "Men are disposed to society. . . . The general tendency of the law of gravitation is, to cause bodies

to approach to each other; as the tendency of the law of society is to cause men to produce public good, or to abstain from public harm. But the external result is opposite in opposite circumstances. Heavy bodies are not always falling, nor social natures always acting for the common good. . . . And thus the operation of the law of society, like that of gravitation itself, is always real, though the external result is not always the same." [The Newtonian parallel requires no comment.]

(3) The law of estimation or progression. "Men are disposed to better themselves . . . it is an ultimate fact in the nature of man, and not to be explained by anything that is previously or better known."[47]

Ferguson's discussions of the sentiments, desires and volitions of men add nothing noteworthy to any of the contemporary analyses. In his discussion of the propensities, or instincts, however, he was more detailed than Hutcheson, for example, and said extremely well what was the best of eighteenth-century thought on the instinctive basis of man's life. His expression here sounds very modern, if by modern we may mean, in this instance, the last decade of the nineteenth century and the first quarter of the twentieth, when making lists of instincts was still a major activity of psychologists. For the last few years, as is well known, we have reversed the process and have been getting rid of all the instincts save two or three, and some psychologists have abandoned them all. But let us get into his thought by the use of his own words:

Man, we have observed, though in general let loose from the trammels of instinct, and left to observe and to chuse [sic] for himself, yet, in some respects also, but a variety among the animals, is directed by instincts that precede the knowledge of his ends, or any experience of the means to be employed in obtaining them. Of such instinctive directions, in human nature, there are several examples . . .

and he goes on to speak of the instinctive efforts involved in breathing, in suckling, in avoiding a fall from a precipice. He continues:

But the more general character of man's inclinations, or active dispositions . . . is not that of a blind propensity to the use of

means, but instinctive intimation of an end, for the attainment of
which he is left to discover and to chuse, by his own observation
and experience, the means that may prove most effectual. . . .

But the precise material with which hunger is to be gratified,
and the precise expedients with which he may be secured from
harm, are left, in a great measure, to his own choice in the result
of his observation and experience.

Man is thus, even in the practices of his instinctive life,
somewhat "let loose from the trammels of instinct." He is

so far from being limited by his instincts to any particular species or form of materials for every purpose . . . that he is disposed to innovate on every practice, whether of nature or art; and
finds occasion to diversify his manner wherever he is placed, or to
whatever situation he is enabled to advance himself. Hence the
multiplicity of arts which he is disposed to practise, and in which
his inventions so frequently varied continue to accumulate almost
without end.

In another sense man is more free from the trammels of
instinct than are other animals to whom "appetite continues to be the sole motive to action, and the animal, in
every moment of time, proceeds upon the motive then present": man generalizes from the repeated experiences of
gratifications and frustrations and "in the intervals of
any particular appetite or instinct, he can take measures
to secure his good, or to avert his evil."

In the same fashion Ferguson treats man's instinct to
associate with his fellows and the instinct to better himself.
Man feels these as desirable ends, it is part of his constitution to entertain these values, but his ways of realizing
them are not narrowly channelized as if he were a mere
animal. Man makes conceptions of situations and then
moves to realize the desirable situation and to avoid the
undesirable. In this way his instinctive life differs from
that of the other animals.[48]

Candid judgment must admit that Ferguson's discussions compare favorably with those offered a century later,
in the sense that they are interesting anticipations of the
later. Starting out in the *Institutes* with the term "propensities," when he published his *Principles of Moral and*

Political Science in 1792 he was using the word "instincts" far more frequently, and we do not know how much earlier that practice had been begun in his lectures. True, he does not name all of the instincts specifically, nor does his list approach the fifty-two items of William James, the one hundred and ten of Woodworth or the hundreds of Thorndike. But it is worth putting his discussion with the definition of William James, the philosopher, who first in the United States made the term popular: "Instinct . . . the faculty of acting in such a way as to produce certain ends, without foresight of the ends, and without previous education in the performance."[49]

Another interesting thing is to find that the psychologist who has been regarded as the leader of the instinctivists turned in his later years to the use of the old term "propensity." William McDougall, in his *Energies of Men*, tells us quite frankly that he has reverted to the older terminology because it has no such definite and specific physiological implications and, therefore, will avoid the controversy which has, since the early nineteen twenties, marked the discussion of instinct. Like the later eighteenth-century writers, McDougall wants to free psychology from its overintellectualistic bias and have it interpret the whole active life of man in terms of all the springs of action. Of "propensity" he writes that it is "the name given in these pages (in accordance with old usage) to any part of the innate constitution whose nature and function it is to generate upon occasion an active tendency"; and a tendency is "an active energy directed towards a goal." His phrase "the mind in action" suggests the familiar dichotomy of the cognitive and active powers, the understanding and the will, or the understanding and the desires.[50]

We should not leave our account of Ferguson without noting one other emphasis of his which anticipated William James, namely, his discussion of habit. Along with his concern with inborn tendencies, Ferguson was equally taken up with the deep grooves which habit makes. Indeed, habits often can "scarcely be distinguished from original propensity," so ingrained are they, so "natural" do they seem. Yet they are acquired forms of behavior, which follow the patterns they do largely because of the nature of human association and the suggestions or requirements thrown out by one's fellows as to what is acceptable conduct.[51] If separation could be made it would probably be found that in any human activity habit plays a larger part than instinct. But such separation cannot be made, and what we have actually operative is a greatly modified native tendency. How this modification occurs interests Ferguson greatly. As Lehmann says, though the terms "conditioned response," "repression," "emotional transfer," "complexes" are not used by Ferguson, he has the conceptions very definitely.[52] Ferguson was as certain as Hume that psychology, or the science of man, was the basic study for an understanding of society, but it itself was ununderstandable without taking into account the facts of human association.

Closer analysis would reveal other parallels with Ferguson and his contemporaries afforded by McDougall and psychologists of his following, but such analysis is not the object of this discussion. Nor is it in place to point out the positions of attack on the instinctivists by both behaviorists and sociologists.[53] The thing to be noted is that here again, in the account of human nature and its functioning, the social sciences have had a legacy from the eighteenth century with which they have had to deal as they have reshaped themselves in this century.

What, in general, can be said of the psychology of these Scottish writers? By all of them, first, it was regarded as the most fundamental portion of any knowledge they might have or might achieve regarding man. As Dugald Stewart put the case, psychology is "the centre whence the thinker goes outward to the circumference of human knowledge." Or, to change the figure, it is the groundwork on which all other discussions of man's life and activity rest. As Hume saw it, "the science of man is the only solid foundation for the other sciences. . . ."[54]

In the second place, they believe that human nature could be known as truly as any other set of phenomena could be known; knowledge of it could be arrived at by following empirical methods in the spirit of Bacon and Newton. This meant for them observation of their own minds at work, introspection on their own sensations, ratiocination and emotions. This gave them an atomistic psychology—one which tended to break up knowledge or experience into little bits, each bit thereafter treated almost as if it were an independent entity. Hume, for example, in his effort to be rudely empirical, to accept nothing as a whole which could be experienced or analyzed in its parts, was as atomistic as any thinker of the century. But this method gave them considerable confidence in their ability to achieve a true philosophy of mind.

For, in the third place, it was a philosophy of mind, and not a psychology, that they wanted, primarily, to construct, and it was such a philosophy that they did construct. Their concerns with epistemology outweighed their concerns with psychology, but, for their day, this was the first field for clarification, it would seem, and it could be said, of course, that the time was not quite ripe for further physiological emphasis. Even so, they themselves were persuaded that they were proceeding empirically. By way of consciousness, that inner sense which allowed them to perceive the self in its various states, they felt that they could discover the laws of the human mind. And among their discoveries they (Hume excepted, here) thought they observed principles which were above observation, which were universal and eternal. These they called by various names: Reid, the principles of common sense; Stewart, the fundamental laws of thought and belief; Hamilton, Stewart's pupil, reason in the first degree. But this insistence on the presence and activity of a principle beyond which investigation could not go, and into which it could not penetrate far, was one of the chief reasons for the later charge that the Scottish school was dogmatic, conservative and, in spite of its proclamations, unempirical. In any case, it offered a sort of balance to the atomistic analysis which, otherwise, would have overweighted their approach.

Their very certainty as to some integrating principle, however, was what made them popular in their day and in the next generation in France and in the United States. As Professor Gardner Murphy puts it, practically using their own words, "they appeared to save the individual and society from intellectual and moral chaos." And it was because "of its insistence upon the unity and coherence of mental life, and because it pictured the individual as an acting entity, not as a mere field in which capering ideas assembled and reassembled, [that] the greatest contributions of the Scottish school were necessarily general rather than specific."[55]

The reference to ideas assembling and reassembling themselves suggests, of course, the associational psychology which is usually said to have come into prominence in the century with the work of Hartley and Condillac and to have given the character to the psychology of the period. Associational psychology was not altogether new; aspects of it are to be found in Aristotle, but in the eighteenth century the first efforts were made to establish a physical basis for the theory. Not until the nineteenth century was the physical basis acceptably established by Alexander Bain, and then, shortly afterward, the popularity of the school waned. But we may ask here, what was the relation of the Scottish group to the associationism they knew?

To Hobbes they were all, with the exception of Hume, hostile, because of his mechanistic materialism. Locke they lauded, for his efforts to be empirical and his effort to do away with the doctrine of innate ideas, even while they regretted that the logic of his position had resulted in the subjectivism of Berkeley and the scepticism of Hume. Both Hutcheson and Hume wrote their principal psychological works before Hartley's *Observations on Man* appeared in 1749, so they were not influenced by it. Hutcheson's reference to an earlier associationist psychology is very brief.[56] Hume's system rests heavily on association—recall his discussions of substance and causality—and his position here mirrors closely that of Aristotle.[57] Reid did know the work of Hartley, and criticized it chiefly for its "exploded method of hypothesis," for its teaching that all knowledge comes from the senses, and for its position that judgment, in principle, does not differ from any other complex idea. As fantastic as Hartley's theory of vibrations was, it was an attempt to provide a physical basis for an explanation of mental operations, and it was done as consciously in the method of Newton as any bit of Scottish introspection. By scorning it, Reid listed himself among those who failed to recognize the more profitable empirical procedures. Reid probably did not know the work of Condillac, the *Treatise on Sensations*, though it appeared in 1754.[58] Reid's chief ground for rejecting the doctrines of association was his belief in the fundamental inductive principle of the mind, which is active, which of itself brings together, sorts out and tests ideas, but which is independent of and superior to the ideas which it integrates.

The Scottish school, thus, with the exception of Hume, stood to the side of the main road of the psychology of their day, that is, of the psychology which was later, at the hands of the Mills and Bain and Spencer, to be a psychology provocative of further fundamental physiological research. And ironically enough, that section of the Scottish school which was represented by Reid and his followers was brought to a close when Thomas Brown, a student of Stewart's, became eclectic and borrowed some ideas from the associationists, and when Sir William Hamilton, under Kantian influence, began to point the way for the idealism of T. H. Green and Bradley.[59]

A fourth characteristic they had in common. They all wanted to break away from the Cartesian rationalism, with its emphasis on abstract intellectualism and innate ideas. The essence of the mind was to them more than thought, and, set in the direction of empiricism as they were, the a priori character of innate ideas was not acceptable. In this aspect of their philosophy they were good followers of Locke. This accounts, then, for the attention given by them to sensation and perception, the source of our knowledge of the external world, and for the adjectives "empirical" or "sensationalist" which are frequently attached to the school. In all of this they were interested; moreover, they wished to emphasize the fact that man is a sensitive being, as well as a thinking being, and that man lives far less by certain and demonstrable truths than the Cartesian position would lead us to believe. Hence, the attention to feeling, to impulse, to passion—all unintellectualistic—and the attention to the active life of man. It is ironical that in his argument against the Humean scepticism, Thomas Reid should have built up as his organon a set of principles which was as inexplicable, as ultimate, as God-inspired as were Descartes' innate ideas. True, Reid's common sense was a blend of judgment and feeling, it was itself a belief, but it was inspired by God as were the Cartesian innate ideas, and in no sense were its dicta arrived at by induction and generalization.[60] And, after the period of his popularity, this weapon which he thought would defend philosophy from scepticism was turned against its forger, as being too unphilosophical for consideration, and the indictment was laid on the whole group save, as so often was the case, David Hume.

One last comment might be made on their common efforts. Though these Scots were so intent on getting to the heart of epistemological problems, the connotation of the term "human nature" was for them far wider than would be indicated in any theory concerning the resources within us for our coming to knowledge of the world. They were far more interested in the life of men, the life of activity, than they were with the purely intellectual processes. They would not have opposed the statement popular with us that man is not born human, but becomes human by virtue of his societal life. And so we find in all their writings great attention to communication, sympathy, imitation, habit and convention, which take us, on mention of the words, into the realm of our associated life. Epistemologists, yes, offering new solutions, empirically based, they thought, to traditional problems; but no one can deny that they were forerunners, too, into new fields of investigation which were later to be named sociology and social psychology.

V I

SOCIETY

IN the long history of the literature dealing with the life of human beings in groups, perhaps no word offers less precision in usage than the word "society." We have not yet seen the resolution of the problems involved in the use of that term and the concepts related to it; almost any discussion reveals the consciousness of equivocal usage when it offers definitions of "society," "a society," "societal," "social." Even in the field of sociology, which in the nineteenth century stated its claims to be "the science of society," there is as yet no complete unanimity in the use of the term. Is society "a whole, a substance, a unity, . . a being," either in ideal or in actuality? Do we mean by the term a whole summation of human groupings, each group of which is, within itself, also a society?[1] Or, when we use the term, are we employing "a completely verbal concept" denoting "a happening, a process," and are we indicating by its use no "fictitious substance," but "the sum of those occurrences which have elsewhere been termed social processes"?[2] And if we of the twentieth century are so far from unanimity in our usage, what may be expected of the eighteenth?

We have already seen that that century was, markedly, a transitional era: its enlightened authors knew, though unevenly, the classical philosophers and expounders of ethics; but most of them were much more concerned to transfer to a new science of man the methods and findings of natural science which had begun to flower in the seventeenth century. These two modes of thought were not always reconciled; but in general it may be said that, for most Scottish and English writers, at least, a simple empiricism provided them with conclusions as to the innate sociability of man and the naturalness of society. This the Galilean mechanical-mathematical method which they praised, with its formula of resolution and composition, atomism and individualism, would not have encouraged, and it is true that traces of that Galilean method are here and there to be found, particularly in some early expositions of the social compact. But even the hold upon them of the concepts of Natural Jurisprudence, emphasizing as it did the rights and obligations of individuals in the abstract, and disregarding the particular social organization in which those individuals happen to find themselves living, did not serve to break the emphasis on socialized life, for Natural Jurisprudence prescribed rules of right conduct. These rules were enunciated on a basic presupposition concerning uniform traits—needs, capacities, obligations—of men anywhere.[3] What we need to underscore is this: that in the eighteenth century, by many British authors, society ceased to be viewed as an artificial creation; instead it came to be called a natural relation. Simple proofs of its naturalness were found in the helplessness of babes and in the fact that the most primitive peoples as yet discovered lived in some sort of organized life.

This cannot be called a completely new position; it had indeed been one persistent theme since antiquity. Cicero had written:

Nature . . . by power of reason associates man with man in the common bonds of speech and life; she implants in him above all . . . a strangely tender love for his offspring. She also prompts men to meet in companies, to form public assemblies and to take part in them themselves; and she further dictates, as a consequence of this, the effort on man's part to provide a store of things that minister to his comfort and wants.[4]

And near the opening of the eighteenth century, Shaftesbury, who was both indicative of trends and so influential in giving new directions (particularly to the Scots), had ridiculed the idea of Hobbes and his followers that "civil government and society" are "a kind of invention and creature of art." "For my own part, methinks," he wrote,

this herding principle, and associating inclination, is seen so natural and strong in most men, that one might readily affirm 'twas even from the violence of this passion that so much disorder arose in the general society of mankind. . . . All men have naturally their share of this combining principle. . . .[5]

What was new was that in the course of the century that position was adopted by many, and that analysts devoted themselves less incidentally than had been customary to the concerns of society. They set themselves to compass in thoroughgoing fashion, with the aid of new methods of thought, the many problems of human relationships. Their attention to group life rather than to individuals, their emphasis on society as being the primordial and natural habitat of man, became so marked that not a few historians of social theory are now saying that in that period, and particularly in Adam Ferguson's *Essay on the History of Civil Society*, we climbed to the first step of sociological knowledge. There was, of course, as yet no analysis of group-composition, group-functioning or group-processes. What writers were concerned to emphasize was the fact of the social nature of man and their belief that primordial life must have been group life. As James Dunbar put it, society was not "the sickly daughter of calamity, nor even the production of an aspiring understanding, but the free and legitimate offspring of the human heart"; and Adam Ferguson, "both the earliest and latest accounts collected from every quarter of the earth, represent mankind as assembled in troops and companies," and this fact "must be admitted as the foundation of our reasoning relative to man."[6]

Society, however, was difficult to encompass intellectually, to conceptualize satisfactorily. Of the variety of social organization the century was becoming aware, but the differences presented by them, the divergences of primitives' practices from those of the particular society known best by any writer made it almost impossible to speak of those societies and the writer's society in any inclusive and universal way. Metaphorical language could be drawn on, as in the Dunbar quotation just offered; and there was widespread acceptance of the fact on which

Ferguson insisted, that human beings are and have always
been found in "troops and companies." But beyond that,
what was to be done?

Several procedures were followed. One procedure was
to enumerate the advantages and corresponding responsibilities brought by highly organized life. Here the writers
waxed eloquent on the subjects of defense; of the division
of labor, with its accompaniment of increased wealth and
improved technology; of the achievement and conservation
of culture, and of elegance and progress of all kinds.
Another procedure, very similar to the first, was to identify
society with politically organized society, the kind they
knew best, and to enlarge on its values. Citizenship was
highly prized in this century—perhaps, since the revolution of 1688, more by British than by others—and the
advantages of that status were favorably contrasted with
the conditions prevailing in societies dominated by familial
ties. On the theory of progress, so popular in the century,
it was easy to hold that political society was the inevitable
form of organization to be achieved, since so many advanced peoples of the world were already enjoying it. Under this conception which, in a slightly different guise, was
as old as Aristotle,[7] political organization would be viewed
as a mature condition for all human groups, a natural
condition to be arrived at in time, and easily to be taken,
therefore, as the normal expression of society at its best;
it represented, in the words of Thomas Rutherforth, "a
complete or perfect society."[8] A third way out of the conceptual difficulty was offered. If society is an undefinable
product, why not emphasize, instead, the elements of which
it is made, the parts which go into the composition of the
whole? And so we find in the literature discussions of the
family, of education, of religion, of economic, juridical
and political institutions. In two ways these treatments
manifest the older atomistic psychology: the institutions
are, from one point of view, products of the "propensities"
of individuals, fairly direct projections of those instincts
and needs which are found universally; from another

point of view, they themselves are taken as the units of a structure, of a whole larger than themselves, and description of them is allowed to suffice for a description or analysis of that whole.

Whichever alternative was followed at the moment, in each type of procedure the attention to interhuman relationships was prominent—a definite anticipation of a later sociological focus. The very ethical aims with which most writers began and closed their disquisitions made it inevitable that relationships between individuals, between groups, between individuals and groups would have to be kept to the fore in their thought. No discussion of sympathy, for example, would have been possible except in terms of the relationships and interactions of human beings; the concern with the obligations of political life certainly expresses another aspect of the idea. The relationships evident in the exchange of commodities and in the division of labor which creates a condition wherein exchange is possible and profitable, are other aspects frequently dealt with. But when those items have been noted, it must still be said that relationships were treated almost as if they were static structures; there was little that was mobile, fluctuating or processual about them; pattern, rather than action, received the emphasis—to use Leopold von Wiese's terms from a later day.

In all the discussion concerning society there were, as Professor Lovejoy has pointed out,[9] several distinct issues on which eighteenth-century opinion was divided: 1. Is man "naturally" (i.e., originally) a gregarious animal? 2. Has he "natural" (i.e., unreflective and spontaneous) impulses and feelings which make him act in a "social" manner (in the eulogistic sense), and, if so, what are these? 3. Is the political state "natural," in the sense that it evolved out of a prepolitical stage without any deliberate and reflective design? 4. Is the state a necessary corrective of nonsocial or antisocial propensities of man in a juristic state of nature?[10] In scanning the offerings of the Scottish group on the subject of society, we should keep in mind these issues and the resolutions given by the Scots.

The earliest of them, Francis Hutcheson, opens his attack in unequivocal clarity. When in 1730 he assumed the professorship of moral philosophy at the University of Glasgow the subject of his inaugural lecture was *De naturali hominum socialitate*. This lecture was concerned primarily with the facts of human gregariousness, but he speaks also of the society of animals as having relevance for consideration of human association. Elsewhere he writes:

One can scarce deny to mankind a natural impulse to society with their fellows, as an immediate principle, when we see the like in many species of animals; nor should we ascribe all associating to their indigence. Their other principles, their curiosity, communicativeness, desire of action, their sense of honour, their compassion, benevolence, gaiety, and the moral faculty, could have little or no exercise in solitude, and therefore might lead them to haunt together, even without an immediate or ultimate impulse, or a sense of their indigence.[11]

But men are not "perfectly wise and good," nor do they always know how to promote the "general happiness of their race"; other measures, then, are required, and civil society (political organization) is, in time, inaugurated to be an aid. Can we say, then, that men are naturally political, when there seems to be no "immediate instinct" for political union? Hutcheson answers in this fashion:

As men are naturally endued with reason, caution, sagacity; and civil government, or some sort of political union must appear, in the present state of our nature, the necessary means of safety and prosperity to themselves and others, they must naturally desire it in this view; and nature has endued them with active powers and understanding for performing all political offices.[12]

Thus, an admittedly "adventitious" state might still be thought of as a "natural" outcome of man's using all his abilities, and not only his spontaneous and unreflective ones, to solve his problems. In this enlarged conception of what could be viewed as natural, Hutcheson was not alone; Adam Ferguson wrote:

While this active being [man] is on the train of employing his talents, and of operating on the subjects around him, all situations are equally natural. . . . If the palace be unnatural, the cottage is so no less; and the highest refinements of political and moral apprehension, are not more artificial in their kind, than the first operations of sentiment and reason.[13]

Hutcheson often speaks of mankind as constituting by nature one great society, a body, a system; yet there are many societies, too. Thus there seems to be a series of microcosms in a macrocosm: the great society, particular societies, and the individual who is himself a system. The parts of the great system are held together by virtue of the plan and purpose of the whole cosmic scheme; in the case of man his social impulses provide the bonds, and, when he lives in society, that experience calls out and strengthens in him honor, benevolence, compassion, gaiety, and the moral judgment; these, in turn, serve the good of the whole as well as the individual himself.[14]

All is not, however, completely sweet and fair: "the general tenor of human life is an incoherent mixture of many social, kind, innocent actions, and of many selfish, angry, sensual ones; as one or other of our natural dispositions happens to be raised, and to be prevalent over others." Fortunately, some of the unlovelier aspects really constitute a bond of society: anger, resentment and indignation, for example, when not carried to excess, are as necessary for a just and balanced regime as are pure benevolence and generosity. Though these feelings of anger and resentment are uneasy and unlovely in themselves and to the persons experiencing them, they are nevertheless valuable for society. In all of these ways the secret chain between a man and his fellows is forged. The ideal seems to be a sort of balance between the good of the individual and the good of the whole; or, rather, in the phrasing of the period, because the individual is a part of the whole, he becomes the object of his own benevolence when he acts for the good of the whole. Because, however, the happiness and duration of the whole depends on that

of the parts, the system may exercise certain perfect
rights, as Hutcheson calls them, over individuals; for
example, the prevention of suicide, the preservation of
the race, the prevention of monstrous lusts, the prevention
of destruction of useful things, the prevention and punishment of injuries, the requirement of public use of helpful
inventions, the preservation of ideas of the dignity of the
race—all of these are society's perfect rights.[15]

Adam Ferguson again supports Hutcheson when he
too recognizes all the animosities and the dissensions which
seem to be "seeds" in the mind, and which flower when men
are in contact; no more than Hutcheson does he deplore
them in the fashion that might be expected of a moralist.
Rather, he sees them as productive of certain social values
such as a liberal spirit, patriotism, political ability and
the conservation of property, with all the concomitants
of the latter. He does not regret the fact that dissensions
between groups frequently lead even to wars, for out of
wars nations are made:

> Without the rivalship of nations, and the practice of war, civil
> society itself could scarcely have found an object or a form. Man-
> kind might have traded without any formal convention, but they
> cannot be safe without a national concert.[16]

Hume is one of the earliest and most insistent critics of
an individualistic interpretation of society. "Man, born in
a family, is compelled to maintain society from necessity,
from natural inclination, and from habit."[17] Alone, man
is a very inadequate and defective creature, and it is only
in society that these weaknesses are compensated and that
we achieve ability, security and force. But this good
estate was not effected by man's wisdom: it came about
more or less accidentally, developing from family circles
until after long ages large groups, nonkinship groups, became as concerned with peace and justice as were families.
On this analysis, Hume calls sex a first and original principle of human society; next come the ties between parents
and children which have peculiar potency through infancy,
and which accustom the children to expect everywhere the

same system of co-operation and restraint. This precludes any talk of a "state of nature" regarded as an unsocial or antisocial state, unless one realizes that he is using a "mere philosophical fiction." What happens is that individual and community interest become increasingly intertwined and in that relationship men appear to have operating within them a principle of fellow-feeling and a concern for the interest of society, as well as a consciousness of the benefits to be expected for individuals from society.[18]

This principle, or propensity, is sympathy, considered not as a virtue, but as a psychological tendency to share others' feelings. We have, says Hume, a "propensity . . . to receive by communication their [other persons'] inclinations and sentiments, however different from or even contrary to, our own." And, in other contexts: "As in strings equally wound up, the motion of one communicates itself to the rest. . . . So close and intimate is the correspondence of human souls, that no sooner any person approaches me, than he diffuses on me all his opinions, and draws along my judgment in a greater or lesser degree." Evidently this is a "powerful and insinuating" principle. The result is that "the minds of men are mirrors to one another. . . ."[19]

Another notion of which Hume made considerable use, and which has innumerable sociological implications, is the power of custom. True, as he discusses it he is frequently accounting for our mental operations and not for social phenomena, but the implications are there, and they are often made explicit. Typical of some of his statements is this:

Such is the effect of custom, that it not only reconciles us to anything we have long enjoyed, but even gives us an affection for it, and makes us prefer it to other objects, which may be more valuable, but are less known to us.[20]

Now, as Professor Lovejoy says, this is in a way an old story on which Herodotus, Montaigne and Charron, among others, had had much to say; what was rather new in Hume's further discussions was the recognition of the social value of custom, whereas the older tendency, at least in Montaigne and Charron, had been to regard it as an irrational, and therefore evil, factor in human thought and behavior.[21] But in Hume there is considerable anticipation of Sumner's concept of the folkways. The folkways are those group ways of behaving which begin in acts, not thoughts, which arise out of immediate interest or need, sometimes unconsciously and even by accident; their efficacy is judged by results in pleasure or pain; they commend themselves by way of suggestion to suggestible human beings; in time they are regarded as the only true and right ways of doing things, and a large element of force enters into them working through rituals and discipline of all sorts; in short, the folkways constitute a societal environment without which, though it is coercive, men could not live.[22] The sway of custom, analyzed in considerable detail, was Sumner's topic; the sway of custom Hume, too, knew and he credited it with much value for the common life.[23]

The "system" or "scheme" of society Hume describes several times, and in various figures of speech. It is a vast play of mutual dependence, involving buying and selling, co-operative planning, protection of some by others in return for service of another kind, the use of some people as tools while the tools in their turn use still other people and devices. It is, as he sees it, a network of reciprocal services. Now all of this involves something more than the simple, natural social impulses of benevolence and humanity; it presupposes the social virtues of justice and fidelity. These latter virtues are natural only in the sense that man has, by his intelligence, come to see the need for mutual reliability and mutual services if the common need is to be met. It is not that men have ever contracted with one another to work for the common good, but that their good sense indicates what the common good is and, often, a plan for effecting it, just as two rowers "pull the oars of a boat by common convention, for common interest, without promise or contract . . . thus speech, and words, and language, are fixed by human convention and agreement."[24] Individuals come to recognize some common interests and to support certain institutions, customs and conventions, when often their first inclination may be to do otherwise. In this case it is not love of mankind which is operative, but a regard for the conventions and systems of relationships which have been established, tacitly or by law, and which have been seen to have useful results.

In all of this system of mutual obligation and demand Hume finds that there are varying degrees in the reciprocity of services.

> Whoever is united to us by any connexion is always sure of a share of our love, proportioned to the connexion, without inquiring into his other qualities. . . . Nor has consanguinity alone this effect, but any other relation without exception. We love our countrymen, our neighbors, those of the same trade, profession, and even name with ourselves. Every one of these relations is esteemed some tie, and gives a title to a share of affection.[25]

Here he approaches the sociological concept of social distance, which suggests degrees of intimacy of contact, and degrees of acceptance of one group by another which, usually, regards itself and its values as superior.[26] Hume then goes on to say that acquaintance, even, without any degree of kinship, may give rise to preference. Writing on the general resemblance among men, he thinks that likeness

> must very much contribute to make us enter into the sentiments of others, and embrace them with facility and pleasure. Accordingly we find, that where, beside the general resemblance of our natures, there is any peculiar similarity in our manners, or character, or country, or language, it facilitates the sympathy. The stronger the relation is betwixt ourselves and any object, the more easily does the imagination make the transition. . . .[27]

Here is an approximation to Giddings' theory of the "consciousness of kind": "a state of consciousness in which any being, whether low or high in the scale of life, recognizes another conscious being as of like kind with itself."[28] This latter approximation is not surprising, in view of Giddings' own admission of his debt to Hume's close friend

Adam Smith,[29] whose theory of sympathy is so similar to Hume's.

What has Hume to say on the origins of political government? His argument runs along the line that, though men cannot change their natures to lift them out of "narrowness of soul," they can "change their situation," and through government make it advantageous for all to "observe the dictates of equity through the whole society."[30] The results far exceed anything that could be called "simple regulation," for, under government, all sorts of public works and public benefits can be achieved which overcome the limitations of individuals.[31]

In discussing the advantages of society (and here it is definitely political society that is meant), Hume lays great emphasis on the security of property which government guarantees. This security was not possible until it had become the custom to recognize the possessions of others, and to refrain from infringing on those claims. This simple "convention of abstinence" led to ideas of justice and injustice, and still later came the more abstract ideas of property, property right and obligation. "The remedy, then, [for instability of property, et cetera] is not derived from nature, but from artifice; or more properly speaking, nature provides a remedy in the judgment and understanding, for what is irregular and incommodious in the affections."[32] In time, after the social organization is operating well and men reflect on what it does for the preservation of common interests, it becomes a chief source for the promulgation of many other moral ideas beyond those that have to do with possessions. Men become aware of their debt to society, and, in turn, the claims of society are met with less reluctance. Men, in other words, become more and more society-minded: in another of Hume's famous phrasings, "the next generation must imbibe a deeper tincture of the same dye."[33]

To Adam Smith, society is "the peculiar and darling care of Nature," and "justice . . . is the main pillar that upholds the whole edifice," while benevolence is merely "the ornament which embellishes the building." Justice, the acquired virtue, is more to be trusted even than man's natural sympathy, since sympathy requires "particular connections" before it works adequately. He reminds us how unwilling we are to punish criminals for the good of society; we punish more readily and with more conviction if we know particular persons who have been injured by the criminal—"a particular connection" here has worked, but is the result complete justice?

Smith's discussion of sympathy is interesting. With him, as with Hume, sympathy is not primarily a virtue to be acquired; it is a natural and universal human trait, a power of the imagination which allows a person to put himself in another's place, to see the world through that other man's eyes, to feel its pressures and rebuffs through his sensitivities. It is a fellow-feeling, but it is not pity nor compassion, which are feelings with another over his sorrows and adversities; sympathy allows us to participate in any passion or experience of another. It is the ability we have as human beings to receive communications, subtle as well as overt, from and about our fellows, and that reception makes of us, in varying degrees and for shorter or longer time, persons different from those we were.

We acquire from other persons our first notions of ourselves as selves, and we are constantly molding and remolding ourselves to win their approval. In turn we judge all persons who come into communication with us: "Every faculty in one man is the measure by which he judges of the like faculty in another." Society presents itself to us, thus, as a vast network of interstimulation and response (using terms of our day), in which individuals are greatly controlled by the wishes, the judgments, the praise and disapproval of other individuals. Indeed, in these discussions of Smith's—as in those of Hume—which prefigure so much of modern social psychology, there sometimes seem to be no individuals at all, so organic is the relation of person to person conceived to be.

One of Smith's analyses which follows Hume, and which sounds like a page out of Charles Horton Cooley or any social psychologist influenced by him, is that of society as a mirror into which we look. Speaking of the dire condition of a person brought up in isolation without communication, he says:

Bring him into society, and he is immediately provided with the mirror which he wanted before. It is placed in the countenance and behaviour of those he lives with. . . . This is the only looking glass by which we can, in some measure, with the eyes of other people, scrutinize the propriety of our own conduct.[34]

Here is the picture of "the individual conscience as only emerging from the social conscience, the idea of society as the whole from which the individual disentangles himself"; and this it is which Selby-Bigge considers the central idea of Adam Smith's system, "a notable return to a more concrete method of thought" after the methods of a "facile individualism," in which "men started from a conception of society as built up of individuals equipped each with a complete moral faculty."[35]

We may note, in passing, that Smith opposes the doctrine of contract as the foundation of allegiance to the civil magistrate. He takes his position bluntly, whereas his teacher Hutcheson had wavered between regarding the contract as an actual historical fact and as a useful speculation. Smith remarks that the doctrine is peculiar to Great Britain and yet that "government takes place where it [the contract] was never thought of"; and he is sure that most Britishers would not think of mentioning the contract as the foundation of their civil obedience. On one point he agreed absolutely with John Locke: "Till there be property there can be no government, the very end of which is to secure wealth, and to defend the rich from the poor."[36]

For Adam Ferguson the fact of society is one never to be called into question. In his "elegant" moods he writes of society as

the element in which the human mind must draw the first breath
of intelligence itself; or if not the vital air by which the celestial
fire of moral sentiment is kindled: we cannot doubt but it is of
mighty effect in exciting the flame; and that the minds of men, to
use a familiar example, may be compared to those blocks of fuel
which taken apart are hardly to be lighted: but if gathered unto
heap are easily kindled into a blaze.

And, still more elegantly,

Society . . . may be considered as the garden of God, in which
the tree of knowledge of good and evil is planted; and in which
men are destined to distinguish, and to chuse [sic], among its
fruits.[37]

More realistically he writes, "Mankind have always
wandered or settled, agreed or quarrelled, in troops and
companies." Man is "a man in every condition" and "with
him society appears as old as the individual, and the use
of the tongue as universal as that of the hand or the foot."
And, as if to settle the matter, he quotes from Montesquieu, whom he so much admired: "Man is born in society,
and there he remains."[38]

Now certainly this is no nominalism with reference to
society but a genuine, almost a passionate, insistence on
its reality. The picture Ferguson presents throughout his
writings is not that of an artificial grouping of individuals
who behave artificially toward each other, mechanically,
spiritlessly; nor are his individuals motivated by self-
interest or benevolence exclusively. What he gives us is a
description of group life which has existed from primordial
time, in which all human motivations and relationships are
lived out. Man lives in society because he always has lived
in it, and must continue to live in it. The seeds of it are
in his nature: they are seen in his propensity for alliance
and union which man everywhere displays; in his propensity for dissension—"our species is disposed to opposition as well as to concert"; and in his propensity to
preserve himself. It is the latter propensity which, in its
ramifications, gives "rise to his apprehensions on the subject of property"; and while man has no such specific

instinct toward property as beavers, squirrels, ants and bees have for accumulating their little hoards for winter, inadvertently he becomes, "in process of time, the great storemaster among animals,"[39] and, by that fact, very able in his measures toward self-preservation.

Though the fact of man's being in society is rooted in his nature, there are many charms, as Ferguson calls them, which hold him to this union. With man, the affection for parents does not die when the offspring are old enough to shift for themselves, but lasts on, mixed with gratitude and the pleasure of shared experiences. But even such bonds

are of a feeble texture, when compared to the resolute ardour with which a man adheres to his friend, or to his tribe, after they have for some time run the career of fortune together. Mutual discoveries of generosity, joint trials of fortitude, redouble the ardours of friendship, and kindle a flame in the human breast, which the considerations of personal interest or safety cannot suppress.

Then there is the affection which grows up from "mere acquaintance and habitude," and there are all those situations which make a man forget his own individual concerns and act more freely and more vigorously than he knew he had it in him to do. All of these factors, apart from any reckoning of advantages and conveniences, hold man in society. The roots of society are in man, and man would not be man but for his life in society. "Send him to the desert alone, he is a plant torn from his roots; the form indeed may remain, but every facility droops and withers; the human personage and the human character cease to exist."[40]

Ferguson takes account of convention in these words:

Convention, though not the foundation or cause of society . . . may be supposed almost coeval with the intercourse of mankind. Men do not move in the same company together, without communications of mind or intention. These communications become objects of mutual reliance, and even that party may be charged with breach of faith who has belied the expectations he gave by his amicable looks or pacific behavior. From the first steps, therefore, that are made in society, conventions may be supposed to go on accumulating in the form of practice, if not in the form of statute or express institution.[41]

We should note here that Ferguson combats as vigorously as Hume had done earlier in his *Essays* the popular theory of the origin of society and government in a contract. Man was born in and for society, he insists; as for political institutions, they often originated in force, but when people for long periods availed themselves of the benefits thereof and complied with the general requirements, they consented to the government:

> Here is a compact ratified by the least ambiguous of all signs, the whole practice, or continued observance of an ordinary life. The conditions here are ratified, in every age, and by every individual for himself; not merely stipulated, in any remote age, and for a posterity over which the contracting part had not any control.[42]

This was a far cry from the idea of the contract as a definite and crucial agreement entered into at a certain time and place. Though he speaks of civil society representing a concerted plan of political force, he is emphatic in stating that he is not meaning that specific concerted act to which some theorists give so much attention:

> No constitution is formed by concert, no government is copied from a plan. . . . The seeds of every form of government are lodged in human nature; they spring up and ripen with the season.[43]

As the establishing of political government is not deliberate, neither are some of its results. Liberty, for example, and the public welfare are often by-products rather than avowed objectives; casual relationships may result in conditions which appear to have been planned. The tone and character of a nation are determined quite as much by the casual subordination connected with the unequal distribution of property and influence as they are by the particular kind of subordination required by the constitution itself. Once established, however, certain ideals and achievements may be deliberately maintained, sometimes even by the energy and idealism of one man or one party in the state. One must not expect much rationality and conscious planning in the affairs of these human beings, since men

pass on, like other animals, in the track of their nature, without perceiving its end . . . and nations stumble upon establishments, which are indeed the result of human action, but not the execution of any human design.[44]

Buddeberg's judgment of Ferguson's notion of society is very fair. He points out that Ferguson had clearly seen the difference

zwischen einer rein äusserlichen, summarischen Anhäufung von Einzelmenschen und der "Gruppe" als einer neuen soziologischen Einheit. . . . Die Gruppe ist nach Ferguson ein soziologisches Eigengebilde von besonderer Struktur. Sie ist ein ursprüngliche Verbundensein, das "mit der Natur des Menschen" gegeben ist; sie ist ein emotionales Gebilde, beherrscht und zusammen gehalten von den "Banden des Gefühls." Die Gruppe wurzelt, wie Ferguson hervorhebt, nicht in den Schichten des Bewussten, der Zwecke und Interessen, sondern in der Welt irrationaler Motive.[45]

Thomas Reid is as eulogistic as his fellow Scots when writing in general terms of society, but he does not enter into very close analysis of what is involved in societal living. On the subject of our social nature he writes:

The Author of our being intended us to be social beings, and has, for that end, given us social intellectual powers as well as social affections. Both are original parts of our constitution, and the exertions of both no less natural than the exertions of those powers that are solitary and selfish.

And, elaborating one of Ferguson's "elegant" analogies:

Human society may be compared to a group of embers, which when placed asunder, can retain neither their light nor heat, amidst the surrounding elements; but when brought together, they mutually give heat and light to each other; the flame breaks forth, and not only defends itself, but subdues everything around it.[46]

He makes much more of benevolence than do Smith and Hume; he is sure that all the security, happiness and strength of human society spring solely from reciprocal benevolence. He criticizes Smith, particularly, for his doctrine that sympathy is something different from benevolent affections, and in taking this position, he becomes much more particularistic than his two friends, and much less realistic than were they and Ferguson. But they would all agree with Reid and with us when he writes:

> I am very apt to think, that, if a man could be reared from infancy, without any society of his fellow creatures, he would hardly ever shew any signs, either of moral judgment or of the power of reasoning.[47]

Dugald Stewart is one of those whose thought constantly seems to play between the notions of political organization and of generic society without ever coming to a focus for distinction. We are somewhat surprised to find, for example, that when he undertakes a discussion of man as a member of a political body he proceeds to a treatment of marriage and the character of the sexes, property, the arts and sciences—items not all of which we regard as political, but which for him make up the "history" of political society. True, private property, except in possessions such as clothing and tools, is seldom recognized among nonpolitical peoples, and primitive conditions of life do not call for an elaboration of the arts and sciences. The inference would seem to be that, for Stewart, political society was the only kind worthy of analysis. But he, too, can be "elegant" and write that we were made for society

> by the same comprehending wisdom which adapts the fin of the fish to the water, and the wing of the bird to the air, and which scatters the seeds of the vegetable tribes in those soils and exposures where they are fitted to vegetate.

Even the principles of political union may be said to be universal and essential principles of our human constitution, since "man . . . excepting in his rudest state, has always been found connected with a political community."[48]

When we come to the two judges in this group of friends and philosophers, we meet some variations on the usual themes. Lord Kames naturally says all that is expected on the appetite which man has for society, on the benefits of it and the conflicts within it. He makes a good deal of the point that man's capacity for these feelings is limited, that his affections lessen gradually in proportion to the distance of the object, so that family and friends come first and other groups command less and less of a person's good will. There is another angle to be considered, however, and

here comes in a happy contrivance of nature . . . which is to give power to an abstract term, such as our religion, our country, our government, or· even mankind, to raise benevolence or publick [*sic*] spirit in the mind. The particular objects under each of these classes, considered singly and apart, may have little or no force to produce affection; but when comprehended under one general term, they become an object that dilates and warms the heart.[49]

The part of Kames's discussion which is new is his attention to animal society, in terms which go beyond mere gregariousness. Others had made casual references to this and had offered apt analogies, but Kames was genuinely interested in the thought that "the social laws by which . . . animals are governed, might open views into the social nature of man"; and he was disappointed to find little discussion of animal societies in the literature of natural history. To meet the need somewhat he puts together, then, "a few dry facts," "the fruit of casual observation"; he was eager, as always, "to blow the trumpet, in order to raise curiosity in others." Thus he may, without too much stretching of the interpretation, be thought of as anticipating somewhat the discussions of Wheeler, Alverdes, Yerkes, Zuckerman, in our day.

He makes clear that not all animals are found in society; wolves, vultures, lions, tigers, bears—the animals of prey—have no appetite for it. Though they frequently unite for an attack on man or animal, the objective is food and not the company of their kind. It is mostly the harmless animals that show the appetite for society, and the appetite serves them well by strengthening their defense and facilitating the procuring of necessities. Sheep, swine, beavers, bees and baboons are among the animals to which society seems necessary. Other animals live in society for no other reason, apparently, than the pleasure it gives them. Horses afford an example of this imperfect society— imperfect because it is not provided by nature for defense or food-getting—and nothing, says Kames, is "more common in a moon-light night than to see hares sporting together in the most social manner." After this little pastoral touch, he goes on to discuss whether some animals do not really show some proclivities even for civil society. He speaks of the sentinels among monkeys, beavers, seals and elephants; of the monarchical organization of apes and the horned cattle, of the republican form of government among herons and rooks. However simple or complex animal government appears, it is

perfect in its kind; and adapted with great propriety to their nature. Factions in the state are unknown; no enmity between individuals, no treachery, no deceit, nor any other of those horrid vices that torment the human race. In a word, they appear to be perfectly well qualified for that kind of society to which they are prompted by their nature; and well fitted for being happy in it.[50]

In one of the stories illustrating his points in this discussion Kames would seem to be set to rival Monboddo and his delightful orang-outangs. He is commenting on the misunderstood nature of sheep—and M. Buffon, no less, was among those in error—and insisting that they have a sort of military instinct and can very well defend themselves. He then tells the story of a very soldierly ram:

A ram, educated by a soldier, accompanied his master to the battle of Culloden. When a cannon was fired, it rejoiced and ran up to it. It actually began the battle, advancing before the troops, and attacking some dogs of the highland army.

Bleating, we suppose, "Pro Patria!"

For Kames, too, as well as for most of his contemporaries, civilization is practically synonymous with a highly organized political society. It has been wrought out from that state of degeneracy and savagery into which the whole race was thrown after Babel. For the most part there has been a slow, gradual, progressive change, not always intended by man; yet, as a lawyer, Kames knows that legislation has occasionally made drastic changes in the life of a people; and he knows, too, that wars and commerce and migrations have resulted in a blend of cultures, so that it is difficult to trace out original culture patterns.

When Monboddo discusses group life he agrees with his contemporaries that society is necessary, but he will have none of the popular talk that it is a state natural to man; Grotius was quite wrong in reintroducing the teaching that man is by nature not only rational, but even political. The truth is that man has formed social groupings when he has seen the inescapable need for providing sustenance and defense, and he has now his intelligence to meet these needs by group action. Even today man is only partly gregarious:

> . . . man participates so much of the gregarious animal as to have no aversion to the society of his fellow-creatures, far less to be the natural enemy of his own species, as certain species are of others; and . . . he also has so much of the nature of the solitary wild beast, that he has no natural propensity to enter into society.[51]

Since man is a "mixt kind," his society would probably be somewhat "mixt," too. And so Monboddo views it: bad for the best of the animal in man, but necessary for the cultivation of man as a being of mind. He may argue that society is unnatural, but he does have to grant that it is by means of it, the civil form of it, that man has been restoring himself to the approximation of his original status, to the recapturing of all those arts and sciences he lost as a result of his intellectual sin and fall.[52]

Society is not pure gain, by any means, however. It may be well, metaphysically, that man by becoming civil manifests himself as a microcosm within the macrocosm of the great system animated by Mind; but civil society presents many difficulties:

> In this state, every man has within his clothes a little kingdom, but which is not easily governed; for in civil society they [sic] are so many wants and desires, and so many opportunities, which

the civil life furnishes, of gratifying those desires, that our intellectual mind, or governing principle, is very often led astray. . . .

Consequently, civil life leads to many weaknesses and perversions; it tends to exaggerate the desirableness of ease, convenience and pleasure, with their train of money-madness, war and depopulation. So, though it has offered the necessary means of rehabilitating man as man, and though in it man has made wonderful progress, Monboddo is glad that the teachings of the classics and the Scriptures point to a cataclysmic ending of the life of man on earth and to a brighter future in the epoch of the new heaven and the new earth.[53]

As we read the Scots on the subject of man in society we may with reason suspect that several concessions, as it were, were granted by them, though grudgingly, to Mandeville, that "Lord High Bogy-man" of their century, as Professor Kaye calls him. What matter that Hutcheson himself wrote two books against him and that Adam Smith spoke disparagingly of his system "which once made so much noise in the world"? If, as some of the critics of the Scots felt, the Scottish account of human nature was painted a bit too rosy, at least it admitted with Mandeville that complete dispassionateness was not to be expected of man and that some of his egoistic promptings resulted in undeniable social good. Besides, Mandeville did not have to be fought on the point of man's being unsociable by nature, for he had it that though man was always self-seeking he was even more sociable than any other animal, and that was one contention to which all of the Scots except Monboddo held fast.

It must have become apparent from the discussion offered here that society was not conceived very exactly by these philosophers. Civil society meant for them the political state in some form, but *society*, without the adjective "civil," meant variously, as Professor Lehmann has pointed out for Ferguson, any kind of group, any association serving a purpose, or any collectivity as contrasted with a single individual[54]; we may add that it frequently meant sociability. Of one thing they were sure: society, in any of its meanings, was both real and functional. Most of them would have said that it had existed ever since there had been men, and all of them would have agreed that it was, in large measure, a maker of men. Buddeberg's judgment of Ferguson's theory applies to the conception of all of these writers whom we have considered: "Nicht das Individuum, sondern die 'Gemeinschaft' ist . . . der Träger der Kultur und die Geschichte."[55]

By those who were interested in political organization—and most of them were—there was considerable anticipation of Sir Henry Sumner Maine's conception of the differentiation between societies in which the major principle of organization is status, based on kinship relations, and those in which the major principle is contractual relations.[56] There was an even closer approximation to Tönnies' concepts, *Gemeinschaft* and *Gesellschaft*.[57] Whereas *Gemeinschaft*, "community," is seen by Tönnies as a product of nature and propensity, of kinship and necessity, characterized by a common will, dominance of community interests and common property, *Gesellschaft*, "society," is seen as an artificial mechanism, in which individual interests predominate and the solidarity of the group is achieved by contractual relations, both juridical and economic. These eighteenth-century authors are not concerned to labor the distinction, but it is there implied, and brought into the open when they dwell, for example, upon the division of labor which characterizes advanced political societies. Most of them do not emphasize the artificiality of the advanced state, since they are concerned to show that all of man's development is natural, to be expected in the course of time, once we grant man's propensities to meet varying situations and to progress. In their anticipation of Tönnies' conceptions they simply saw a not very complex kinship-group giving way to a larger, more complex group which was required in the later conditions of life, dominated by political bonds rather than blood bonds,

and by the reciprocity of economic services required in
such a complex organization. But much of the sentiment
and loyalty of the older *Gemeinschaft* carries over into
the *Gesellschaft*, especially in small groups and small
communities; in more senses than the historical, then, the
former represents for them the basic social form.

Many details of the Scots' accounts of society have not
been dealt with here; some of them will appear in the following chapters which treat of social institutions as they
viewed them. In this chapter what has interested us chiefly
has been their concern with gregariousness, with man's
bent for society, with the benefits of societal life and the
relation of political to prepolitical society. In talking so
freely of society, what the authors were accepting, without question, was the fact of the social nature of man.
They were conscious of different societies over the face
of the earth and that in each of them there was a web of
relationships, both interpersonal and institutional, among
the beings making up the groups. In this they anticipated
slightly the recent conception of society as functional, as
verbal, and the conception of the group; but their emphasis was put on the common-human qualities of man
and on the social heritage of those born in civil societies.
The most distinctive features in their discussions are,
perhaps, their almost unanimous refusal to accept the
contract as the origin of government, and, more important, and again almost unanimous, their extension to political society of the idea that it, too, though it came late in
history, was as natural to man as any other achievement
which characterizes man's maturity. This marks the enlarging of the conception of the "natural" faculties of
man to include not only the spontaneous and nonrational,
but the rational and deliberative as well. In the words of
Adam Ferguson:

> If the palace be unnatural, the cottage is so no less; and the
> highest refinements of political and moral apprehension, are not
> more artificial in their kind, than the first operations of sentiment
> and reason.[58]

VII

SOCIAL INSTITUTIONS: MARRIAGE
AND FAMILY;
EDUCATION; LAW AND GOVERNMENT

For the most part, society was viewed by eighteenth-century writers as a great structure, the parts of which could be fairly clearly seen in their functioning. These parts, as substructures, were the institutions. The analogies of organism and organ, body and members, fire and embers, orchestra and individual instrument, were constantly drawn on to suggest the relationships involved between the larger whole and its segments. This analysis of the total structure in terms of its substructures was in line with the prevailing atomistic psychology, which tended to see every activity of man rooted in a specific need and an ability to meet that need. Institutions are socially approved ways of meeting human needs and, viewed quickly, seemed to the eighteenth century related very closely to human psychology, especially to a psychology dealing not with the whole man but with his parts.

It seems to us now rather natural that a century like the eighteenth should have been so concerned with institutions. Institutions are procedures socially accepted; they are conventions made not by one but by many; they are arrangements for making easy and felicitous man's life in groups. The century was absorbed in procedures, conventions, arrangements; at the same time it was concerned with the spontaneous, the preconventional, the natural. The bridge which it made between the two sets of apparently antithetic concepts was the belief that it was natural for man to make an order of life different from that in which the race was nurtured earlier, that it was in the nature of his equipment that it should react intelligently and creatively to the situations in which he found himself, however new and different and difficult they might be. If some new solution came to light it was not to be called unnatural just because it had not always been in use; it was as natural, if man devised it to meet well a real need, as was the first instinctive response of man to man. Ferguson offered a neat statement on this point when he wrote:

If we are asked therefore, where the state of nature is to be found? We may answer, It is here; and it matters not whether we are understood to speak in the island of Great Britain, at the Cape of Good Hope, or the Straits of Magellan. While this active being is on the train of employing his talents, and of operating on the subjects around him, all situations are equally natural. . . . But if nature is only opposed to art, in what situation of the human race are the footsteps of art unknown? In the condition of the savage, as well as that of the citizen, are many proofs of human inventions; and in either it is not any permanent station, but a mere stage through which this travelling being is destined to pass. If the palace be unnatural, the cottage is so no less; and the highest refinements of political and moral apprehension, are not more artificial in their kind, than the first operations of senti-ment and reason.[1]

Perhaps no age before or since the eighteenth century has had such confidence in institutions for their efficiency and sufficiency. It was an age of confidence in man, man's achievements and man's future. In England the political institutions had weathered the storms of the Civil War and the bloodless revolution, to the satisfaction of the liberals, at any rate; and in France the whole emphasis of the Encyclopedists and other kindred groups was on the molding power of institutions. If institutions could be correctly devised, then the future was guaranteed to the race of man. Institutions could provide what, in the words of a later generation, could be called the environment, which could suggest, stimulate and call out the best reactions of men.

Institutions everywhere embody most of the social values of the people who live their lives in them. The eighteenth century viewed institutional life as so many fields for the application of moral law, moral law itself being seen as one

of the requirements of man's nature. Discussions of institutions, then, are largely in terms of the individual and
social needs to be met, and of the most ethical ways of meeting those needs for a whole group. Frequently the reader
of today feels that the discussion is too rhetorical and too
much a matter of rationalization and justification; but
here it must be remembered that the larger framework of
discussion in which these particular discussions found
place was that of moral philosophy, the ultimate question
of which was, What ought man to do? How should his
life, both personal and social, be organized?

From our earlier discussions we should expect that
questions of the origin and history of institutions would
assume large proportions, and so we find. The questions
which James Beattie asked concerning government were
asked, with pertinent changes, of all institutions:

. . . for what reasons and by what steps is it probable that men,
not subject to government, would think of it, and submit themselves to it? . . . What may reasonably be presumed to have
been the actual origin of government according to best lights that
may be had from history, tradition, or conjecture?[2]

The openings for rationalizing and for providing conjectural instead of actual history are clearly indicated.
That the same sorts of considerations were uppermost in
the minds of the Encyclopedists is evidenced by the space
devoted by them, too, to origins of society itself, religion, politics, morals, jurisprudence, economics, arts
and sciences.[3]

All the institutions received their fair share of attention. In an age when politics and jurisprudence were
undergoing great changes it was only natural that discussions in those fields should loom large; only natural,
too, that religion should be noticeably to the fore, especially "natural" religion, conceived as that fundamental
rational and emotional response to the universe which lies
back of institutionalized religions. The economics discussed
relates still, for the most part, to the economy of the
household, in the same sense in which it was used by

Xenophon in his instructions to young homemakers. After the publication of Adam Smith's *Wealth of Nations*, political economy, by name, took its place among the discussions. Language was an institution which quite rightly was regarded as the most fundamental of all, as the most necessary for man's life in groups. By all who considered themselves "polished" the arts were much discussed and praised. But at this point it might be well to take account more concretely of the treatments accorded the several institutions by the Scots, remembering as we do so that here, again, they were representative and typical of the thought of the century.

For orientation let us look first at Hutcheson, the leader of the group in point of time. In his prefatory instructions to students in the universities he reminds them that philosophy among the ancients was divided into three fields, the rational or logical, the natural and the moral. Continuing, he writes thus:

Their moral philosophy contained these parts, ethics taken more strictly, teaching the nature of virtue and regulating the internal dispositions; and the knowledge of the law of nature. This latter contained, 1) the doctrine of private rights, or the laws obtaining in natural liberty; 2) Oeconomics, or the laws and rights of the several members of a family; and 3) Politics, shewing the various plans of civil governments, and the rights of states with respect to each other.[4]

Accordingly, Hutcheson's own presentation was divided into Three Books: I, Elements of Ethics; II, Elements of the Law of Nature; III, Principles of Oeconomics and Politics.

The same traditional division is clearly made by Adam Ferguson when he writes that men are governed in two ways; first, by casuistry (which, in his usage, means ethics), when they are not bound by a community organization which sets rigid rules and standards; and second, by laws, when they live in a community which is organized politically. According to Ferguson's scheme, then, ethics consists of two divisions: the ethics of person with person,

abstracted from the network of obligations socially instituted; and the ethics of those relationships which a complex society has already fairly well defined.[5] Adam Smith
delivered lectures on natural religion and ethics, and also
on jurisprudence, domestic law, political and economic
theory.[6] In like manner the field was viewed by practically
every writer who set himself to write systematically in
moral philosophy.

In other words, there were in moral philosophy two
types of ethical discussions: a first, dealing with the in-
wardness of virtue, with the most general principles governing moral choices; and a second, dealing with what
Cicero had called the "offices," or practical duties of life,
the social relationships in which moral obligations disclose
themselves.[7] In this second type of discussion is to be
found mirrored the thought of the day with respect to
institutional behavior. In a real sense, then, these discussions represent a sort of matrix from which emerged
in the nineteenth century the several social sciences.

Let us turn now to several treatments of several institutions, looking first at marriage. Of this institution Pufendorf, in the manner of Plato, had written: "we must . . .
before treating of civil government, consider matrimony,
which is the source of families and furnishes, as it were,
the material for the establishment of governments and
states."[8]

Hutcheson's discussion follows that on the "Elements
of the Laws of Nature" in which he had treated "of the
rights and obligations of that state of liberty constituted
by nature." He proceeds then, under the heading of "Principles of Oeconomicks and Politicks," to discuss "the adventitious states, founded upon some human deed or institution." Such states are "either *domestic*, regarding the
utility of a few, so many only as can subsist in one family;
or *public*, respecting the utility of a whole nation or
state, or even of many states." Discussion of the domestic
relations makes up the field of "oeconomicks," and the

relationships to be centered on are those of husband and wife, parents and children, masters and servants.

In connection with the first relationship we note his discussion of the reasons for marriage among human beings, in which he emphasizes the factor of long infancy. He passes on to what he calls "the chief articles" in the covenant of marriage: the necessity of fidelity of wife to husband, and equally of husband to wife. On the second point he deals in this fashion with the "double standard," so widely observed in the century:

. . . it is a natural iniquity that a wife's conjugal affection, and all her cares and fortune, should be devoted to one man and his offspring; while the affections of the husband are allowed to be intercepted by, or dispersed among several women and their children, and along with it his fortune.

Other "articles" are the necessity of joint endeavor in the education of and provision for children; and the requirement that the bond be perpetual.

He passes on next to the hoary discussion of impediments to marriage, of which our twentieth-century laws are still full—those conditions which render the marriage void *ab initio* and those which render the contract voidable. Here he discusses nonage and disparity of ages, impotence, diseases which thwart true marriage, consanguinity, affinity and prior contract. His Presbyterianism crops out in a number of places, as in his discussion of the low age at which marriage was allowed by the Roman Church and, subsequently, by the common law. He writes:

This doctrine was sprung from that fruitful source of all corruption and superstition, the church of Rome; and for securing it she has taken care to blind men's eyes so as not to use the resources and exceptions justly allowed in other foolish or iniquitous contracts, by cloathing this one with a cloud of the mystical nonsense of a sacrament.

Though he holds for the perpetuity of the marriage bond as an ideal, he acknowledges that there are situations which justify divorce, such as "adultery, obstinate desertion, capital enmity or hatred, and such gross outrages as take away all hopes of any friendly society for the future." In the event that a marriage is dissolved, he thinks that the guilty party should be punished with the severest punishment, since injuries to marriage do greater mischief than such offenses as robbery. The innocent party should not be refused the right of remarriage, however, "for it should be strangely inhumane because one has suffered injury, that the law should inflict another hardship, by depriving them [sic] of a new marriage and offspring."

Hutcheson recognizes that "the powers vested in husbands by the civil laws of many nations are monstrous"; and he anticipates the doctrine of woman's "indirection" by writing that many wives practice a "disingenuous and ungrateful conduct" when they win an ascendancy over their husbands, as if "in resentment of the unequal condition in which the laws have placed them, and out of ostentation of their art and spirit, by which they have broken through them."

The note which surprises the reader throughout the discussion is his emphasis on compatibility and companionship as basic to a right relation—a very modern note. Even the attraction of the sexes, modified as it is by "appearances of virtue and constancy," "plainly shew[s] it to be the intention of nature that human offspring should be propagated only by parents first united in stable friendship." Polygamy should not be allowed for the reason, among others, that it destroys all friendship in marriage. The bond of union should be perpetual, "to make marriage a state of friendship." As for the right of command vested in either party, "it seems opposite to that tender affection, the spring of marriage; which rather points out an equal friendly society." The whole relationship, for Hutcheson, seems to sum up as "a friendly society for life," with all the mutual consideration and assumption of responsibilities which that involves.

Such an "amiable society" comes usually to include children. Parental power is founded in the weakness and ignorance of childhood and belongs equally to father and mother. It does not rest in the fact of "mere procreation," for though the "bodies of children were formed in their first state out of some parts of the parents [*sic*] bodies," it was "not by any wisdom or art of the parents; nay sometimes contrary to their desire and intention." The conclusion is that

children cannot be deemed accessions or fruits going along with the property of their parents [*sic*] bodies. They commence rational beings, parts of this great system, with the same natural rights which their parents enjoy, as soon as they have reason to use them. Generation no more makes them a piece of property to their parents, than sucking makes them the property of their nurses out of whose bodies more of the matter of a child's body is sometimes derived, than was from both parents.

Away then, for all time, with talk of *patria potestas* such as the Romans knew—the father is in no sense a deputy magistrate.

The third relationship to be treated within the framework of domestic economy is that of master and servant—a rather sterile little discussion in Hutcheson. It ends on a homiletic note addressed to masters, the conclusion of which is this:

all are of one blood, and naturally allied to each other, and . . . fortune is inconstant, . . the souls and bodies of servants are of the same stuff with our own, and of a like constitution; and . . . all of us must give an account of our conduct to God, the common Parent and Lord of all.[9]

With constant debt to Hutcheson, whose lectures on moral philosophy he had attended when he was a student at Glasgow, Adam Smith limits himself to the same three relationships when he discusses domestic economy.[10] Characteristically, he injects much more of the factual and historical than does Hutcheson, so that his lectures read a bit more like our contemporary descriptions and analyses. His pages are full of references to the ancients, to Orientals, to Americans, and, especially in his discussion of the property rights of husband and wife he makes many specific references to the laws of England and Scotland. His treatment of the parent-child relation is arid, but when he comes to the master-servant relation he is again full of illustration from the present and from history. Smith gives some attention to the status of free servants and apprentices, to the relationship of guardians and wards, and, with very slight mention of various domestic offenses and the punishments allotted them by law, he brings to a close his discussion of man "considered as a member of a family."

Since the topic of marriage, with its related consideration of the place of women in society, was so much in the writing of the day, it is to be expected that Hume would have something to say, and in the urbane and gallant mood he so loved to affect. We shall note only two papers: "Of Love and Marriage," which was omitted from editions of his essays after 1760, and "Of Polygamy and Divorces." In the first, after a few facetious remarks, he proposes to tell women the truth as to what it is in marriage that men most complain of. It is the "love of dominion" which women express, even to the point of making their husbands look like incompetent fools. He is quick to admit that this tyranny of wives has probably been the result of their rebellion against the earlier authority of husbands, and he devoutly wishes that, instead, "everything was carried on with perfect equality, as between two equal members of the same body."

In the essay "Of Polygamy and Divorces,"[11] he begins with the point of view afforded him by his knowledge of history and of other cultures, and notes that circumstances and laws of various peoples lead to great variety in forms of marriage and in the duties expected of the marriage partners toward each other and their offspring. This variety is as it should be, since man possesses reason by which he can adjust to particular requirements, and all regulations devised by man are, therefore, to be taken as equally lawful and conformable to the principles of nature. But they are not all equally convenient or equally

useful, and with that general comment in mind he sets
out to examine polygamy and divorce. He cites the usual
defenses of polygamy, but finds that they do not carry
weight against the criticisms. Polygamy is unnatural in
that it

destroys that nearness of rank, not to say equality, which nature
has established between the sexes. We are, by nature, their lovers,
their friends, their patrons; would we willingly exchange such
endearing appellations, for the barbarous title of master and
tyrant?

No wonder, he says, that Solomon, sitting among his
seven hundred wives and three hundred concubines, but
without one friend among them, could write pathetically
concerning the vanity of the world! But added to this
major criticism is that that the system is bad for the education of children, especially children of favored circumstances, who are likely to forget the natural equality of
mankind and to have little attention from a father of a
brood of fifty. And when the frightful effects of the jealousy inculcated by the system are taken account of somewhat luridly, there is no verdict possible for him but that
polygamy must be rejected.

Monogamy, then, is the preferred form of marriage.
Shall it be a perpetual union? To this his first answer
seems negative:

Let us separate hearts, which were not made to associate together. Each of them may, perhaps, find another for which it is
better fitted. At least, nothing can be more cruel than to preserve,
by violence, a union, which at first, was made by mutual love, and
is now, in effect, dissolved by mutual hatred.

He meets this anticipation of a modern point of view,
however, with three objections which he considers to be
unanswerable. First, he offers the problem of the children
of separated parents; then he argues that the impossibility
of divorce would diminish the desire for it as a remedy;
and a third argument is that, in a relation so close, it
would be dangerous not to have the union complete and
total in every way, including the element of time.

No great contribution to this problem certainly, from the great philosopher, but only a pleasant manner-of-the-day discussion of one of the recurrent topics of conversation and polite writing.

Kames, with his usual vigor and his zest for the "whimsical," undertakes a longer discussion.[12] He begins by making clear his belief that nature has bestowed different talents on men and women, so there should be no rivalry once it is understood that they are different and that men were intended by the Creator to take the lead in all active enterprises; especially is this true in the choosing of a mate and the governing of a family. His first real topic is the question whether marriage was instituted by nature or whether it appeared late in the history of man as an achievement of municipal law. Great authorities to the contrary notwithstanding—Cicero, Pliny, Herodotus, Justin—Kames insists that matrimony is and was "an appointment of nature," since in the human race the child is so long a helpless infant, and the mother, under primitive conditions of a life sustained by hunting and fishing, unable to provide for herself and it. The same argument from final cause suggests, too, in line with Westermarck's contention later, that marriage was of the single-pair type, since promiscuity would undoubtedly have depleted the race in strength and number. Then Kames inserts a most ingenious illustration to prove that marriage was not of relatively late human invention but original and natural. He resorts to an appeal to the knowledge of children, who, supposedly, are closer to natural knowledge than their elders:

If undisguised nature show itself anywhere, it is in children. So truly is matrimony an appointment of nature, as to be understood even by children. They often hear, it is true, people talking of matrimony; but they also hear of logical, metaphysical, and commercial matters, without understanding a syllable. Where then their notion of marriage but from nature? Marriage is a compound idea which no instruction could bring within the comprehension of a child, did not nature cooperate.

Kames is no sociological relativist, as is Hume, when it comes to the acceptance of polygamy as right for some social systems. To him it represents a gross infringement of the law of nature. Single pairing was evidently the intention of nature or Providence, as seen in the nearly equal number of males and females in all countries in all ages. Too, in primordial time, all men were of equal rank, so that no man would have the social privilege of more than one wife. Polygamy, finally, is not calculated to perpetuate the race either in number or character. He does have to admit that polygamy was once fairly universal in the race and is still widespread among savages, even though the practice be against nature; the reasons given are savage tastes for variety and ostentation, and voluptuousness in hot climates.

After treating briefly of divorce, adultery and the rights of female succession, he ends his sketch by writing more fully on the subject of the causes of the different degrees of restraint which have at various times and in various countries been imposed upon married women. Some of his explanations, offered with many illustrations, are as follows: where luxury is unknown, there is likely to be great freedom; ripening of "sensibility" leads to jealousy, which is a sign of increasing esteem for women, and is followed by increasing exclusion of women from the society of men other than those of their own family; women are trusted with their own conduct in civilized societies, and are treated as friends and companions. The sketch closes, curiously enough, with an appendix devoted to the discussion of propagation of animals and their care of their progeny.

Intimately connected with the institution of the family in the writings of the century were the discussions of education. This was natural, since so much of the education of a child was still under the direct supervision of his parents or of tutors chosen by them; natural, too, because of the expansion of knowledge and the questions that raised for the methods of imparting the new learnings. With increasing secularization, inevitably questions of schools, subjects and methods would have to be debated. It is a fair question, however, whether we are really discussing an institution when we discuss eighteenth-century writings on education, since their import was almost totally the decrying of the inadequacies of schools and colleges, and the placing of reliance on tutors and moral instruction.

Locke had started the ball rolling anew with his *Thoughts Concerning Education* (1690). His theory is frequently called "the disciplinary theory of education," but the discipline he advocated was of the emotions and the understanding, rather than of the memory, which the schools of the day set out to train. His work made an appeal to the gentry and the clergy, and did a great deal to spread the idea that the best method of instruction was at the hands of a wise, learned and traveled tutor who could be a real mentor to his pupil. It is of interest to recall that of the group of Scots we have been discussing, three—David Hume, Adam Smith and Adam Ferguson— were for a time tutors to various young gentlemen and traveled abroad with them to improve their learning, manners and taste.

The great flurry over education was doubtless due to the writings of Rousseau more than to any other one person, especially to his *New Hélöise* and *Émile*. Except for Fénelon of the preceding century very little had been written on the education of girls, and the *New Hélöise* carried forward that particular discussion in much the same manner. Fénelon's *De l'éducation des filles* was a combination of the psychology of learning current in his day, of critical comment on the common failings of women and the ways in which these might be offset, and of suggestions for moral, religious and civic instruction.[13] His *Télémaque* was even more popular, but to us today is almost unreadable because of its unctiousness of tone. Both Fénelon and Rousseau were further popularized in countless "conduct books," which have a history all their own in connection with the development of the novel of the eighteenth century.[14]

Two works considerably quoted were George Turnbull's *Observations upon Liberal Education* (London, 1742), and Dr. John Gregory's *A Father's Legacy to his Daughters* (Edinburgh, 1788). Turnbull, at the time of his writing, was Chaplain to his Royal Highness, the Prince of Wales, and a person of some prestige in the circles of the Church of England. His book is written in the form of letters and conversation with a sage, a form beloved of the century. In keeping with the favored position of the century, too, is his insistence that the rules he offers are founded on the experimental knowledge of human nature. His book contains a résumé of the teachings of the ancients, Milton, Locke, Montaigne, Fénelon and others influential in education; a general essay on education in the art of right living; and much discussion of the methods of teaching languages, the use of fables and the Socratic dialogue, the necessity of instruction in poetry and the fine arts for the forming of an elegant taste, and the resort to travel for the completion of an education.

Dr. Gregory's book is of less moment, except as it illustrates the popularizations of Fénelon. It is done in the form of letters to his motherless daughters. He declares that he considers women the companions and equals of men, though it would seem that they were designed in a rather special manner to soften the hearts and polish the manners of men. On the subject of happiness and marriage, he advises his daughters as follows:

> In short, I am of opinion, that a married state, if entered into from proper motives of esteem and of affection, will be the happiest for yourselves, make you most respectable in the eyes of the world, and the most useful members of society. But I confess I am not enough of a patriot to wish you to marry for the good of the public. I wish you to marry for no other reason, but to make yourselves happier.[15]

Throughout, the tone is one of fatherly guidance, with a little less of the unctiousness and saccharine quality of

Télémaque. Even so, the book brought down upon itself the wrathful denunciation of Mary Wollstonecraft for the efforts of "the amiable Dr. Gregory" to encourage women to dissimulate high spirits and energy for the effect on their men.[16]

Coming to Lord Kames' writings on education, after noting these other efforts, we are not so surprised to find them lying almost altogether in the field of an unphilosophical morality. Ramsay of Octertyre writes of Kames' "unwearied attention to form the minds of young people of both sexes," but notes that he was criticized severely "for going, as a judge over seventy, with young girls of eighteen or nineteen to public places and philandering with them with all the sprightliness of an ensign of the guards." Ramsay goes on to say that when Kames was "in very high spirits the levity of his talk was sometimes reprehensible."[17] Be that as it may, there is no questioning the amount of time and effort he spent in directing the development of some of his young friends. Among his letters is one to John Bell, bookseller in Parliament Close, Edinburgh, in which he writes:

I was informed the other day of a thing published for the use of children by a remarkable female hand Mrs. Barbold. Enquire for it. It is not impossible but it may furnish me with hints. . . . In my young years I had packs of cards for teaching history and geography to children. Please enquire if such things can be got now. I want a pack of historical cards for a present to a young girl.[18]

For nearly three years (May 12, 1764, to March 12, 1767) he carried on a steady correspondence with young Catharine, daughter of Thomas Gordon the younger, of Earlston near Air.[19] Kames at this time was in his late sixties and early seventies, and not only very gallant but more than a little flirtatious in tone at times. He, however, maintained that his idea of the relationship was, as he wrote in the first letter, that he was her mentor and she his female Telemachus. There is much talk about good government and women's part in it; there is advice that

she could profitably enliven her conversation with passages
from plays; he urges that she read steadily in French
literature, since "there are more good books in that language for your purpose than in all the other language of
the world beside." But apparently young Catharine was
"desperately afraid of the character of a learned lady,"
and the reader of the letters feels that the correspondence
yields Kames very little satisfaction on any score other
than that of offering advice freely to a young and fair
Télémaque.

His two published works that may be classified as belonging to the field of education were his *Introduction to
the Art of Thinking*, which appeared in 1761, the year
before Rousseau's *Émile*, and his *Loose Hints upon Education, Chiefly Concerning the Culture of the Heart* (1781).
In the former his plan was to illustrate his moral maxims
by stories, fables and incidents from history. The chapters were headed as follows: Observations tending to explain Human Nature; Prejudices and Biasses founded
on Human Nature; Peculiarities that depend on Character and Condition; Rules for the Conduct of Life; Exhor-
tations to Virtue and Dissuasives from Vice; Reflections
and Inferences; and, finally, his Illustrations, Historical
and Allegorical. If this seems arid matter to our generation, and puzzling in its free use of maxims drawn from
other moralists, we may let Kames' biographer quote us
a very warm judgment of it from Dr. Benjamin Franklin:

In your truly valuable *Art of Thinking* . . . you sow thick in
the young mind the seeds of goodness concerning moral conduct.
Permit me to say, that I think I never saw more solid useful matter contained in so small a compass; and yet the method and expression so clear, that the brevity occasions no obscurity.[20]

The *Loose Hints upon Education* was dedicated to the
Queen—and the culture of the heart. His discussions cover
the authority of parents, the management of children in
successive stages of their growth, peculiarities respecting
education of females, education relative to religion, marriage, knowledge, et cetera; and he ends with two ap-

pendices: I, "Things to be got by Heart for improving the Memory"; and II, "Excerpts from a young Gentlemen's Commonplace-book; being the History of his first Excursion after completing his College Education."

One aspect of the discussions of education produced throughout the century is the effort to interest women in some studies, but to determine, first, what studies are suitable for them. The very serious Dugald Stewart turned his attention to the problems involved. He took the position that, though women as a group appeared to be inferior intellectually to men, the differences were due to education. He means by that term, he says, not only the formal instruction received by them, but the habits of mind imposed by situations or by women's physique. He finds women less strong and energetic, more sedentary and more timid, more mobile in their muscular systems, and therefore more sympathetic, more prone to hysteria, to mimicry and to religion of the "enthusiastic" brand. Women are not trained to think with steady and concentrated attention to some particular intellectual objective, and it is not surprising, therefore, that they show no particular taste for the philosophy of mind and even less for mathematics. Women have, however, a greater facility of association, which shows itself in the ease with which they learn foreign languages and in their ease of conversation and letter writing. And Stewart ends his little excursion by remarking on the greater docility of women.[21]

Hume felt moved to recommend to his female readers the study of history.[22] After facetiously remarking that from it ladies will learn that men are not such perfect creatures and that love is not the only passion which rules men, he passes on to note the more solid advantages offered by the study: it amuses the fancy, it improves the understanding and it strengthens virtue. Quite characteristic of Hume's usual point of view in such matters is the comment:

A woman may behave herself with good manners, and have even some vivacity in her turn of wit; but where her mind is so unfurnished, 'tis impossible her conversation can afford any entertainment to men of sense and reflection.

What is apparent from even these few examples is the rather dilettantish conversation and correspondence which passed for discussion of education. It is noticeable, too, that almost every writer has some special remarks to throw in the direction of women's special needs. Perhaps the best known product of the century's stand here was the amusing work by Fontenelle, *Entretiens sur la pluralitié des mondes.* Here a philosopher undertakes, as he strolls about in the evening with a female companion, to enlighten her on the newer facts and speculations held about the universe. The efforts to render the matter palatable and easy for assimilation, the desire to whet the Marquise's curiosity and lead her to further inquiry but, above all, to more titillating conversation—here is a pattern for many efforts of the century which were more clumsily contrived.[23]

Throughout Europe in the eighteenth century, writers concerned themselves with discussions of law and government quite as much as they did with religion. The reasons were much the same for the two discussions: both religion and government in the preceding century had faced radical changes, and the issues were not yet altogether clear. For the English, it is true, the way ahead in government looked fair enough after the bloodless revolution of 1688, but, as Laski says, the loss of the dogma of Divine Right led to a comparative barrenness in speculative political philosophy. What was written dealt with method rather than principles, and it was urbane, but hardly exciting, literature.[24] Of course for the Scots the advantages of the Act of Union in 1707 were not undebatable, and for both English and Scots the Stuart uprisings of 1715 and 1745 were, to say the least, disconcerting. On the continent, Maria Theresa and Frederick the Great were giving their subjects enlightened and long reigns, and prospects looked bright for continued political prestige for their successors.

In France the state of affairs was most unhappy. Writings of the Encyclopedists and Economists testify to the deep concern over both political and economic injustice. But though other governments as well as that of France might here and there be sharply criticized for conditions as they actually existed, there was everywhere almost unanimous praise for the state of culture achieved under that social organization known as civil society.[25] Here and there a nostalgic mood for the simpler primitive life was expressed, as we have noticed in Rousseau and Monboddo, but for the most part there were in the considerations of civil society only paeans of praise. No significant new political theories were originated, but much weighing of those already in the field went on. Much of the discussion with respect to governmental institutions was in the hortatory mood. That was to be expected, given the temper of the century, and given the fact that so much of the writing for centuries concerning government had found itself as a section within the general framework of a system of moral philosophy. Janet's statement is true to all the facts when he writes:

Les publicistes anciens n'ont jamais mis en doute cette alliance de la morale et de la politique; et les plus grande d'entre eux ont été aussi les plus grands moralistes de leur temps: Platon, Aristote, Cicéron . . . . ces deux études n'ont jamais cesse d'influer l'une sur l'autre, et elles ont une histoire commune.[26]

The general thought had long been, aside from Machiavelli, that government or politics was simply one of the fields in which the operation of moral laws could and should be seen at work. And, further, the thought was that those moral laws were in origin and essence natural, that is, "coëval with the human constitution, from which positive institutions derive all their force."[27] Most writers give credit for the reintroduction into western thought of this Stoic idea to Grotius, who used it to combat both Hobbes and the church. Most of them credit Grotius, consequently, with having been the first to formulate a system of natural jurisprudence, "a system," as Adam Smith

puts it, "of those principles which ought to run through
and be the foundation of the laws of all nations."[28] Enough
has been said throughout this work of the concept of "the
natural," "law" and "natural law" for us to omit further
discussion here. Suffice it to recall the judgment which
several modern analysts have made of the complex concept. Laski speaks of "the mountain of metaphysical right
which they never related to legal facts or political possibility." Barker points out the unhistorical, but moral,
value of the concept and calls it a "confusion of 'history'
and *raison d'être.*' " Kocourek and Wigmore write of
"natural laws" as "that dromedary which has carried the
burden of many a caravan of juridical delusion from the
days of the ancient Greeks up to the present."[29]

Let us once again turn to Ferguson for a shorthand
statement of the relations of general moral laws and specific applications of them in social relations, as typically
conceived by his contemporaries.

Moral laws may be considered under different aspects, and distinguished by different titles.

Considered in respect to their source, they may be distinguished
as original, or natural, and adventitious or conventional.

Considered in respect to their subjects, they may be distinguished by denominations taken from their subjects; as laws of
religion, or of society; as laws of peace or war; as laws political,
civil or criminal.

Considered in respect to the persons to whom they are applicable, they are laws of nations, or the laws of particular states.

The obligation of every law, whether original or adventitious,
general or partial, may be resolved into an obligation of the law
of nature.

The first or fundamental law of nature relative to mankind, is
an expression of the greatest good competent to man's nature.

Subsequent laws are branches and applications of this.

Summarizing another section of Ferguson's discussion,
we find him differentiating types of conduct in this fashion:
Laws of morality are applicable to the conduct of single
parties or of collective bodies. Single parties such as individual persons may operate under the compulsions of
duty, in which case the study of those compulsions and

the conduct affected is called casuistry; or they may operate under the sanctions of compulsory law, in which case
the study is called jurisprudence. Politics, further, is the
study of conduct which is prohibited or required because
it affects the community and state. States, however, having
no common authority above them, find themselves in relation to each other acting as single parties, that is, they
are governed only by duty and the considerations of man-
to-man obligations.[30]

These two passages, considered together, provide the
interpretation for Adam Smith's statement that Grotius'
De Jure Belli et Pacis is "a sort of casuistical book for
sovereigns and states, determining in what cases war may
justly be made and how far it may be carried on"[31]—war
being the only method of redressing injuries among entities which have no common sovereign to compel their
conduct. They indicate to us, too, the confusion to be
expected in discussions of politics, when many of the concepts of natural law and right and morals were carried
over into analyses of governments.

Let us note the formulation of Smith's own lectures on
Juris Prudence[32]—to use the title given by his Glasgow
student to the handwritten notes on Smith's lectures, and
doubtless so given by Smith himself.

Jurisprudence is that science which inquires into the
general principles which ought to be the foundation of the
laws of all nations.

The four great objects of law are justice, police, revenue and
arms.

The object of justice is the security from injury, and it is the
foundation of civil government.

The objects of police are the cheapness of commodities, public
security, and cleanliness. . . . Under this head we will consider the opulence of a state.

It is likewise necessary that a magistrate who bestows his time
and labor in the business of the state should be compensated for
it. For this purpose and for defraying the expenses of government, some fund must be raised. Hence the origin of revenue. . . .

As the best police cannot give security unless the government can defend themselves from foreign injuries and attacks, the fourth thing appointed by law is for this purpose. After these will be considered the laws of nations, under which are comprehended the demands which one independent society may have upon another, the privileges of aliens, and proper grounds for making war.

After a brief introduction in which he notes several writers on natural jurisprudence, beginning with Grotius, he enters on his discussion of justice. Here his major subdivisions are Public Jurisprudence, which deals with principles and actualities of state government; Domestic Law, of which we have already taken some notice; and Private Law, under which topic he discusses property, pledges and mortgages, contracts and delinquencies. Next comes the topic Police, which, strangely to us, involves discussion not only of Cleanliness and Security but of Cheapness and Plenty—the core of the *Wealth of Nations*, when the next sections on Revenue and Arms are added. Finally comes the topic the Law of Nations, the discussion, usual since Grotius, of when war is lawful, of what is lawful in war, of the rights of neutral nations and the rights of ambassadors.

Here is a good Stoic mood reflected by Smith:

Every system of positive law may be regarded as a more or less imperfect attempt towards a system of natural jurisprudence, or towards an enumeration of the particular rules of justice. . . . In no country do the decisions of positive law coincide exactly, in every case, with the rules which the natural sense of justice would dictate.[33]

He may have been remembering Cicero's comment on the discrepancy between the universal law of nature and the civil laws: "we possess no substantial, life-like image of true law and genuine justice; a mere outline sketch is all that we enjoy."[34]

Or take Hutcheson's formulation. It may seem artificial to talk of laws in connection with our conduct, he admits, but "yet it has in all ages been so obvious and familiar to men that it may also be called natural." It is clear that the will of God and the very structure of our

nature give us notions of right and wrong on which to
act: "all these precepts or practical dictates of right reason are plainly so many laws, enacted, ratified by penalties,
and promulgated by God in the very constitution of nature." We discover natural laws by allowing our reason
to observe the nature of things; we discover positive laws
when they have been written down for the government of
a particular people in its particular or adventitious circumstances. Rights, likewise, may be known by consulting
our own good and the good of the group. Rights may be
classified as perfect, imperfect, external; alienable, in-
alienable; private, public, common. His chief concern,
however, is to discuss property, which is a real, natural
right, that is, a right pertaining to some definite goods
rather than to a person, and a right constituted by nature
rather than by some human deed or institution such as
establishes adventitious rights.[35] He discusses the methods
of acquiring property; real and personal rights; rights
of entail and transference. Then he passes on to contracts,
oaths and vows, the values or prices of goods—all those
matters of interpersonal relationship which may or may
not be governed by state law but which originally were
dictated by nature.[36] To prevent violence and to guarantee
the highest values for all, recourse is usually had to political union, which puts the power of the state behind such
arrangements as the state deems best for men in their
relations with each other and with the state itself. His
discussion of politics includes chapters devoted to the
origin of civil government, the internal structure of states,
the various plans of polity, the rights of supreme power
and the ways of acquiring it, the nature and execution of
civil laws, the laws of war, treaties, ambassadors, and the
conquest and dissolution of states.[37]

Kames, the judge, when offering a generalized discussion of politics, takes account of the origin of political
organization, compares different forms of polity in great
and small states, discusses war, peace and patriotism, and
spends considerable time on taxation as the chief source

of revenue for states.[38] It can be seen from even a glance at the topics how much opportunity was allowed the writer to offer his own opinions, speculations and moral judgments, and Kames never missed the opportunity; for, as he said in another volume, "I pretend not to say what our law actually is, but what it ought to be."[39] He did from time to time discuss actual governmental arrangements, as for example, in his *Essays upon Several Subjects Concerning British Antiquities* (1747), in which he discoursed of the introduction of feudal law into Scotland, the constitution of parliament, rank and privilege, and the rights of succession. Scottish legal peculiarities always were of interest to him, as may be seen in a series of essays on entails and royal boroughs in Scotland, appended to his *Sketches of the History of Man*. His more than occasional practicality is once again evidenced in the same essays in his proposals for improving and preserving Scottish highways and thereby encouraging commerce. In an earlier chapter we took some notice of his *Historical Law Tracts*, that strange mixture of philosophy and history; yet Kames had his moments of historical and logical clarity. He early stated:

I never was satisfied with the description given the law of nations, commonly so called, that it is a law established among nations by common consent for regulating their conduct with regard to each other. This foundation of the law of nations I take to be chimerical. For upon what occasion was the covenant made, and by whom?[40]

We have already seen the enthusiasm which Ferguson has for the institutions and achievements of civil society. We have seen, too, his anti-rationalistic point of view which gives credit to instinct and habit always before reason, to concerns of practical consideration rather than to concerns for refinement as such. His essential position on the origin of political organization is that, just as the commercial arts originated in the necessities of man's animal nature, so the political arts originated in the wants and defects of instinctive, or, as we would say, familial society. As men found themselves living in groups it was inevitable, given the inequalities in age, capability, leadership, courage, that some would be looked to for guidance and command. Subordination, thus, is a trait found in rudest societies, and the history of government has largely been one of elaborating, making specific and correcting the requirements of domination and subordination. Want of order within the group or want of security against invasions from abroad has continued to be the impelling motive for accepting the arrangements, but almost never with more of deliberation and planning than characterized the first rude men.[41] Divergences in form and practice, then, are due to the situations groups find themselves in, to their peculiar needs and action-before-reflection techniques, and not to any rationalistic or idealistic programs.

As he was realistic about inequalities of ability and rank in the first societies, so he was realistic on the point of the fact and function of dissent and conflict. Instead of insisting that men once lived in harmony and ought always to live in harmony, Ferguson points out that opposition and strife have characterized human society from the beginning of time and will always do so. Not only so, but the results of such energy and conflict in the social group are beneficial, and historically they have served to hammer out political institutions.[42]

Turning to some comparative studies, Ferguson discusses, with respect to the advantage and disadvantage of the states concerned, the topics of population, the political character and aptitudes of a citizenry, wealth and civil and political liberty. He anticipates Malthus (1798) with the statement that "it is indeed commonly observed or admitted, that the numbers of mankind in every situation multiply up to the means of their subsistence." He anticipates modern social psychology when he insists that "human nature no where exists in the abstract, and human virtue is attached, in every particular instance, to the use of particular materials or to the application of given

material to particular ends." In other words, the particular
political character of a people will be considerably molded
by the type of political institutions under which they
live. He debates the desirable degrees of liberty possible,
and decides that liberty is possible only under political
government; true liberty is "the operation of just government, and the exemption from injury of any sort, rather
than merely an exemption from restraint."

He discusses the legislative, judicial and executive
powers of government from the point of view of their
efficacy to restrain disorder in a state and maintain liberty. He thinks it highly important for governments to
encourage wide participation on the part of their citizens,
and does not shrink from the possibility that such participation will mean divided counsels and even conflict. Such
a situation is to be expected and welcomed, since "the
congregation of men is not, in any instance, to be considered as an aggregate of still or quiescent materials,
but is a convocation of living and active natures"[43]—another expression of Ferguson's own philosophy of activism.

Hume, of course, had been the earliest of the Scots of
this group to write at length on political topics, his first
discussions being embodied in the *Treatise of Human Nature* (1739). Here the character of the discussion was
philosophical, concerned for the most part with the question of whether justice is a natural or artificial virtue;
with the origins, justification and transference of property; with questions of allegiance. It is well known that
his analysis makes of justice an artificial virtue, arising
from the "selfishness and confined generosity of men, along
with the scanty provision nature has made for his [*sic*]
wants." Self-interest is thus the motive, but it is supported by sympathy for others who are treated unjustly
and a concern for public interest—which brings the matter
close to morality. But it is important to note that justice
arose in connection with men's desire to be guaranteed
stability in their possessions, and in no abstract idealistic
regard for virtue. The stability and permanence of posses-

sion, which in time were guaranteed, were never guaranteed formally, but only by convention: some men held property and others withheld their efforts to wrest it from the holders, and all agreed that it was better so than to be continually in conflict and uncertainty.

This convention is not of the nature of a *promise*. . . . It is only a general sense of common interest; which sense all the members of the society express to one another, and which induces them to regulate their conduct by certain rules. . . . Two men, who pull the oars of a boat, do it by an agreement or convention, tho' they have never given promises to each other.[44]

To this point the analysis sounds as if a simple society, made up of individuals so unargumentative and so willing to make concessions, might proceed harmoniously without further artifice being introduced. But such a judgment reckons inadequately with human nature; men cannot resist the impulse to act for near, rather than remote, ends, and this propensity blinds them to issues of justice which are involved. As Hume puts it:

Men are not able radically to cure, either in themselves or others, that narrowness of soul, which makes them prefer the present to the remote. They cannot change their natures. All they can do is to change their situation, and render to observance of justice the immediate interest of some particular persons, and its violation their more remote. These persons, then, are not only induced to observe those rules in their own conduct, but also to constrain others to a like regularity, and inforce the dictates of equity through the whole society.

Such an innovation marks the beginning of government. The advantages turn out to be greater, however, than those of simple regulation; further conventions are made and co-operative enterprises on a huge scale can be undertaken:

Thus bridges are built; harbours opened; ramparts raised; canals formed; fleets equipped; and armies disciplined; everywhere, by the care of government, which, though composed of men subject to all human infirmities, becomes by one of the finest and most subtle inventions imaginable, a composition, which is, in some measure, exempted from all these infirmities.[45]

Hume passes next to the discussion of allegiance and sees it rooted, for the most part, in exigencies of war—a situation which accounts for the fact that most governments are at first monarchical and become republican only from the abuse of power by the monarch. But though the first submission to a governor in time of war may have partaken of the nature of mutual contracts, in the course of time allegiance "takes root of itself, and has an original obligation and authority, independent of all contracts." He thus takes his stand against the "fashionable system of politics" of his day. He does allow some resistance to authority, however, not on the score of promises broken by rulers, but on the score that the interest of the greater part of the people, that is, the public interest in security and protection, is not being served and that the bond between ruler and subject, therefore, is broken. He cannot say too strongly, however, that resistance to supreme authority is in most cases pernicious and criminal, and that only the most grievous tyranny and oppression can justify it. He discusses the principles by which lawful magistracy is determined: after the original promise of obedience on the part of subjects, long possession of the succession, or at least present possession, is useful in the assumption of power; so also is conquest, or the right of succession; and positive laws which set the form of government and determine the method of choosing rulers can establish almost any ruler on the throne. "Time and custom give authority to all forms of government, and all successions of princes," and "power becomes in time legal and obligatory."[46]

Most persons think of Hume's political discussions as appearing chiefly in his essays—an opinion not surprising in view of the fact that the essays were one of the channels by which he determined to capture popular interest after the *Treatise* fell dead-born from the press. It should be remembered, however, that very extended expression of his political theories is to be found in his *History of England*. Reference to that would, at this point, carry us too far afield, but we shall take account briefly of the *Essays*, though they make no effort to present a systematic discussion or theory. Many of them, as he tells us himself, were written with a view to their being published as weekly papers in journals like the *Spectator* and *Craftsman*; and, though he called them trifles, Hume was very proud to display in them that moderation and impartiality becoming a philosopher, and in some moods he was more than willing to have them read in place of his ill-fated *Treatise*.[47]

Those essays which are political divide themselves into three groups: one group debating general theoretical problems, usually with some reference to a situation in British politics; one dealing pointedly with British situations or personalities or both; one dealing with what we today call economics. The last group will be discussed in the following chapter.

Among the essays debating theoretical issues are those entitled "That Politics may be reduced to a Science"—a trifle, truly; "Of the First Principles of Government," which repeats the substance of the discussion in the *Treatise* dealing with government and public interest, government and property; "Of the Origin of Government," in which he reiterates the *Treatise* opinion that obedience is the new duty invented to support justice, thereby inaugurating and maintaining government. There are "Of Civil Liberty," "Of Eloquence," and "Of the Rise and Progress of the Arts and Sciences," in all of which the core of the discussion concerns the comparative advantages of free and absolute governments for the development of the cultured life. The most aggressive of the group are the "Of the Original Contract" and "Of Passive Obedience," neither representing interests new with Hume since the *Treatise*, but they are more popularly presented than in that book, and neither sounds at all aggressive in its opening paragraphs. Nevertheless, these two essays are key essays in Hume's political thought and served, along with the essays discussing English politics and his *History*, to give him the name of Tory which was not so sought after in that age.

What he here admits in the way of contract is a voluntary submission on the part of people to one of their own equals and companions, for the sake of peace and order; but, as he hastily goes on to say, there could have been no compact or agreement for general submission, since that idea would be beyond the comprehension of savages. Rather,

Each exertion of authority in the chieftain must have been particular, and called forth by the present exigencies of the case: The sensible utility, resulting from his interposition, made these exertions become daily more frequent; and their frequency gradually produced an habitual, and if you please to call it so, a voluntary, and therefore precarious, acquiescence in the people.

But when the people's party undertake to say that a mature government today rests on a contract with each citizen, and that unless that citizen receives justice and protection from his sovereign he is free to resist the government, they are being entirely unrealistic and are lacking in knowledge of history, both past and contemporary—for practically all governments have their origin in usurpation or conquest or both. Even the bloodless revolution of 1688 cannot be analyzed as a contract in the free way the people's party would like to make it seem, for the only thing changed by that event was the line of succession, and the persons who determined the changes were only the majority-group of a parliament of seven hundred, as against a citizenry of nearly ten millions. Very little contract there, and certainly very little freedom to resist after the decision was made by the parliamentary group, but most of the citizenry conformed to the decisions and the younger generations were trained to accept the situation and did accept it, additionally, for the sake of stability. Such is Hume's answer to Locke and his disciples who had carried the implications of their doctrine of contract so far from facts.

Logically, then, his transition is easy to "Of Passive

Obedience," where his effort is to "draw the bond of allegiance very close, and consider an infringement of it, as the last refuge in desperate cases, when the public is in the highest danger, from violence and tyranny." The practical consequences of resistance, except in such cases, are too grave to risk harm to public utility, and public utility is, after all, the objective of government.

The essays analyzing British situations seem to have grown directly out of the Walpole-Bolingbroke struggle, in which Walpole had stood for the power of the crown and Bolingbroke for parliament and people. Journal controversies were carried on, the *Craftsman*, the *Patriot*, and the *Thistle* being spokesmen for the Bolingbroke party. Hume entered the field, apparently hoping to win laurels for his own analytical acumen and elegance, but doubtless hoping also to encourage a tone of moderation and objectivity in the principals to the dispute.

In "Of the Independence of Parliament" he discusses the check which operates to keep the House of Commons from overrunning King, lords and people, and seems to remind Bolingbroke that his party is not more restrained and more patriotic than others in staying within bounds. What holds them in leash is the fact that the influence and patronage of the King, with reference to individual members, makes them unwilling to forfeit such favors, so in self-interest the majority hold themselves in check and thus balance, with the crown, other parts of the constitution. But this influence of the King is used in various degrees, as kings come and go, so that a government like Great Britain's is not very determinate in its operations; and, in "Whether the British Government inclines more to Absolute Monarchy, or to a Republic," he avers that an absolute monarchy is not undesirable, since certainty of its operations can be taken for granted over long periods.

Coming to the discussion "Of Parties in General," he identifies parties with factions and declares that they "subvert government, render laws impotent, and beget the fiercest animosities among men of the same nation, who ought to give mutual assistance and protection to each other." Parties are either personal, that is, founded on friendship or animosity as the basic principle, or real, that is, founded on some significant difference in position. After further analysis Hume takes occasion to point out how many struggles of religion have been fostered by real parties in which, however, self-interest was the motive. Turning to the situation at home, in "The Parties of Great Britain," he notes that though a discernible difference in principle has been apparent from time to time, especially in the Roundhead and Cavalier struggle, for the most part self-interest has drawn the party lines and always when religious leaders are involved. But now Whig and Tory confound and distract the government, and how can one distinguish between them? Hume undertakes to give something of the historical setting of the parties and their shifts in principle, but points out that here, too, self-interest, degree of affection for the royal family and other factors enter in to confuse the issues. Again he cannot forbear, by taking an example from Scotland, to point out the pernicious effects of religious factions. In still another essay, "Of the Coalition of Parties," he seeks to correct some misconceptions as to party history and position in England, and to urge that old, and frequently false, enmities be laid by. Particularly in "Of the Protestant Succession," he urges that all hot feelings in behalf of the dispossessed Stuart line be allowed to cool off. He weighs the merits of the two lines, Stuart and Hanover, with the nicest balance, but his final shot against the Stuarts is at their religion—the real reason they were excluded by the British people:

The Roman Catholic religion, with its train of priests and friars, is more expensive than ours: Even though unaccompanied with its natural attendants of inquisitors and stakes, and gibbets, it is less tolerating; And not content with dividing the sacerdotal from the regal office (which must be pre-judicial to any state), it bestows the former on a foreigner who has always a separate interest from that of the public, and may often have an opposite one.

Such is the kind of balanced, elegant attack which Hume makes on matters political in his *Essays*. But the style was acceptable to the century, and the form also, and the *Essays* were molders of opinion—and of his popularity—in a way that was never true of the *Treatise* until a later day when the issues were already settled.[48]

VIII

SOCIAL INSTITUTIONS (*CONTINUED*):
POLITICAL ECONOMY; RELIGION; LANGUAGE

ONE aspect of political problems was not hackneyed in the treatment given it, nor did it represent a mulling-over of theories no longer at white heat, as was the case with theories of the origin and forms of government. This aspect was that which soon grew into the study known as political economy. Here, of course, the great name is that of Adam Smith. No one will today maintain that Adam Smith was the first man to write on the subject of governmental economy; but, as Ingram remarks, earlier writings had been concerned with special exigencies and particular questions, usually of a practical kind, and were designed to offer counsel to governments. What Smith did was to weld together, with original ideas of his own, the theories of some of his predecessors, and to present in sustained philosophical tone an extensive and comprehensive discussion of many topics relevant to the economy of states. The name itself, "political economy," was not new. It had been used as early as 1615 by Montchrétien de Watteville in his *Traité de l'Économie Politique*, and as late as 1767 by Sir James Steuart in his *Inquiry into the Principles of Political Economy*. Two groups of financial advisers to governments, the mercantilists and the cameralists, had, by their insistence on treating government financing as an independent subject of inquiry, paved the way for the emphasis which Adam Smith gave to this section of his discussions in the general framework of moral philosophy; and contemporary with him the Physiocrats were enunciating their doctrines applicable, as they thought, to the situation in France.[1]

But though in Smith's *Wealth of Nations* there is much factual information offered on the situation in Great

Britain, his starting point and orientation are not with
reference to Great Britain alone. He writes, rather, as the
moral philosopher he was, who, at a definite point in his
discussion, has come to make an abstraction of the economic motive in human activity whenever and wherever
found, just as at an earlier point he had made an abstraction of the specifically ethical motivations or the religious.
John Theodore Merz is quite right when he states that in
England—only he should have said Great Britain—political economy started as a province of moral philosophy.[2]
That provincial or subordinate position meant that there
would be apparent in Smith's treatment more systematic
discussion such as characterized the whole reach of moral
philosophy. Professor Viner, when discussing Smith's claim
to originality, speaks of

his detailed and elaborate application to the wilderness of economic phenomena of the unifying concept of a coordinated and
mutually interdependent system of cause and effect relationships
which philosophers and theologians had already applied to the
world in general.

The result of this was, as Professor Viner goes on to say,
that Smith "gave to economics for the first time a definite
trend toward a logically consistent synthesis of economic
relationships."[3]

One other feature of this systematic treatment we may
note. Guido de Ruggiero writes: "The ultimate cell of
modern economic society is not the family with its property, but the business"[4]; and while it was, ultimately, the
business of a state that was Smith's major concern, his
discussions include much material on all kinds of business,
small as well as great, agricultural as well as industrial
and commercial. But that shifting of attention to business,
rather than continuing to talk in terms of the estate with
all that that involves of legal and familial matters, is the
aspect in Smith's discussion which makes him, above any
contemporary of his, seem rather one of ours.

Let us see how Smith defined his undertaking when he
turned to the discussion of the regulations made by states

to increase their power and efficiency. We have seen that his lectures on moral philosophy included natural theology, ethics in the narrower sense, jurisprudence and doctrines based on expediency. Jurisprudence really was a large category including discussion not only of justice—public, domestic and private—but of police, of revenue, of the military and of the law of nations. Police and revenue are obviously the titles which pertain most closely to political economy, but since the first term is obsolete with us, let us note Smith's definition. Police, he tells us, is

the second general division of Jurisprudence. The name is French, and is originally derived from the Greek πολιτεια, which probably signified the policy of Civil Government, but now only means the regulation of the inferior parts of government, viz., cleanliness, security, and cheapness or plenty.

And then he adds quickly, "The two former [cleanliness and security] . . . though useful, are too mean to be considered in a general discussion of this kind." In the same lectures he states that under the head of police he will discuss the opulence of states.[5]

Such a definition he doubtless used again and again from the time he began to lecture on moral philosophy in the University of Glasgow in 1752. When he came to write the *Inquiry into the Nature and Causes of the Wealth of Nations* he had organized his thoughts to advantage and we find him defining his terms with more definiteness. His discussions are now labeled political economy:

Political economy considered as a branch of the science of a statesman or legislator, proposes two distinct objects: first, to provide a plentiful revenue or subsistence for the people, or more properly to enable them to provide such a revenue or subsistence for themselves; and secondly, to supply the state or commonwealth with a revenue sufficient for the public services. It proposes to enrich both the people and the sovereign.

Worth noting is the second form of the statement regarding the first objective of political economy. In another place he uses as equivalent terms "political economy" and "the theory of the nature and causes of the wealth of nations."[6]

But how does he set about his inquiry? His first task is to seek the causes leading to improved and increased production on the part of labor; they are found in industrial organization (Book I). This quickly turns into a discussion of the division of labor as the chief cause of increased wealth; division of labor, in turn, he analyzes not as the product of human wisdom but as rooted in a propensity in human nature to truck, barter and exchange one thing for another. This propensity, like all others, bespeaks self-interest, but, when normally pursued, it involves not antagonism with one's fellows, but co-operation and assistance. Thus, an individual man is usually a better judge of what his own interest is than is any legislator for him, and, if allowed to pursue it, will find himself co-operating with others to achieve his end; and the others, operating on the same propensity, will be satisfied, too. The situation is like this, as he sees it:

Give me that which I want, and you shall have this which you want . . . it is in this manner that we obtain from one another the far greater part of those good offices which we stand in need of. It is not from the benevolence of the butcher, the brewer, or the baker, that we expect our dinner, but from their regard to their own interest.[7]

The division of labor is a characteristic primarily of industrial society. One of the results of industrial organization, as contrasted with an agricultural society, is the appearance of money, stocks, credit. So to these new economic institutions he next turns his attention and discusses their nature, the manner of their accumulation and use (Book II).

But not all countries are equally advanced in wealth nor in the degree of the division of labor which both makes wealth and is a concomitant of invested wealth. His discussion at this point undertakes to account for the different rates in what he is pleased to call the progress of opulence. The difference is due to the fact that some countries follow a course marked out by nature, while others invert the intended plan (Book III). Human institutions sometimes thwart natural inclinations, as in modern European states where foreign commerce, manufactures and agriculture have become the order of preference for the investment of capital—a complete inversion of the natural order of things. He goes into considerable historical detail to call attention to the measures which have allowed Europe to prosper while violating this natural order, and points out that wealth acquired by commerce and manufacturing must still be held precarious and uncertain unless it be made secure by a comparable improvement in agriculture.[8]

The varying progress of opulence in different countries has given rise to two main systems of political economy, one advocating priority of commerce as a means of enriching a country, the other, agriculture. Book IV he devotes to an analysis of these systems, the mercantilist and, very briefly, the agricultural, the latter of which was popular with the French Physiocrats, or as he chooses to call them here, the Economists—a name favored by the theorists themselves. He points out the strengths, weaknesses and inconsistencies of each, especially the devices of preference and restraint adopted by each, and concludes by lauding "the obvious and simple system of natural liberty" which would, with restraints and preferences removed, establish itself of its own accord. Under it

every man, as long as he does not violate the laws of justice, is left perfectly free to pursue his own interest, in his own way, and to bring both his industry and capital into competition with those of any other man, or order of men.[9]

Such a system of natural liberty would leave a sovereign with only three duties to attend to: the protection of his people from invasion by other peoples; the establishing of justice within his country; and the erecting and maintaining of "certain public works and certain public institutions, which it can never be for the interest of any individual, or small number of individuals, to erect and maintain." But such duties involve an ascertainable cost, and this cost requires a guaranteed revenue. Smith turns, then, in Book V to a consideration of necessary expenses of a state and how they may be met, in part by particular individuals and groups, in part by contributions from the whole society. Here occur those discussions of the maintenance of militia, of the courts, of educational institutions, and of the carrying forward of public works such as roads and harbors; here, too, the discussion of trading companies and of colonial possessions which were not always profitable; and, finally, the discussion of the means of financing these various national necessities.

Far too much has been written of Smith's economics for us to repeat detailed discussion here. His three basic doctrines, as emphasized by Gide and Rist, are: the division of labor, by means of which the economic world is kept a natural community; his naturalism and optimism, which allow him to view the economic mechanism as spontaneous activities motivated by self-interest, which, in turn, is seen as having been planted firmly within us by the invisible hand that thus continues its guidance; and, as a practical conclusion, his doctrine of economic liberty and free trade between nations.[10] Even the mention of these doctrines shows how much of a piece they were with the whole pattern of thought we have been discussing throughout this book. Hasbach's judgment on Adam Smith therefore seems just: "Er ist kein Pfadfinder der Wissenschaft, sondern ein im höchsten Masse receptiver Kopf . . ."; and, on the *Wealth of Nations*: "eine im grossen und gangen vollendete Zusammenfassung alles desjenigen. . . ."[11]

Though we shall go no further into analysis and interpretation of these doctrines themselves and their implications, we shall, nevertheless, make several comments with the intention of pointing out the intellectual setting of the work and some items of Smith's indebtedness.

Professor Edwin Cannan reminds us that in Smith's own time Dr. Samuel Johnson and Malachi Postlethwayt seriously debated whether a trader could be a gentleman. (Incidentally, it may be recalled that Smith said of Johnson: "Of all the writers, ancient or modern, he that keeps off the greatest distance from common sense is Dr. Samuel Johnson."[12]) Adam Smith's doctrines helped make such debate impossible. His gospel of the mutual service which is unintentionally given when each man follows his own interest provided a comfortable philosophy for those soon to be caught up in the machine age which he had barely glimpsed. Professor Cannan, who does not object to Smith's being hailed as the father of "bourgeois economics," has this to say of the generosity of that gospel: "the modern trader can practice virtue as well as a Greek philosopher, a mediaeval begging friar, or a twentieth-century social reformer."[13]

Certainly no one today, and very few ever, would agree with Ruskin's heated judgment that Smith himself was a "half-bred and half-witted Scotchman who taught the deliberate blasphemy: 'Thou shalt hate the Lord thy God, damn his laws and covet thy neighbour's goods.' "[14] On the other hand, as recently as 1934 a book was published which declares that one of Smith's reasons for writing *The Wealth of Nations* was "to record his disgust with the chicanery which the merchants and manufacturers practiced."[15] Though there has been such variety of judgment as to Smith's intention, there is considerable agreement that his doctrine of the natural order, which bespoke freedom of economic enterprise motivated by self-interest, has been consistently used as a rationalization and justification of capitalism, even though Smith may not so have intended it.

We now have good evidence that Adam Smith was not simply a British edition of the Physiocrats. Long before his visit to France or the publication of any significant French treatise by the Physiocrats, the essentials of Smith's political economy were already being taught in his lectures in the moral philosophy class in Glasgow.[16] True, back of him lay many authors from whom he gleaned

ideas and points of view. Pufendorf's discussions carried
great weight with him, as with others of the Scots, particularly Pufendorf's discussion "Of Value," in the *De Officio
Hominis et Civis* (1673). This doctrine was mediated to
Smith by his own instructor at Glasgow, Francis Hutcheson, who, in his turn, had had as instructor Gershom Car-
michael, who had done the English translation of Pufendorf. Again, like others of the Scots, Smith knew well
the writings of John Locke; and there were Sir William
Petty, Thomas Mun, Simon Clement and Sir James
Steuart who had had somewhat to say in this field. But
two contemporaries and one near-contemporary (namely,
Hutcheson, Hume and Mandeville) were more useful to
him than were all the others, including the Physiocrats.

We are reminded by Benn that Smith recovered,
rather than discovered, the principle of the division of
labor. It had been used by Plato in *The Republic* and,
even before Plato, Anaxagoras and Diogenes of Apollonia
had talked of progressive differentiation as the world-wide
principle by which order is evolved from chaos.[17] More
consciously in Smith's mind, however, was the fairly recent use of the idea by Mandeville in his *Fable of the
Bees* (1705). Hutcheson had sought to disprove Mandeville's doctrine of self-interest. Smith himself had said
that Mandeville had .destroyed the distinction between
vice and virtue, and that the effects of his teaching were,
therefore, wholly pernicious and led to vice's flaunting
itself audaciously.[18] Yet when Smith describes the making
of a laborer's coat, for example, not only is the concept
of the division of labor which is employed very close to
that of Mandeville's, but the language itself is Mandeville's. Mandeville had likewise made systematic the idea
of *laissez faire*. As Mr. Kaye points out, every practical
aspect of the argument had been anticipated before Mandeville even, but Mandeville had forcefully identified the
good of the state and the good of the individual.[19] What
Smith did was to elaborate on that identification and on

the beneficent results. The idea thus formed one aspect of his doctrine of economic individualism.

Another aspect of Smith's individualism, the logical form, was a heritage from Cartesian days, and had become firmly entrenched in English methodology by way of Hobbes and Locke. According to this method not only are individuals separated from their social group and examined as if *in vacuo*, but within the individual more minute entities are isolated and then projected as active agents which account for man's activities and relationships. Thus, self-interest with Smith is isolated as a force accounting for all the economic activities of man. No matter that the quality of the entity studied is not of the quality of reason, as with the Cartesians, but of the instinctive and emotional type, we have to say that it is used, in quite the manner of the Rationalists, as an original fact from which other facts, representing developments in the course of time, may be deduced. This results in a considerable abstraction, an abstraction so neglectful of other factors that actually are in operation that Vaihinger has included Smith's "economic man" among his "fictions."[20]

Because the abstraction was what it was, that is, an isolation of economic motivations and processes, Smith's theory is labeled materialistic. Lange, in his *History of Materialism*, is fair enough to point out that for Smith himself "this market of interests was not . . . the whole of life, but only an important side of it"; it was Smith's successors who "forgot the other side and confounded the rules of the market with the rules of life, nay even with the elementary laws of human nature."[21] But those successors had broken away from the comprehensive demands of the older moral philosophy and had no check on their theories while they considered economic motives in complete isolation.

In the amiable Hutcheson, as well as from Mandeville, Smith had a precedent for resorting to self-interest as an explanatory principle when he came to an analysis of economic processes. Hutcheson had taught and written:

> General benevolence alone is not a motive strong enough to industry, to bear labour and toil, and many other difficulties which we are averse to from self-love. For the strengthening therefore of our motives to industry, we have the strongest attractions of blood, of gratitude, and the additional motives of honour, and even of external interest. Self-love is really as necessary to the good of the whole as benevolence; as that attraction which causes the cohesion of the part, is as necessary to the regular state of the whole as gravitation.[22]

Indeed, what has to be said again is that much of Smith's economic theory is to be attributed not to Quesnay and the Physiocrats, nor even to Hume, but to Francis Hutcheson, who antedates both. The system of natural liberty, with its concomitant of optimism, is in Hutcheson. So is the theory of the division of labor, and the theory that labor is the chief creator of value—the latter theory occasionally cited to make Adam Smith out a socialist. There is the same point of view on money and interest, and, in the *Lectures* of Smith, the same silence on distribution as in Hutcheson. What would seem to be true is that in the years when he was teaching at Glasgow, before he had been to France or read any of the Physiocratic writings, Smith's basic formulations of political economy were molded by the positions of Hutcheson more than by any other one man.[23]

Of course, as always, there was Hume, the father of positivism, as Windelband somewhere called him. In whatever field one undertook to write after the middle of the century, Hume was almost certain to have been there first, if only with an essay. His *Political Discourses* of 1752, incorporated later in the *Essays*, preceded not only Smith's publication in the field of political economy but also that of the chief Physiocrats.[24] In essay form though these discussions were, they were as Laski says, together with Hume's metaphysics, "the most powerful dissolvent the century was to see"; Turgot thought so highly of them that he translated several, including "Of the Jealousy of Trade," into French; and Dugald Stewart declares that they "were evidently of greater use to Mr. Smith than any other book that had appeared prior to his lectures."[25]

For the sake of brevity and cogency we may use the summary of a modern critic who knows the century well, and who begins by saying that, for one to whom the study of such phenomena was but a casual inquiry, it is marvelous how much Hume saw:

He is free from the crude errors of mercantilism; and twenty years before Adam Smith hopes, "as a British subject," for the prosperity of other countries. "Free communication and exchange" seems to him an ordinance of nature; and he heaps contempt upon those "numberless bars, obstructions and imposts which all nations of Europe, and none more than England, have put upon trade." Specie he puts in its true light as merely a medium of exchange. The supposed antagonism between commerce and agriculture he disposes of in a half-dozen effective sentences. He sees the place of time and distance in the discussion of economic want. He sees the value of a general level of economic equality, even while he is sceptical of its attainment. He insists upon the economic value of high wages, though he somewhat belittles the importance of wealth in the achievement of happiness. Before Bentham, who on this point converted Adam Smith, he knew that the rate of interest depends upon the supply of and demand for loans. He insists that commerce demands a free government for progress, pointing out, doubtless from his abundant French experience, that an absolute government gives to the commercial class an insufficient status of honour. He pointed out, doubtless with France again in his mind, the evils of an arbitrary system of taxation.

And then Laski—for it is he who has been quoted—adds, "*The Wealth of Nations* would less easily have made its way had not the insight of Hume prepared the road for its reception."[26]

One other of the Scottish group helped to spread Smith's teachings and that was Dugald Stewart, from his chair of moral philosophy in the University of Edinburgh. Popularizing and making concrete Smith's teachings were definite objectives Stewart set himself, though

he talked a great deal of other economists, too.[27] Lord
Cockburn gives a rather nice picture of the situation:

> The opening of these classes made a great sensation. The
> economical writings of Hume and Smith, though familiar with
> the liberal youth, had so little impregnated the public mind, that
> no ordinary audience could be collected to whom the elements
> and phraseology of the science were not matters of surprise. The
> mere term "Political Economy" made most people start. They
> thought it included questions touching the constitution of govern-
> ments; and not a few hoped to catch Stewart in dangerous propo-
> sitions. It was not unusual to see a smile on the faces of some
> when they heard subjects discussed upon seemingly beneath the
> dignity of the Academical Chair. The word *corn* sounded strangely
> to the Moral class, and *drawbacks* seemed a profanation of Stew-
> art's voice.[28]

In his zeal to do justice to political economy, Stewart
left the discussion of politics proper almost unattended.
In his published *Works* the theory of government covers
one hundred and two pages, while the theory of political
economy covers seven hundred and sixty-three. But he
was not content to discuss population, wealth and trade
merely as resources of the state. His general philosophical
and ethical interests were always to the fore and his aim
was to put before politicians the standards by which the
wisdom and expediency of every institution should be
checked. A political economist must know human motives
and aspirations and must safeguard and balance the
concerns of various groups of people and various localities.
One of the economist's major problems becomes the ascer-
taining of what the state should take upon itself and
what it should leave to individual initiative, and the solution cannot be approached without an adequate knowledge of the human mind. And always the economist must
seek to serve not simply the financing of the state, but
the welfare and happiness of the state's citizens.[29]

Gide and Rist may, perhaps, be too generous in their
judgment when they declare that "Smith persuaded his
own generation," but with the latter part of their statement we can agree: [he] "governed the next."[30] How his

doctrines were taken up, not only by Stewart, but by Say, Malthus and Ricardo, and repeated until recently is well known; well known, too, how his teachings influenced the statesmanship of men like Lord North and Pitt, to mention only the Britishers. It is only in our own day that a book can be written with the title *The End of Laissez-Faire*,[31] and whether or not the practice, as well as the theory, has come to an end will have to be reported by analysts in the next generation and later.

An analyst of the writings of Bishop Butler says of the eighteenth century that it "had a facile interest in religion, its sins were vulgar, and its virtues were dull."[32] While agreeing with the last two of the charges and somewhat with the first, we must remind ourselves that the constant and trenchant criticism of Hume, the vitriolic attacks of Voltaire, the emergence of nonconformist Quakerism, Unitarianism and especially Methodism, bespeak something more than an interest that is merely facile. It is true that, as in the case of political conflicts, the issues had been at white heat in the preceding century when in England James II tried to restore Catholicism and in France Louis XIV tried to destroy Protestantism, and when the greatest authors in literature and philosophy, as well as in theology, took part in the controversy. But the eighteenth century is, after all, roughly the century of English Deism, unexciting though that may be and facile enough in some hands, but the interest aroused at the time was enough to give character to the succeeding century; and in France, though the Catholic reaction quickly set in, Bayle's Dictionary did its share in preparation of the revolution which dethroned God as well as the king. In Scotland, as we have already seen, it was the century when "a new face was put on theology" and when the "New Light" appeared.

Without claiming too much for the ardor of the century we may, however, wonder whether the very phrase most often used in describing the newer approach to religion may not have led to misunderstanding concerning

the hold of religion on the people. To speak of a religion
as "natural" religion does make it sound easy and elementary, and may very well suggest merely facile interest
in such a system of thinking. But we may doubt whether
that was the significance of the term for the men of the
day, when they were as deeply interested as they were in
nature, particularly human nature, and all the products
that were labeled "natural." We have seen their efforts
to hammer out the natural laws of morality, to discover
the natural principles of taste, to outline a natural jurisprudence, to discover the natural progress of opulence
and the natural history of every institution they knew.
What more probable, then, than that they should devote
a good deal of interest to Natural Religion, in the same
effort to get at universal elements in all religions? Thus
they would have a scientific (or, as they would have preferred to say, a philosophical) approach to a basic social
phenomenon.

A living Scottish philosopher gives an excellent definition of the theology of Natural Religion at its best:

> It is the doctrine of God and the divine seriously taught by
> scientific philosophers as an integral part of a reasoned theory
> of φύσις, *natura*, the reality of things. It thus makes a definite
> claim, well founded or not, to be genuine ἐπιστήμη, to give us
> truth, in the same sense in which geometry or arithmetic does so.[33]

We might expect, then, that wherever thinkers interested
themselves in nature, whether physical or human, Natural
Religion would be one of their avenues of investigation.
And so it has been. The Ionian natural philosophers of
the sixth century B.C., with their knowledge of the physical world and its orderliness, found the polytheistic religion of their people untenable, not only because of the
multiple gods involved, but because of the disorder and
whim which would have resulted in the running of the
universe by such erratic beings. Not many of them were
concerned to state a positive teaching with respect to
religion, and from these pre-Socratic philosophers the
problem was carried over to Plato, who devotes the tenth

book of *The Laws* to it. The conclusion of the discussion there is that "there are gods, that they are mindful of us, that they are never to be seduced from the path of right." This demonstration is, according to Professor Taylor, "the first attempt in the literature of the world to demonstrate God's existence and moral government of the world from the known facts of the physical order."[34] But it was far from the last. As another commentator puts it, when writing of the eighteenth century:

the conception of Natural Religion . . . which had endured through all the vicissitudes of Greek philosophy, had been accepted as fundamental by the reasoned faith of the Middle Ages . . . was now exposed to view by sceptical denudation as the bedrock of theological belief.[35]

The quotation just given suggests the use to which Natural Religion could be put by a person devoted to revealed religion—it could be the foundation on which revelation could raise a structure peculiar to itself, so long as the structure did not contradict the foundation. It was supposed by many that that foundation would be fairly similar and substantial among all peoples, no matter how primitive. But what Benn says of Cicero's Natural Religion could be said of many another thinker's: "nothing more unnatural, in the sense of remoteness from primitive conceptions, has ever been devised."[36] Be that as it may, the fact remains that many an orthodox Christian found himself held quite as much by what was natural in his religion as by what was revealed, or, to put the matter another way, his revealed religion might be vindicated to him by his natural theology.

But the true Deist left no place for supernatural revelation. We cannot here trace the history of the Deistic movement from the days of Herbert of Cherbury and John Locke, both of whom did cling to the unique features of Christianity, through those members of the school who trusted only in reason as formulator of religion and the guide of life, to the time, a century after its beginning, when Hume blasted the foundations of the movement by attacking the validity of the reasoning process itself on which Deism rested.[37] We need only note that the distinctions between Deism and Natural Religion could not always be neatly drawn, for there was no strict consensus of the writers in the use of terms, though the feeling prevailed that Deism was much more tinged, to its disadvantage, with Rationalism; and we can note, too, that among the orthodox real hostility was directed toward those regarded as Deistic destroyers of Christianity.

Before examining Hume's arguments which were to prove so devastating to believers, we may recall several statements from others of the Scottish group. First, let us look at Hutcheson, on Natural Religion:

As the order, grandeur, regular dispositions, and motions, of the visible world, must soon affect the mind with admiration; as the several classes of animals and vegetables display in their whole frame exquisite mechanism, and regular structure, evidencing counsel, art and contrivance for certain ends; men of genius and attention must soon discover some intelligent beings, one or more, presiding in all this comely order and magnificence. . . . Thus some devotion and piety would generally obtain, and therefore may justly be called natural to a rational system. . . . Notions of Deity and some sort of worship have in fact as universally obtained among men, as living in society, the use of speech, or even propagating their kind; and thus may be counted as natural.[38]

We may remember that, while he was professor at the University of Glasgow, Hutcheson gave public lectures on Sunday on the "Evidences of Christianity," in the manner of Grotius' *De Veritate Religionis Christianae.*

In his *History of Ancient Physics* Adam Smith writes as follows:

As soon as the Universe was regarded as a complete machine, as a coherent system, governed by general laws, and directed to general ends, viz., its own preservation and prosperity, and that of all the species that are in it; the resemblance which it evidently bore to those machines which are produced by human art, necessarily impressed those sages with a belief, that in the original formation of the world there must have been employed an art resembling the human art, but as much superior to it as the world is superior to the machines which that art produces.

And then he adds: "thus . . . science gave birth to the first theism that arose among those nations, who were not enlightened by divine Revelation."[39]

While Smith began his lectures in the course on moral philosophy by discussing Natural Theology, he did not see fit to use his Sundays as his predecessor Hutcheson had done, to sermonize to the public and students on Christian Evidences. Ramsay of Ochtertyre has a story to the effect that Smith objected to another of the Glasgow customs, that of opening classes with prayer, and asked to be excused from such practice. Ramsay records that the request was refused, and then adds dryly, "His prayer savoured strongly of Natural Religion."[40]

Adam Ferguson, after enlarging on the evidences of design in the universe, deals with a question not raised by every author:

> Whether this lesson, to be taken from the aspect of things, be obvious to every beholder, or only to a few of superior discernment, and from them communicable and easily received by the ordinary class of men, we may not be able to determine, and is not of moment to our present argument in accounting for religion as the gift of nature, to every nation and to every age. For, in every nation and in every age, the few may be found who are fit to receive and communicate to others the apprehension of design in the works of God.

And then, characteristically, he adds:

> This conception . . . is, like other articles in the progressive and variable nature of man, a foundation on which he may build; a germ which, in the progress of his nature, may wax to indefinite magnitude and strength; or, if we may still vary the image, it may be considered as one of the rude materials on which he himself is to exert his talent for art and improvement.[41]

Dugald Stewart devoted one-fourth of his lectures on the active and moral powers of the mind to an inquiry into the principles of Natural Religion. Therein he discussed the proofs for the existence of God, both a priori and a posteriori proofs being used; evidences of the moral attributes of the Deity; arguments for life after death; and finally, the duties owed to the Deity by man.

When he came to publish his disquisitions he seemed to feel that he owed his readers some explanation for having spent so much time on this topic. His defense includes the following items: first, the lectures, from their inception in the University of Edinburgh in 1792-1793 until twenty years later, were attended by students from England, the United States, Germany, Switzerland, France and other countries; we infer that Stewart felt it was more courteous to discuss Natural Religion than any specific religion in the presence of such a heterogeneous group. Second, it was a revolutionary epoch and the country was inundated with sceptical and atheistic publications; Stewart wished to demonstrate that a person could show an "enlightened zeal for political liberty" as did he, without going to the lengths of "the reckless boldness of the uncompromising free-thinker." Third,

> Certain divines in Scotland were pleased, soon after this critical era, to discover a disposition to set at nought the evidences of Natural Religion, with a professed, and, I doubt not, in many cases, with a sincere view to strengthen the cause of Christianity.[42]

He is reminded of Locke's judgment of such a situation, which he approves:

> He that takes away Reason to make way for Revelation puts out the light of both, and does much the same as if we would persuade a man to put out his eyes, the better to receive the light of an invisible star by a telescope.[43]

Thirty years after beginning his course Stewart rejoices that the more general diffusion of knowledge among all ranks has now made such emphasis less necessary. He rejoices particularly that the way in which scientific knowledge is now presented leads to contemplation not only of nature, but of God.

When Kames came to consider Natural Religion[44] the most dangerous obstacle to be met, he thought, was his friend David Hume's arguments on the connection between cause and effect. Those arguments, with their insistence that we can know nothing of cause and effect save the facts of sequence, ultimately struck at the root

of the effort to prove the existence of God from nature—
nature viewed as the effects He caused. Kames, therefore,
set himself to examine Hume's argument—and had to
accept it, to the extent, that is, of admitting that reasoning can never actually demonstrate causal connection.
Going a step further with Hume, he falls back on the
function of belief, which, without formal proof, convinces
us that such a connection does exist even though it cannot
be demonstrated. Belief is a feeling, an internal light
accompanying our perceptions, and it is irresistible in
the commendations it makes to us of the world. Reason
may support it, but is not the essential element in belief.

But Hume was not the only obstacle. Kames was just
as much irritated by Dr. Samuel Clarke's *Discourse Concerning the Attributes of God, the Obligations of Natural
Religion, and the Truth and Certainty of the Christian
Revelation*. These Boyle Lectures of 1704-1705, embodying the discourse, exemplified the highest degree of a
priori reasoning, in good Cartesian fashion. Kames sus-
pected that such arguments were "slippery and far-
fetched," but his chief objection was that such procedure
would seem to indicate that knowledge of God was "re-
served for persons of great study and deep thinking"—a
position analogous to the protest against rationalistic
ethics. But even the vulgar have the advantage of perception and feeling and the beliefs that spontaneously
arise in the heart, and surely, in an affair of religion,
these are the avenues to follow to come to knowledge of
God. So, an appeal to arguments a posteriori may be
made by any and all, if only they completely refuse to
argue and simply accept the evidence of belief. His conclusion is:

When, at last, we take in at one view, the natural and moral
world, full of harmony, order and beauty; happily adjusted in
all its parts to answer great and glorious purposes; there is, in
this grand production, necessarily involved, the perception of a
cause, unbounded in power, intelligence and goodness.

And then he proceeds to discuss the attributes of Deity as unity, power, intelligence and benevolence—comprehensions which, to our way of thinking in the twentieth century, seem rather°difficult to be arrived at by natural man, but not for Kames' century.

Kames ended this discussion with a prayer which, in addition to embodying praise and petition, in Protestant fashion set forth an intellectual position:

> Where reason is unavailing, instinct comes in aid, and bestows a power of divination, which discovers the future, by the past. Thus, thou gradually liftest him up to the knowledge of thyself. The plain and simple sense, which in the most obvious effect, reads and perceives a cause, brings him straight to thee, the first great cause, the antient of days, the eternal source of all. Thou presentest thyself to us, and we cannot avoid thee. We must doubt of our own existence, if we call in question thine . . . everything thou hast made is good.[45]

Very obvious throughout, of course, is Kames' delight in reasoning on the evidences of final cause or design. No matter what objections had been raised by Hume, Descartes and Bacon, the common sense of the procedure was, to him, too clear to be denied; and most of his century was with him rather than with the critics.

What did Hume do with the popular discussion of religion? One answer we can make with certainty, and that is that it was a lifelong interest with him, one which he could not let alone. Even in the *Treatise*, his first publication, there were many obiter dicta related to religion; throughout his life he debated with friends the wisdom of publishing certain of his "pieces"; after his death appeared the *Dialogues Concerning Natural Religion*. Another thing to be said with certainty is that, much more than over his metaphysics and ethics, even, the controversy has continued as to what Hume really intended to say. Some commentators have felt that, from time to time at least, he would have wished to be as orthodox as the most "vulgar" of his fellows and that, in some moods, he was intent on establishing whatever could be established by the mind of man, if nothing more than a very pale Theism. Deist he should never be called, though he has been; for, with his shafts directed against the efficacy of reason, he was destroying the foundations on which that brand of religion was built. Again, it has been urged that Hume's most consistent attitude was, as Professor A. E. Taylor thinks, an amused and detached contemplation, with some of the foibles of "a very clever man" apparent in it. And, finally, there is the contention, upheld by the colleague of Professor Taylor at the University of Edinburgh, Professor Norman Kemp Smith, that, in spite of his many warm friends among the Moderates, Hume very definitely regarded religion as a malign influence to be exposed for all that it is and is not.[46]

Taking his several papers on religion, let us see the aspect of belief or practice with which each concerns itself and what would seem to be its contribution to the current discussions.

His essay "Of Miracles"[47] was suggested to him while he was in France on his first visit, when, in the cloisters of the Jesuit College of La Flèche, where Descartes had been educated, he engaged in conversation with a priest concerning the alleged miracles at the tomb of the Abbé Paris. The avowed purpose of this essay is to "silence . . . bigotry and superstition, and free us from their impertinent solicitations." The weakness and the contrariety of evidence offered in support of miracles are enough to convince him that, in the face of the laws of nature, "no testimony for any kind of miracle has ever amounted to a probability, much less to a proof"; and "we may establish it as a maxim, that no human testimony can have such force as to prove a miracle, and make it a just foundation for any such system of religion." But in treating of miracles specifically, Hume is treating of revealed religions generally, and when he proves that reason and evidence invalidate miracles he is really saying that a revealed religion in the same way is invalidated. And then, at the very conclusion, he gives a characteristic

Humean fillip to the argument: Our most holy religion, Christianity, does not have to be tested by reason, indeed should not be so tested by friends or enemies, since it is founded on faith! And finally, after the devastating argument against miracles, comes this:

> We may conclude, that the Christian religion not only was at first attended with miracles, but even at this day cannot be believed by any reasonable person without one. Mere reason is insufficient to convince us of its veracity; And whoever is moved by faith to assent to it, is conscious of a continued miracle in his own person, which subverts all the principles of his understanding, and gives him a determination to believe what is most contrary to custom and experience.

Two essays, written about 1757 but not published until 1777, and then suppressed, are entitled "Of the Immortality of the Soul" and "Of Suicide."[48] In the former he again attacks the arguments of reason, this time as being inadequate to prove immortality, whether those arguments be derived from metaphysical, moral or physical considerations. It is perfectly clear that, as he rehearses these arguments, Hume does not believe in immortality, but, again, note the reference to revelation, and, in this instance, its teaching on life after death:

> Nothing could set in a fuller light the infinite obligations which mankind have to Divine revelation; since we find, that no other medium could ascertain this great and important truth.

In "Of Suicide" his object is to attack the "superstition" which deters men from suicide, and to free from every imputation of guilt or blame any person resorting to suicide. To that end he shows that suicide is not criminal, for it does not transgress our duties to God, neighbor or one's self. It represents no transgression of our duty to God, since "the life of a man is of no greater importance to the universe than that of an oyster" and since the physical elements of which the living body was composed will still be equally useful in the grand fabric of the universe. It is, indeed, a kind of blasphemy for men to think that they can disturb the order of the world. As for the supposed injury to society: a man who chooses to put an end to his life only ceases to do some possible good to society, and such a flimsy justification for living should not be counted more heavily than the man's own burdens of age or illness or anguish of any kind. As for the individual's wrong to himself, Hume's belief is that "no man ever threw away life while it was worth keeping"; and, far from considering as criminal a person who commits suicide, we should instead applaud the prudence and courage of him who can command his own life.[49]

Turning to *The Natural History of Religion*,[50] we have one of Hume's two sustained discussions in the field of religion. From what we have already seen of the procedure adopted when any investigation labeled "natural history" was under way, we may expect to find far more discussion of human nature than of history, and such history as does enter will be generalized, incidental and illustrative. The question he examines here is not concerned with those aspects of physical nature which speak to the reason of man, and which, at this point he declares, lead to genuine Theism, but rather with man's own nature and the kinds of religion it produces. It is, thus, an inquiry concerned with both Natural Religion and the natural history of religion, and based on all the assumptions regarding nature and what is natural which were shared by the century. But there the similarity, as stated in general terms, ceases, for whereas most writers using those assumptions had written that men everywhere and always had held a belief in an invisible, intelligent power, Hume shows that such is not the case; and whereas the others held that there could not but be considerable uniformity of belief, since belief had its springs in human nature, Hume shows the great diversity which obtains. Quickly, then, he states his first significant conclusion: the first principles of religion are not primary as the instincts are, but are secondary, "such as may easily be perverted by various accidents and causes, and whose operation, too, in some cases, may, by an extraordinary

concurrence of circumstances, be altogether prevented."
His investigation turns then, to ask what it is that leads
men to believe the things they believe—in other words,
what are those first principles and circumstances that are
necessary to the various creeds. His results were devastating, not only for revealed religion but for Deism with
its foundation in reason, and for all optimistic defenders
of Natural Religion of whatever brand.

First, the clear testimony of history convinces him that
polytheism, and not pure Theism, was the original religion of men. This is to be expected, given the natural
progress of human thought: "the ignorant multitude
must first entertain some groveling and familiar notion
of superior powers, before they stretch their conception
to that perfect Being, who bestowed order on the whole
frame of nature." Order, regularity, harmony, are not
the aspects of nature which would appeal to primordial
man, "barbarous, necessitous animal" that he was; "not
. . . a contemplation of the works of nature, but . . . a
concern with regard to the events of life, and . . . inces-
sant hopes and fears" give rise to religion. Particularly
in the face of uncertainty, accident and catastrophe, men
are baffled by the unknown causes at work, and, in the
human way, conceive that those causes are more or less
like themselves, personal agents. Polytheism, thus, is not
only the first religion, actually, but it is the natural one
for untutored man to achieve. Allegorical religions and
hero-worship are simply variations of polytheism, and
when Theism itself is achieved it represents no more of
reason than its parent form, but only a concentration of
the hopes and fears of men on a particular deity. The
vulgar among a theistic people will always be found to
have carried over many sentiments more appropriate to
polytheism; indeed, one of the phenomena in the realm of
religion is the fluctuation from polytheism to Theism and
back again to polytheism.

One merit of polytheism, understandable when one
knows its principles, is that it is more tolerant of other

religions than is Theism. It encourages spirit, activity
and courage, as a religion whose deity is infinitely superior
to men cannot do. And since it is not bound by a scripture
and a scholastic philosophy, polytheism sits more easily
and lightly on men's minds and does not lend itself to
demonstration as does Theism. Still, Hume admits, Theism
stands for advancement:

> A purpose, an intention, a design is evident in everything; and
> when our comprehension is so far enlarged as to contemplate the
> first rise of this visible system, we must adopt, with the strongest
> conviction, the idea of some intelligent cause or other.

But before we are lost in admiration of man's achievement of this belief, he goes on:

> What a noble privilege it is of human reason to attain the
> knowledge of the supreme Being . . . But turn the reverse of
> the medal. Survey most nations and most ages. Examine the re-
> ligious principles, which have, in fact, prevailed in the world.
> You will scarcely be persuaded they are anything but sick men's
> dreams: Or perhaps you will regard them more as the playsome
> whimsies of monkies [sic] in human shape, than the serious, posi-
> tive, dogmatical asseverations of a being, who dignifies himself
> with the name of rational.

And then, his conclusion, which has infuriated so many
of his readers, whether religiously persuaded or not:

> The whole is a riddle, an enigma, an inexplicable mystery.
> Doubt, uncertainty, suspense of judgment appear the only re-
> sult of our most accurate scrutiny, concerning this subject. But
> such is the frailty of human reason, and such the irresistible con-
> tagion of opinion, that even this deliberate doubt could scarcely
> be upheld; did we not enlarge our view, and opposing one spe-
> cies of superstition to another, set them a-quarreling; while we
> ourselves, during their fury and contention, happily make our
> escape into the calm, though obscure regions of philosophy.

Hume's other sustained discussion is contained in the
Dialogues Concerning Natural Religion (1779). This is
the work which he wrote probably as early as 1751, certainly before 1761, which he did not publish in his lifetime, though on several occasions he discussed with his
friends his desire to publish it, and which, after his death,
when both Adam Smith and Strahan, his publisher, re-

fused to sponsor it, was brought to publication by his nephew and heir. David Hume wanted this work in print, he revised it several times at several points, and just before his death put the finishing touches to it. Professor Norman Kemp Smith, who has examined the completed manuscript in the library of the Royal Society of Edinburgh and noted the tenor of the revisions, offers the judgment that "the teaching of the *Dialogues* is much more sheerly negative than has generally been held. . . . He [Hume] is consciously, and deliberately, attacking the religious hypothesis, and through it religion as such."[51]

The treatment follows the model set by Cicero's *De natura deorum*. The youthful auditor of the conversation characterizes the positions maintained as "the accurate philosophical turn of Cleanthes," "the careless scepticism of Philo," and "the rigid inflexible orthodoxy of Demea." In the light of Professor Smith's researches it seems less possible than ever to try to identify Hume with Cleanthes, and we simply accept as a bit of Humean humor the ascribing of carelessness to the sceptic who raises all the Humean questions and, at the close, the comment of Cleanthes' pupil that Cleanthes' arguments are nearest the truth.

At no point in the discussion does the question concern the being of God, but only the nature of God and the ways of knowing that nature. Specifically, the discussion starts with a question as to the contribution of reason to the solution of the obscurities and uncertainties inherent in religious problems.

Cleanthes leads off with the argument from design: the world appears to be one great machine with all its parts so admirably contrived as to suggest a contriver with a mind somewhat similar to the mind of man, though of course incomparably greater. Demea at once protests against Cleanthes' effort to envisage Deity from so mean a thing as human experience and against his omission of fine a priori arguments. Philo's protest, on the other hand, deals with the defects in the analogy between the universe and a thing like a house or a machine which a man might contrive, and with the inference as to causes which is involved:

> A very small part of this system, during a very short time, is very imperfectly discovered to us; And do we thence pronounce decisively concerning the origin of the whole?

And when Philo insists that it would be necessary to push even beyond the cause as attributed to the mind of God, Cleanthes can only reassert:

> The whole chorus of nature raises one hymn to the praises of its Creator. . . . You ask me, what is the cause of this cause? I know not; I care not; this concerns not me. I have found a Deity; and here I stop my inquiry.

After pushing Cleanthes on how he could prove the true creativeness of the Deity or his unity or perfection, Philo proposes another analogy as an alternative to that of created mechanism, but drawn, likewise, from observation: "The world, . . I infer, is an animal and the Deity is the soul of the world, actuating it, and actuated by it." The advantage of this suggestion is that it explains the order and law in the world as being due to natural processes of vegetation or generation, without having to resort to reason; as "a tree bestows order and organization on that tree which springs from it, without knowing the order. . . ." The determinism in this position is at once apparent; and if we must seek for priority,

> Judging by our limited and imperfect experience, generation has some privileges above reason: For we see every day the latter arise from the former, never the former from the latter.

Demea, who has contributed nothing of any moment to the dialogue, becomes alarmed at the implications of such argument, especially when Cleanthes has to admit the aptness of Philo's argument—at least so far as to agree to the principle of vegetation, if not of generation— and seeks to introduce the a priori arguments so simple and sublime, so full of the talk of necessity. But in that effort Demea comes off rather badly at the hands of

Philo who, by example from algebra, shows how the doctrine of necessity may land one on ground far from religion. Demea then retreats to the less philosophical argument that man, "from a consciousness of his imbecility and misery, rather than from any reasoning, is led to seek protection from that Being, on whom he and all nature is dependent." But that argument, too, Philo turns, to ask of them if this scene of human misery would not destroy that faith; it is evident to him that there is no concern for human happiness manifest in the universe. The preservation of individuals and the propagation of the species seem to be the only purpose discernible in nature, and

There is no view of human life or of the condition of mankind, from which, without the greatest violence, we can infer the moral attributes, or learn that infinite benevolence, conjoined with infinite power and infinite wisdom, which we must discover by the eyes of faith alone.

Very tardily Demea perceives, when Cleanthes points it out to him, that their friend Philo has been amusing himself at their expense; and, as Cleanthes says, "the injudicious reasoning of our vulgar theology has given him but too just a handle of ridicule." Demea then leaves the group, and Cleanthes and Philo proceed amicably to the conclusion of the discussion.

Philo freely admits, after all that he has said, that the universe does speak of purpose and design and that, if one wishes, one may speak of the supreme cause not only as Deity but as Mind or Thought. But Philo is disgusted with verbal disputes about degrees of quality or circumstance, in this instance degrees of Reason in that First Cause and the degree of completeness of the analogy from which the argument has proceeded. In particular, he is sure that the analogy is not nearly so applicable to the question of virtues as to contrivance; consequently such religious faith as one may achieve by reason would offer no guide to conduct. Here he disagrees flatly with Cleanthes, who thinks that even a corrupted religion, be-

cause of its efficacy in regulating human behavior, is
better than none. Indeed, to Philo, religious control of
conduct is what makes religion's story so sorry a thing,
so much a matter of superstition and vulgarity and unhappiness. He analyzes popular Theism, weighing its
hopes and fears, its comforts and terrors; and he points
out the undignified and unlovely characteristics of the
God of most theists. The wise man, therefore, will refuse
to have part in such a religion and will limit his allegiance
to the thin proposition "that the cause or causes of order
in the universe probably bear some remote analogy to
human intelligence." This constitutes the only true philosophical rational religion and is all that can be claimed
as Natural Theology. But one must not be glib in adopt-
ing even so slight a position, for when one pushes carefully into the reasoning, one must take account of ambiguities, acquired beliefs, and what William James later
was to call "the will to believe." One thing Philo insists
on: such a religion affords "no inference that affects
human life, or can be the source of any action or for-
bearance."

Then comes the usual Humean fillip:

A person, seasoned with a just sense of the imperfections of
natural reason, will fly to revealed truth with the greatest avidity. . . . To be a philosophical sceptic is, in a man of letters,
the first and most essential step towards being a sound believing
Christian. . . .

Such a running summary as here given could take no
account of the twists and turns of the conversation in
which the real traps lay, and the subtleties of the parry-
ing. But even such a summary should show Hume's purpose of exposing the shoddy thought that underlay most
of the discussions of Natural Religion and Deism; the
faultiness of the argument from design; the crimes and
absurdities committed in the name of Theism, not only
by the vulgar, but by supposedly rational believers who
think themselves far from superstition and enthusiasm.
His conclusion, as in the *Natural History of Religion*,

is that "the whole is a riddle, an enigma, an inexplicable mystery," and one would do well to abandon religious discussions and escape "into the calm, though obscure regions of philosophy."

No wonder that Hume continued to be anathema to the orthodox, though most provocative to those among them who would insist on being rational.

When there was such interest in institutions, it was impossible that one so fundamental as language should escape attention. Practically every writer devoted essays to it. The efforts of Smith, Kames and Monboddo are the only ones we can mention, and since we have already noticed that Kames connected his account of the diversity of races and languages with acceptance of the scriptural story of the tower of Babel, we shall not repeat the discussion here.

Smith's discussion was called *Considerations Concerning the First Formation of Languages, and the Different Genius of Original and Compounded Languages*. It was written, apparently, soon after he came to Glasgow and was published as a sort of appendix to the second edition of the *Moral Sentiments*. As Dugald Stewart viewed it, it was "a very beautiful specimen of theoretical history," what Hume would have called "natural history" and the French, *histoire raisonnée*. Stewart's description of the procedure of such an investigation is worth repeating:

When, in such a period of society as that in which we live, we compare our intellectual acquirements, our opinions, manners and institutions, with those which prevail among rude tribes, it cannot fail to occur to us as an interesting question, by what gradual steps the transition has been made from the first simple efforts of uncultivated nature, to a state of things so wonderfully artificial and complicated. Whence has arisen that systematical beauty which we admire in the structure of a cultivated language, that analogy which runs through the mixture of languages spoken by the most remote and unconnected nations, and those peculiarities by which they are all distinguished from each other? . . . In this want of direct evidence, we are under a necessity of supplying the place of fact by conjecture; and when we are unable to ascertain how men have actually conducted themselves upon particular occasions, of considering in what manner they are likely to have proceeded, from the principles of their nature, and the circumstances of their external situation. In such inquiries, the detached facts which travels and voyages afford us, may frequently serve as landmarks to our speculations; and sometimes our conclusions *a priori*, may tend to confirm the credibility of facts, which, on a superficial view, appeared to be doubtful or incredible.[52]

Since we have already had occasion to criticize this type of history, we shall simply note concretely what Smith speculated on. In conjectural fashion he envisaged situations in which early men were placed, and how gradually, naturally, they would first learn to name things, not only individual things but classes of things. Verbs, too, would necessarily be early used. It then became necessary to be able to signify particular things out of a group, so adjectives were invented for distinguishing qualities, and prepositions for expressing relationship. In time it would be useful to be able to express ideas of quality and relation abstractly, hence the invention of substantive nouns; and, in still more time, the distinctions of sex could be expressed linguistically. And so on. The essay ends with a comparison of the relative advantages and disadvantages of simple and compounded languages.

As for Monboddo, it has been shown that language was the social phenomenon with which he was most concerned. He wished to prove that not only was it not natural to man, but that it was not necessary. It was for this purpose that he tried so hard to gain acceptance for his contention that the orang-outangs were of the species Man. Incidentally he sought to demonstrate, thus, that when changes such as language come, they come within the species and not in new and different species. But once language was invented, men could learn really to think and thus invent the other arts and sciences.[53]

We follow a chimera if we expect to find a single parent language, however, for many groups of people have been real inventors, first through their inarticulate cries, then by articulation in imitation of sounds of birds and animals. The process through which the various human groups have gone in the development of the art is very like that through which one individual goes: "first mute; then lisping and stammering; next by very slow degrees learning to speak very lamely and imperfect at first; but at last, from such rude essays, forming an art the most curious, as well as the most useful among men."[54]

One language deserves special treatment—that which came first into full form in Egypt. It had the aid of the Daemon Kings for its perfecting, and that fact renders it almost a supernatural gift. While it was still a system chiefly of monosyllables, it was passed into India and China, forming the root of Sanskrit; and it became, through the colonizings of the Pelasgians, the parent language of many European dialects.[55]

This is not the place to note further details of Monboddo's effort—his speculations as to the number of consonants and the length of words in original languages, the lack of syntax and other items concerning the form, material and composition of languages. From such considerations he passes on to discussions of style in speech and writing and weighs the merits of a succession of writers from the time of the Greeks to his own day. This work thus concludes as a piece of literary criticism.

If this chapter were not devoted to a rehearsal of the efforts to deal with institutions, it would be interesting to go into some account of the renewed interest in aesthetics and the passion for elegance exemplified in this group of authors. We have elsewhere noted a few of the evidences of this phase of the Enlightenment.[56] They all wrote on standards of taste, several of them were involved in the Ossian controversy, and even the sedate Adam Smith devoted some essays to the imitative arts, to music and dancing. In each case the aim was "to discover the springs of our mental pleasures," to use Montesquieu's expression, and to find, by examination of man's mental equipment, what principles or criteria of appreciation he had by nature. It was, in Kames' words, an examination of "the sensitive branch of human nature," and by most authors the study was held to be a "great support to morality."

All of these various relations and institutions we have been reviewing were regarded as so many fields in which natural and moral laws could be seen in operation. When the authors talked of domestic relations they did not introduce matters of political organization; when they talked of contracts and inheritance of property they did not debate the being and nature of God. In other words, they, too, had their abstractions, but always they were bound by two controlling ideas: all relations and institutions were to be shown as rooted in the nature of man, and all were to be shown as depending ultimately for their continued existence on ethical judgments. Ethics, thus, was the final arbiter in the theories of social organization and behavior—a position completely justified when the theorists were, as these men were, moral philosophers. But, along the way, these philosophers anticipated many of the items in our contemporary discussions of institutional life and, in many instances, even some parts of the general framework of what we today call the social sciences.

IX

CONCLUSION

ON coming to the conclusion of this survey of the social theories advanced by the Scottish philosophers of the eighteenth century, the author holds several hopes regarding the usefulness of the study.

One hope is directed toward those persons interested in the history of significant ideas, ideas which have been persistent enough, even when modified, to have influenced thinkers in several fields of thought and over a long period of time. The author's hope is that this study provides those persons with a summary of some of the ideas current in the eighteenth century, complexes of thought at once typical of the century and, at the same time, peculiarly Scottish. In this way, the book may serve as one chapter in the intellectual history of the century and in the story of related ideas on the subject of man and society.

Another hope is directed toward contemporary social scientists who should see in these eighteenth-century Scots their own predecessors in the study of man and his complex social relations. Probably no other group of thinkers before the twentieth century so self-consciously set about encompassing the whole range of discussion which now has become highly elaborated and parceled out among the several social sciences. To be a moral philosopher in the eighteenth century was to take for one's self just such a comprehensive program, within the limits of the knowledge of the time.

In spite of the "mixed mode of thought" which they expressed, these philosophers were very earnestly seeking to be empirical in their approach. By twentieth-century investigators, so given to this same endeavor, this effort should be appreciated for what it was—a concerted effort to find the facts about human association—what enters into association and what it leads to in the making of culture patterns. Many of the ideas indicate, on their faces, the transitional and confused character of the thought of the century; many of them betray Aristotelian colors; others have a medieval and theological tinge. But one is struck, over and over again, with the intent of the authors to follow the empirical procedures already being established in the physical sciences and to be just as "experimental" in their study of man.

Of course, no one who writes today in any of the fields of the social sciences thinks of himself as a moral philosopher. Not even the sociologist, who has had the temerity to include more of the subdivisions of the older discipline than any of his fellows in adjacent fields, considers him-self in that category. But, in view of the fact that the various studies have emerged as recently as they have from the matrix discipline, it would seem to be a valid inference that there would be residual influences still to be seen, heritages traceable to the parent stock. In Europe, and in Great Britain particularly, the break between philosophy, whether general or moral, and the social sciences has not become so complete as in the United States; this is evident in British universities in the grouping of studies, as for example at Cambridge in the moral science tripos. For the United States, the catalogues of the older colleges and universities provide evidence as to dates and places marking the emergence of the new fields of study. The typical procedure was for the professor or department sponsoring courses in moral philosophy to drop those courses and to substitute courses in psychology, economics, political science or sociology.[1] But in becoming independent disciplines the new social sciences did not at once lose all the characteristics true of them as segments of the older and larger field. Judging from current discussions, however, one would suppose that very little attention is being paid to any persistences other than those dealing with value-judgments, and even these ideas are not—and should not be completely, of course—related to their historical antecedents.

No historian of social theory could for a moment overlook the stimulus to theory which the discoveries and movements of thought in the nineteenth century offered, but along with new factual knowledge and new theory there was a carrying-over of ideas from an older matrix discipline. Examination of that earlier formulation, of the immediate foreground, in a period significant for intellectual history, has been the object of this essay. It was a period valuable from any point of view for the history of ideas; but for a true perspective on the history of the social sciences, knowledge of it would seem to be imperative.

The section headed "Conclusion" is not the place to gather up the numerous threads which have woven their way throughout the book itself; we cannot attempt at this point to give a résumé of our discussions. One point to be insisted on is that the heritage from philosophy, especially from the more special moral philosophy, is of greater extent than the persistence in social sciences of value-judgments, overt or unacknowledged. Many other of the controlling ideas of that heritage are still with us. We are not conscious of them as controlling ideas, as were these men of the eighteenth century; with us they hang on as unexamined assumptions, as "ideas ready made," or as refuges to which we sometimes unconsciously repair when hard put to it for a philosophical underpinning or an interpretation which has not yet been satisfactorily worked out.

Another point to be insisted on is that it is not easy to isolate one single idea and trace its influences, for ideas always come in complexes, knitted together in a fairly consistent theory; current terminology would put it that they always have their frames of reference. We have only to remember the related ideas involved in one of the dominant nineteenth-century doctrines to see this, namely, Darwin's theory of evolution. Here the factors are seen to be those of heredity, of variation, of natural selection, and the result is adaptation. But one may start at either end of the series, or in the middle, and find that the four terms belong together, and it is their togetherness that makes the theory. Returning to the complexes of thought brought out in our study, let us isolate for a moment one approach, with the ideas related to it, and see to what lengths that one commitment involved the writers. As we enumerate the several ideas in the complex, we might well take stock of the services and disservices to scientific social study of the employment of that idea. Let us take a beginning from the psychology of the eighteenth century:

1. These moral philosophers believed that a science of man must concern itself at base with the irreducible element in man, e.g., his "original nature." This was a conscious effort on the part of the philosophers to provide an analogue to the chemist's "elements," the scientific objects of his laboratory processes. It offered them, too, a psychological solution to the problem of social origins, otherwise more difficult of solution.

2. These elements of human nature were believed to have their established, ordered ways of behaving, as any physical matter had its way under given conditions. These ordered ways were the laws of nature, positive and normative, and they operated to the glory of the Creator, the satisfaction of the individual, and the greatest good of natural and civil society. All institutions were regarded as the products of the operation of these laws, therefore, ultimately, as the products of a common human nature. The whole ordered system of the universe spelled out to them "Nature's simple plan." It was, as Professor Tinker has called it, a theory of simplicity and, at the same time, a phase of the radical thought of the eighteenth century.

3. This concentration on human nature manifested the effort to abstract from the diversified activities of everyday life something of certain, predictable, similar quality wherever found—an effort common to all scientific procedure following Descartes.

4. Not only was a similar, basic human nature posited, but similar classifiable customs were felt to be the material of science, since they appeared to be normal, natural and widely observed.

5. These similar customs were compared and ranged in series of slight gradations. The conclusion was a judgment that the achievements of the human race could be charted in a unilinear development just as the life of an individual could be charted through the years of his growth. Not only so, but there was believed to be for every custom and every institution a development natural to its kind as growth of a kind is natural to every species. Such thinking produced those varieties of history known to the eighteenth century as "reasoned," "natural," "hypothetical" and "theoretical."

6. The trend of this development was judged to be progressive, of the nature of a continuous movement with no breaks, as growth has no breaks, a movement directed by Nature. The concept of progress was thus a metaphysic, a scientific credo, a value judgment, a philosophy of history. The case for it was to be made out by every writer on the subject of man.

7. Such a notion of natural, slow, continuous, pre-ordained change, judged progress, shut out consideration of what might actually have befallen the people of particular sections in particular times, and the unpredictable turns and twists to particular ideas, customs and events. Yet each of these men knew, and many of them wrote, of the actual life of the Romans, of the Greeks, of the English, and of the career of certain philosophic concepts. But this latter undertaking in actualities was not of the nature of science, they thought, because of its very particularity. There is displayed in their study of man, then, the disjunction of science and history which has continued to plague the social sciences even into our own times.

8. It is evident, even from this enumeration of several related ideas, how largely concepts of God, final causes,

teleology, entered into discussions which were intended
to be scientific.

9. Nor were these philosophers free, even in intent,
from the practice of introducing norms and values into
their science. In truth, right ethical relationships were
not only the ultimate but the immediate desiderata of
their study. They were working as consciously to educate
high-minded administrators and public servants as were
Plato and Aristotle; but sometimes a value-judgment
was mistaken for a scientific fact.

One could take as his starting point almost any other
basic idea—their concern with mathematics, with empirical method, with history, with sociability, with ethics—
and come out with not much more than a rearrangement
of the ideas listed above. In other words, here was systematic thought, the strands of which can never be pulled
apart without losing their meaning, but any strand of
which can lead at once into others of the fabric. Together,
they make up the science of man for the eighteenth century.

Fortunately today there is going on in the several
fields comprising our science of man considerable discussion which bespeaks an awareness that all is not well. We
have become sceptical of the values of overelaboration,
particularly when it results in the sad lack of a common
method in the disciplines. It may be useful, therefore, in
such a time of questioning to attend to the approach made
by a group who were equally earnest but who followed
some false trails. One is reminded of Bacon's apology for
alchemy: "Yet alchemy may be compared to the man who
told his sons he had left them gold buried somewhere in
his vineyard; where they, by digging, found no gold, but
by turning up the mould about the roots of the vines,
procured a plentiful vintage." It is the hope of the author
that this study in moral philosophy, here considered as
embodying the chief theoretical background of our modern
social sciences, may perhaps, with other like methodological efforts, turn up the mould about the roots of the

vines and help to procure a more plentiful vintage for our
own day. Or, to refer to Professor John Dewey's statement with which this study is prefaced, here is presented
an earlier "comprehensive view of the universe and man";
here is one "source in prior philosophic speculation" of
many of the ideas current in our social studies of the
twentieth century. Dewey's question is a pertinent one:
To what degree have our ideas been affected—or infected—by that origin?

NOTES

CHAPTER I

1. Victor Cousin, *Course of the History of Modern Philosophy*, 2nd series, tr. by O. W. Wight (New York, 1852). Reference is to the edition of 1857, I, 319.

2. Adam Smith, *An Inquiry into the Nature and Causes of the Wealth of Nations* (Everyman ed., 1910), II, 278. "Enthusiasm" is here used by Smith, following Shaftesbury, to mean the false feeling of the divine presence. Generally the word was used throughout the century to mean ill-regulated or misdirected religious emotion, or extravagance of religious speculation. Cf. the *New English Dictionary*, and Shaftesbury, *Characteristics of Men, Manners, Opinions, Times* (London, 1711), Vol. I, treatise I.

3. Stewart, "Dissertation Exhibiting the Progress of Metaphysical, Ethical and Political Philosophy Since the Revival of Letters in Europe," in Stewart's *Collected Works*, ed. by Sir William Hamilton (Edinburgh, 1854-1860), I, 550.

4. Henry Grey Graham, *Scottish Men of Letters in the Eighteenth Century* (London, 1901), p. 61.

5. Quoted from the *Caldwell Papers* by H. M. B. Reid, in his *The Divinity Professors in the University of Glasgow, 1640-1903* (Glasgow, 1923), pp. 245-46.

6. Henry Thomas Buckle, *History of Civilization in England* (World Classics ed.), pp. 278-79. It is surprising to find that the one moment of life which even the earlier Scottish religion left untouched was the funeral. Chronicles and general accounts of social life picture the most ribald and drunken scenes.

7. See, for example, the running account given by P. Hume Brown, *Scottish History*, III, 19-32, 35-59, 118-22, 164-70, 174-81, 195-206, 285-88; Sir Henry Craik, *A Century of Scottish History* (Wm. Blackwood Sons, Edinburgh, 1901), I, 126-31, 400-46; II, 1-119; Gerald Berkeley Hurst, *British Imperialism in the Eighteenth Century* (London, 1908); Bishop Pococke, *Tours in Scotland*, ed. by D. W. Kemp, in Publications of the Scottish History Society (Edinburgh, 1887), I, 51-52; *Papers Relating to the Ships and Voyages of the Company of Scotland Trading to Africa and the Indies, 1696-1707*, ed. by George Pratt Insh, in Publications of the Scottish History Society, 3rd series (Edinburgh, 1924), Vol. VI; Graham, *The Social Life of Scotland in the Eighteenth Century* (London, 1899), I, 204.

8. Brown, *op. cit.*, III, 287-88; Craik, *op. cit.*, I, 132-38, 429-31, and II, 21-30, 38-41; Robert Rait, *Scotland* (London, 1911), pp. 301-302.

9. Craik, *op. cit.*, I, 347-99, esp. 367-68; by permission of the publishers, Wm. Blackwood Sons.

10. Graham, *Scottish Men of Letters*, pp. 7-8. Cf. the delightful account of Scottish life given by Harold William Thompson, in his *A Scottish Man of Feeling* (Oxford University Press, 1931), Chs. I, II, and *passim*.

11. Stewart, *Collected Works*, I, 551 and notes; James McCosh, *The Scottish Philosophy* (New York, 1875), p. 108; Alexander Fraser Tytler (Lord Woodhouselee), *Memoirs of the Life and Writings of the Honourable Henry Home of Kames* (2nd ed., Edinburgh, 1814), I, 160-84 and notes. Stewart points out that the philosophy of Locke, as well as that of Newton, was accepted as "a branch of academical education" in the Scottish universities earlier than in others.

12. Merz, *A History of European Thought in the Nineteenth Century* (Edinburgh, 1896-1914), I, 268-72. In the *London Critical Review*, Vol. xv, December 1795, the comment was offered that the Scottish professors were "calculated to rescue the literature and science of Britain from the contempt into which they must otherwise fall."

13. Adam Smith, *op. cit.*, II, 247, 249. Cf. Sir Leslie Stephen, *The English Utilitarians*, I, 43 ff.; A. D. Godley, *Oxford in the Eighteenth Century* (London, 1908); John Richard Green and George Roberson, *Studies in Oxford History* (Oxford, 1901); Arthur Gray, *Cambridge University, An Episodical History* (Boston and New York, 1927); John Venn, *Early Collegiate Life* (Cambridge, 1913).

14. For some account of Leechman, see H. M. B. Reid, *op. cit.*, pp. 243-63.

15. *Ibid.*, p. 253. A few years before this, Christian Thomasius at Leipzig had begun to lecture in German instead of Latin.

16. Lang, *A History of Scotland from the Roman Occupation* (Edinburgh, 1907), IV, 402; Graham, *Social Life*, II, 190.

17. Graham, *ibid.*, pp. 184, 190; P. Hume Brown, *History of Scotland*, III, 210.

18. In the nineteenth century something of a scandal was created when it was learned how little Greek the eighteenth century knew. Andrew Lang suggests that the scant acquaintance may have been due to Scotland's following France fairly closely in university planning, and France was not keenly interested in Greek. Lang, *op. cit.*, IV, 398-400.

19. John Small, "Biographical Sketch of Adam Ferguson," in *Transactions of the Royal Society of Edinburgh*, XXIII (1864), 607, n.

20. Arthur Percival Newton, *The Universities and Educational Systems of the British Empire* (London, 1924), pp. 5-6, 11, 24, 42.

21. John Gibson Lockhart, *Peter's Letters to His Kinsfolk* (1st Amer. ed., New York, 1820), pp. 108-9.

22. Quoted by Harold William Thompson, in his edition of *Anecdotes and Egotisms of Henry Mackenzie, 1745-1831* (Oxford, 1927), Introduction, p. xv. Note a recent popular history of Scottish literature, by William Power, *Literature and Oatmeal* (London, 1935). Adam Smith's biographer narrates a Glasgow incident of 1757 when Smith, on behalf of the University, successfully protested an unprecedented tax on the meal which students brought with them for use during the year; see John Rae, *Life of Adam Smith* (London, 1895), p. 67.

23. Cousin, *op. cit.*, I, 243-44.

24. Ernest Albee, *A History of English Utilitarianism* (London, 1902), pp. 64-65.

25. Gilbert Chinard, "Jefferson and the Physiocrats," *University of California Chronicle*, XXXIII, No. 1 (January, 1931), 19.

26. Carl Becker, *The Heavenly City of the Eighteenth-Century Philosophers* (New Haven, 1932), pp. 29-31, 47, 49, 119.

27. Arthur O. Lovejoy, "The Parallel of Deism and Classicism," *Modern Philology*, XXIX (University of Chicago Press, Chicago, 1932), 281; by permission of the publishers. In the following paragraph we have quoted closely, though not exactly, Professor Lovejoy's analysis.

28. Lovejoy's Preface, in Lois Whitney, *Primitivism and the Idea of Progress in English Popular Literature of the Eighteenth Century* (Baltimore, 1934).

29. Albert E. Baker, *Bishop Butler* (London, 1923), p. 2.

30. In another study of Professor Lovejoy's, in which he had the collaboration of Professor George Boas, there is to be found a highly useful list of some meanings of "Nature"; see the Appendix to their *Primitivism and Related Ideas in Antiquity* (Baltimore, 1935), pp. 447-

56. Cf. also Ernst Cassirer, *Die Philosophie der Aufklärung* (Tübingen, 1932), Kap. II.

31. Boswell's *Life of Johnson*, ed. by Birkbeck Hill (New York, 1904), III, 323. Cf. Hegel's "Encyclopädie" in *Werke*, Bd. 6 (1840 ed.), p. 13, n., for an amusing reference to "The Art of Preserving the Hair, on Philosophical Principles."

32. *Essays on Philosophical Subjects* (London, 1795), p. 20. The purpose of this volume of essays was to discuss "the principles which lead and direct philosophical inquiries," illustrated by the history of astronomy, physics, logic, metaphysics, etc.; principles stressed are curiosity, imagination, simplification, abstraction, conceptualization, etc.

33. *Ibid.*, pp. 115-17.

34. D'Alembert's *Discours* was a much discussed work in Scotland; Dugald Stewart, on whom devolved similar labors of introducing some supplemental volumes of the *Encyclopedia Britannica*, devoted to it his long Preface known as the "Dissertation Exhibiting the Progress of Metaphysical, Ethical, and Political Philosophy, Since the Revival of Letters in Europe."—See Stewart's *Works*, Vol. I. Smith had become acquainted with D'Alembert in 1766 and had the *Discours* in his library; see James Bonar, *A Catalogue of the Library of Adam Smith* (London, 1894), pp. 2-3.

35. Stewart, *op. cit.*, II, 6.

36. On this confusion as to what science is and what criteria it demands, see John Dewey, "Science as Subject-Matter and as Method," *Science* (n.s. 31, 1910), pp. 121-27; Joel M. Hildebrand, "Recent Developments in Scientific Thought," *University of California Chronicle*, Vol. XXXI, No. 4 (October, 1929), 373-92; Karl Pearson, *The Grammar of Science* (2nd ed., rev. and enl., London, 1900), pp. 1-37; Frederick J. Teggart, *Theory of History* (New Haven, 1925), Ch. 13.

37. John Locke, *An Essay Concerning Human Understanding* (1690); in most editions, par. 8. For a succinct statement of the difference between Rationalists and Empiricists in their conception of ideas, see the foreword by Professor Bowman to Olin McKendree Jones, *Empiricism and Intuitionism in Reid's Common-Sense Philosophy* (Princeton, 1927), pp. xix-xx.

38. One of the lesser members of the Scottish school, David Fordyce, Professor of Moral Philosophy in Marischal College, Aberdeen, has a neat statement of the position which gathers up several points enumerated in this chapter: "Moral Philosophy contemplates human nature, its moral powers and connections, and from these deduces the laws of action; and is defined more strictly the 'Science of Manners or Duty,' which it traces from man's nature and condition, and shows to terminate in his happiness. . . . It is denominated an art, as it contains a system of rules for becoming virtuous and happy. It is likewise called a science, as it deduces those rules from the principles and connections of our nature and proves that the observance of them is productive of our happiness."—*The Elements of Moral Philosophy* (3rd ed., London, 1758), p. 5.

39. *A Short Introduction to Moral Philosophy* (Glasgow, 1747), p. 2; cf. *A System of Moral Philosophy*, ed. by his son (London, 1755), I, 1-2.

40. John Laird, *Hume's Philosophy of Human Nature* (New York, 1932), p. 20.

41. *Sketches of the History of Man* (Edinburgh, 1774), II, 236-37.

42. See, for example, a letter from Reid to Lord Kames, in Hamilton's edition of *The Works of Thomas Reid*, I, 8, 11-13, 53; the introductory section to *An Inquiry into the Human Mind*, and pp. 97-8, 200; and on pp. xx-xxii, Hamilton's quotation from Cousin's *Cours d'histoire*

de la philosophie morale au dix-huitieme siècle, 2me partie (Paris, 1840), pp. 241 ff.

43. The sentence occurs at the end of Newton's *Optics,* and is quoted by Stewart in his "Account of the Life and Writings of Thomas Reid, D.D.," in Reid's *Works,* I, 13.

44. Cf. Jacob Viner, "Adam Smith and Laissez Faire," in *Adam Smith, 1776-1926* (Chicago, 1928), p. 116; and Stewart, *Works,* x, 60-64.

45. *Theory of Moral Sentiments,* Vol. I of London ed. of *Works* (1812), pp. 470-71; *Lectures on Justice, Police, Revenue and Arms,* pp. 160-70, esp. 169; *Wealth of Nations* (Everyman ed.), I, 12-15. Cf. Stewart, "Life of Adam Smith," *Collected Works,* x, 60-65.

46. Interpretations of this emphasis in Smith's work may be found in J. K. Ingram, *History of Political Economy* (new and enl. ed., London, 1923), pp. 87-91; Gide and Rist, *A History of Economic Doctrines,* tr. by R. Richards (Boston, 1915), pp. 68-93; Harold J. Laski, *Political Thought in England from Locke to Bentham* (New York, 1920), pp. 296-302. Cf. also A. W. Benn's discussion of the differing concepts of nature held by Quesnay and Smith: Quesnay's knowledge of nature was to be gained from the world about, and his natural liberty to be limited to the wise and good; Smith's nature was to be known from the totality of impulses and instincts of individual members of society, and each man was to be free; A. W. Benn, *The History of English Rationalism in the Nineteenth Century* (London, 1906), I, 289.

47. John Veitch's "Memoir of Dugald Stewart," in Stewart's *Collected Works,* x, xxxiv-xxxv. Note that from Stewart's time forward the word "psychology" comes into use.

48. *An Inquiry* (2nd ed., London, 1726), pp. 125-26. The full title of this work reads: *An Inquiry into the Original of our Ideas of Beauty and Virtue; in Two Treatises, in which the Principles of the late Earl of Shaftesbury are explained and defended, against the Author of the Fable of the Bees, and the Ideas of Moral Good and Evil are established, according to the Sentiments of the Ancient Moralists; with an Attempt to introduce a Mathematical Calculation in Subjects of Morality* (London, 1725).

49. "Naturalism" is here used in the sense of Mr. Sorley's definition: a theory denying to reason any creative or spontaneous function in the human constitution.—*On the Ethics of Naturalism* (Edinburgh, 1885), pp. 16-20. See also George Plimpton Adams, *Idealism and the Modern Age* (New Haven, 1919), p. 230; and Charles William Hendel, Jr., *Studies in the Philosophy of David Hume* (Princeton, 1925), pp. 30, 348, 402, 418.

50. John Herman Randall, Jr., *The Making of the Modern Mind* (Boston, 1926), p. 260. Cf. Edwin Arthur Burtt, *The Metaphysical Foundations of Modern Physical Science* (New York, 1925), pp. 96-127, 204-8, 216-23; Sir Leslie Stephen, *History of English Thought in the Eighteenth Century* (2nd ed., Smith, Elder & Co., London, 1881), I, 23-59; Norman Kemp Smith, *Studies in the Cartesian Philosophy* (London, 1902), pp. 28, 33-34.

51. Quoted by Randall, *op. cit.,* p. 254, as from Fontenelle, *Œuvres complètes* (1818), "Préface sur l'utilité des mathématiques et de la physique," I, 34.

52. Hutcheson's algebra is to be found in his *Inquiry,* pp. 182-83; this section was withdrawn when the fourth edition came to press. Reid's criticism appeared first in *Transactions of the Royal Society of London,* Vol. XLV (1748); reprinted in *Works,* II, 715-19. But there is no doubt that Reid himself was greatly drawn to mathematics; see *Works,* I, 5-6, 10, 24, 58, 452; Jones, *op. cit.,* p. 3. Mr. Jones has examined un-

published manuscripts of Reid, and speaks of a strong mathematical interest predominating in them.

53. Quoted by William Robert Scott, *Francis Hutcheson* (Cambridge, 1900), pp. 31-32, as from Sterne's *The Koran*, in *Works* (Edinburgh, 1799), VIII, 161.

54. Edition of 1779, p. 25; cf. Gordon McKenzie, "Lord Kames and the Mechanist Tradition," in *University of California Publications in English*, Vol. 14 (1943).

55. *Theory of Moral Sentiments, op. cit.*, 413-17, 515-16; *Wealth of Nations* (Everyman ed.), I, 400.

56. George Boas, *Major Traditions of European Philosophy* (Harper & Bros., New York and London, 1929), p. 186; by permission of the publishers.

57. It is well to recall that the word "principle" was not always used consistently. Sometimes it meant not the theory of operating forces, but the actual forces themselves; the latter usage was especially prevalent in treatises on ethics toward the end of the century. Noted by James Bonar, *Moral Sense* (London and New York, 1930), p. 225, n. 2, as from Dr. Walther Eckstein, *Adam Smith: Theorie der Ethischen Gefühle* (Leipzig, 1926), I, xxviii.

58. For example, Smith, *Wealth of Nations* (Everyman ed.), II, 253; Hutcheson, *System*, I, 1, 227, and *Short Introduction*, pp. 1-2, 92; Stewart, *Works*, II, 6; and many other references in Chs. II and V.

59. Cf. John Stuart Mill, *A System of Logic* (London, 1843), Bk. III, Ch. 4.

60. Cf. Arthur O. Lovejoy, "Optimism and Romanticism," *Publications of the Modern Language Association*, XLII (1927), No. 4, 921-45.

61. After considerable thought the author decided to omit entirely a fuller review of the general ethics of the Scots, since much more attention has been given to that aspect of their theories by other analysts than to the discussions dealing with man's social institutions and achievements.

SUPPLEMENTARY BIBLIOGRAPHY

General Works to which no specific reference is made in this chapter:

A. C. Armstrong, *Transitional Eras in Thought* (New York, 1904).

John Grier Hibben, *The Philosophy of the Enlightenment* (New York, 1910).

Henry Laurie, *Scottish Philosophy in Its National Development* (Glasgow, 1902).

W. E. H. Lecky, *History of the Rise and Influence of the Spirit of Rationalism in Europe* (London, 1865).

Sir James Mackintosh, *Progress of Ethical Philosophy* (Philadelphia, 1832).

John Mackintosh, *History of Civilization in Scotland* (new ed., London, 1896), IV, 152.

William Law Mathiesen, *The Awakening of Scotland* (Glasgow, 1910).

Robert Merton, "Science, Technology and Society in Seventeenth-Century England," *Osiris*, Vol. IV (1938).

Francisque Xavier Michel, *A Critical Inquiry into the Scottish Languages with the View of Illustrating the Rise and Progress of Civilization in Scotland* (Edinburgh and London, 1882).

Sir Leslie Stephen, *English Literature and Society in the Eighteenth Century* (New York and London, 1904).

A. Wolf, *A History of Science, Technology and Philosophy in the Eighteenth Century* (New York, 1939).

Several studies which deal with the Scottish School as a group may be mentioned: Victor Cousin, *Philosophie écossaise* (Paris, 1841); S. S. Laurie, *Notes, Expository and Critical, on Certain British Theories of Morals* (Edinburgh, 1868); James McCosh, *The Scottish Philosophy* (New York, 1875); Torgny T. Segerstedt, "The Problem of Knowledge in Scottish Philosophy," *Lunds Universitets Årsskrift*, N. F. Avd. 1, Bd. 31; 2, nr. 6 (Lund, 1935), pp. 1-155; and "Moral Sense-Skolan och dess inflytande på svensk filosofi," *Lunds Universitets Årsskrift*, Bd. 33:2 (Lund, 1937); James Seth, *The Scottish Contribution to Moral Philosophy* (Inaugural Lecture, 1898). In all of these studies attention is centered on metaphysics and epistemology; James Bonar, *Moral Sense* (London, 1930), is obviously concerned with ethics.

Scotland's Relations Abroad:

John Hill Burton, *The Ancient League with France* (Edinburgh, 1862.

——, *The Scot Abroad* (in the same volume).

John Davidson and Alexander Gray, *The Scottish Staple at Veer* (London, 1909).

The Journal of Thomas Cumingham of Campvere, 1640-1654, ed. by Elinor Jean Courthope, in Publications of the Scottish History Society, 3rd series, Vol. XI (Edinburgh, 1928).

Papers Relating to the Scots in Poland, 1576-1793, ed. by A. Francis Steuart, in Publications of the Scottish History Society, Vol. LIX (Edinburgh, 1915).

Matthijs Rooseboom, *The Scottish Staple in the Netherlands* (The Hague, 1910).

Autobiographical and Biographical Works of special significance:

The Autobiography of Alexander Carlyle, ed. by John Hill Burton (Boston, 1861).

John Hill Burton, *Life and Correspondence of David Hume* (Edinburgh, 1846).

Henry Cockburn, *Memorials of His Time* (New York, 1856).

J. Y. I. Greig, *Correspondence of David Hume* (Oxford, 1932).

——, *David Hume* (London, 1931).

William Knight, *Lord Monboddo and Some of His Contemporaries* (London, 1900).

B. M. Laing, *David Hume* (London, 1932).

Ernest Campbell Mossner, *The Forgotten Hume* (New York, 1943).

John Ramsay of Ochtertyre, *Scotland and Scotsmen of the Eighteenth Century*, ed. by Alexander Allardyce (Edinburgh and London, 1888).

William Robert Scott, *Adam Smith as Student and Professor* (Glasgow, 1937).

William Smellie, *Literary and Characteristical Lives of John Gregory, M.D., Henry Home, Lord Kames, David Hume, Esq., and Adam Smith, LL.D.* (Edinburgh, 1800).

Discussions of Eighteenth-Century Ethics:

C. D. Broad, *Five Types of Ethical Theory* (London, 1930).

Rudolf Eucken, *The Problem of Human Life as Viewed by the Great Thinkers from Plato to the Present Time*, tr. from the German by Williston S. Hough and W. R. Boyce Gibson (New York, 1912).

Thomas Fowler, *Shaftesbury and Hutcheson* (London, 1882).

Georg Gizycki, *Die Ethik David Hume's in ihrer Geschichtlichen Stellung* (Breslau, 1878).

Elie Halévy, *The Growth of Philosophical Radicalism*, tr. by Mary Morris (London, 1928).

Wilhelm Hasbach, *Die allgemeinen Philosophischen Grundlagen der von Francois Quesnay und Adam Smith Begrundeten Politischen Ökonomie* (Leipzig, 1890).

Friedrich Albert Lange, *History of Materialism*, tr. from the German by E. C. Thomas (3rd ed., 3 vols. in one, London, 1925).

James McCosh, *Agnosticism of Hume and Huxley* (New York, 1884).

Arthur Cushman McGiffert, *The Rise of Modern Religious Ideas* (New York, 1922).

E. B. McGilvary, "Altruism in Hume's Treatise," *Philosophical Review*, Vol. 12 (New York, 1903).

James Martineau, *Types of Ethical Theory* (Oxford, 1885).

Charles R. Morris, *Locke, Berkeley, Hume* (Oxford, 1931).

Glenn R. Morrow, *The Ethical and Economic Theories of Adam Smith* (New York, 1923).

Edmund Pfleiderer, *Empirismus und Skepsis in David Hume's Philosophie* (Berlin, 1874).

A. K. Rogers, *Morals in Review* (New York, 1927).

Edna Aston Shearer, *Hume's Place in Ethics* (Bryn Mawr, 1915).

Henry Sidgwick, *Methods of Ethics* (1st ed., London, 1874; 6th, 1901).

Norman Kemp Smith, *The Philosophy of David Hume* (London, 1941).

James Hayden Tufts, "The Individual and His Relation to Society as Reflected in the British Ethics of the Eighteenth Century," *The Psychological Review*, Vol. i (May 1904).

CHAPTER II

1. Auguste Comte himself said that Ferguson was the first to hit upon the true principles of group reactions and modifications; see his *Positive Polity*, tr. by Frederic Harrison, ii, 370. See also Harry Elmer Barnes, *Sociology and Political Theory* (New York, 1924), p. 11, and *The New History and the Social Studies* (New York, 1925), pp. 312-13; Frank H. Hankins, "Sociology," in *The History and Prospects of the Social Sciences* (ed. by Harry Elmer Barnes, New York, 1925), pp. 289-90; William C. Lehmann, *Adam Ferguson and the Beginnings of Modern Sociology* (New York, 1930), pp. 25-27 and *passim*. Some useful analyses are offered by Lehmann, though interpretations are not always thorough nor philosophically adequate. German interest in Ferguson is to be seen in such analysts as Hermann Huth, "Soziale und Individualistische Auffassung im 18. Jahrhundert, vornehmlich bei Adam Smith und Adam Ferguson," in *Staats- und Sozialwissenschaftliche Forschungen*, Heft 125 (Leipzig, 1907); Theodor Buddeberg, "Ferguson als Soziologe," in *Jahrbücher für Nationalökonomie*, Bd. 123 (Jena, 1925). Cf. H. Bouet, "Adam Ferguson et ses idées politiques et sociales," in *Journal des economistes*, 5e serie (Dec. 1898). The most useful discussions of all appear in Werner Sombart, "Die Anfänge der Soziologie," in *Erinnerungabe für Max Weber*, herausgegeben von Melchior Palyi (Munich und Leipzig), i, 5-19, and in Hans Proesler, *Die Anfänge der Gesellschaftslehre* (Erlangen, 1935), *passim*. Both Sombart and Proesler, in emphasizing the empirical aims and procedures of Ferguson, and indeed of the whole Scottish group, attribute the origins of modern sociology to them. Sombart, it is true, would include some other opponents of Hobbes' position.

2. The edition of the *Institutes* to which reference is made throughout this book is that of 1773, which is a revision and correction of the second edition. Since the volumes are not available in all libraries it may be worth while to compare the table of contents of the two works,

to note the order of his discussion and the reorganization and elaboration which characterize the second work.

INSTITUTES OF MORAL PHILOSOPHY	PRINCIPLES OF MORAL AND POLITICAL SCIENCE
	VOL. I
Introduction	*Introduction*
Part I. The Natural History of Man	*Part I*. Of the Fact, or the most general Appearances in the Nature and State of Man
Part II. Theory of Mind	*Chapter 1*. Of Man's Description and Place in the Scale of Being
Part III. Of the Knowledge of God	*Chapter 2*. Of Mind, or Characteristics of Intelligence
Part IV. Of Moral Laws and their most General Application	*Chapter 3*. Of Man's Progressive Nature
Part V. Of Jurisprudence	
Part VI. Of Casuistry	VOL. II
Part VII. Of Politics	*Part II*. Of Moral Law
	Chapter 1. Of the Specific Good Incident to Human Nature
	Chapter 2. Of the Fundamental Law of Morality, its immediate Applications and Sanctions
	Chapters 3 and 4. Of Jurisprudence
	Chapter 5. Of Moral Action and the Characteristics of a Virtuous and Happy Life
	Chapter 6. Of Politics

It will be seen that Parts I, II and III of the *Institutes* parallel Part I of the *Principles*, and Parts IV, V, VI, VII of the *Institutes* parallel Part II of the *Principles*.

3. In the *Principles*, under the topic "Of Science" he offers a very neat statement: "In nature all the subjects presented to our observation are individual and marked with their particular qualities and circumstances. In the exercise of imagination or fancy, we proceed after the model of nature and particularize whatever we conceive for any purpose of contemplation, design, or invention. But if we would collect many particulars under one or a few general titles, we must abstract the conditions in which they agree from those in which they differ.

"As imagination, therefore, may be termed the faculty of particularization, abstraction may be termed the faculty of generalization.

"This faculty, applied to matters of description, gives the species and genera of things; applied to the succession of events, gives the laws of nature; and applied to matters of choice, gives the laws of morality."

Ferguson affords us a further glimpse into the conception of science as held by many eighteenth-century thinkers, and into the meaning of their scientific nomenclature when he writes as follows: "The particulars to be explained are termed phenomena," he states, and "A general rule, when applied to explain or regulate particulars, is termed a principle; and explanations or injunctions from principle are termed theory, or system. . . . Theory consists in referring particular operations to the principles, or general laws, under which they are comprehended; or in referring particular effects to the causes from which they proceed. To investigate or to point out any general rule or law of nature in which any particular fact is comprehended is to account for that fact."

4. *Ibid.* Throughout his books Ferguson accepts Newton's idea of hypothesis. Newton had had to say "Non fingo," because in his conception an hypothesis was not arrived at from observation of phenomena but from ratiocination. For discussion of this idea, see Edwin Arthur Burtt, *The Metaphysical Foundations of Modern Physical Science* (New York, 1925), pp. 211-16. Note also, in Ferguson's *Institutes*, Part II, Ch. 2, the parallel he draws between Newton's law of attraction governing the physical world and the principle of universal sympathy which Ferguson thinks governs the human and moral world.

5. Attention is called to the use of the word "history" which, in addition to its connotation of time-perspective, continued to mean throughout the eighteenth century simply an orderly inquiry or description. Cf. *New English Dictionary*, and James T. Shotwell, *An Introduction to the History of History* (New York, 1922), pp. 6-7. Ferguson's own definition is "a collection of facts in description or narration."—*Institutes*, p. 2.

6. *Analysis*, p. 7.

7. The references to the *Institutes* thus far are to the Introduction; to the *Principles*, I, 2, 5, 9, 71-76, 113-19, 157-62, 272, 278-80; II, 180.

8. "Man, though an animal of prey, and from necessity or sport addicted to hunting or war, is nevertheless, in the highest degree, associating and political"; *Institutes*, pp. 21-22. From the *Principles*, I, 24: "To be in society is the physical state of the species, not the moral distinction of any particular man."

9. Note his anticipation of Malthus: "Men, in every secure situation, people up to their resources; and the aid of government is required, not to improve on the laws of propagation, but to bestow security and plenty."—*Institutes*, p. 18.

10. On this favorite topic he anticipated the popular work of his friend, Professor John Millar, *The Origin of the Distinction of Ranks; or, An Inquiry into the Circumstances Which Give Rise to Influence and Authority in the Different Members of Society* (London, 1771).

11. The references of this paragraph to the *Institutes* are to Part I; to the *Principles*, I, 18-25, 48-61, 197-99, and all of Part I, Ch. III.

12. Cf. *Principles*, I, 68: "The mind being destined to know and act, the most general arrangement of its powers is that of understanding and will, or, in the words of Mr. Hobbes, 'The powers *cognitive* and the powers *active.*'" The dichotomy persists for decades.

13. *Institutes*, pp. 12-13, 76; *Principles*, I, 3-4, 77-113, 123-32, 152-56. The term "Pneumatics" is dropped in the *Principles*, but the discussion follows the same lines, and the term did not drop out of general use for many years. Fuller discussion will be offered in Chapter V.

14. *Institutes*, Part II, "Theory of Mind."

15. *Ibid.*, pp. 86-90; *Principles*, I, Ch. III, "Of Man's Progressive Nature," and pp. 26-36, 42, 56, 167, 174-75.

16. *Institutes*, pp. 108-9; *Principles*, II, 403.

17. *Institutes*, pp. 110-29; *Principles*, I, 163-87, esp. 166.

18. *Institutes*, pp. 130-33, 149, 152; *Principles*, I, 157-62; II, 2, 107-13, 134, 149.

19. The term "casuistry," as used by churchmen of the Middle Ages, covered precise rules of duty and conduct, so organized as to be helpful in the practice of auricular confession of communicants to their priests. With the later prominence of Jesuit scholars the formulations came to have a wider, more theoretical use.

20. *Institutes*, pp. 169-73, 212-19; *Principles*, II, 168-90, 315-22.

21. For discussion of the cardinal virtues of justice or probity, prudence, temperance and fortitude, see *Institutes*, pp. 220-38, and *Principles*, II, 315-405. An eighteenth-century moralist's list of cardinal virtues is almost always that of Cicero as given in *De officiis*, Book I.

22. *Institutes*, pp. 239-40.

23. *Principles*, II, 214-25, 230-35, 245. Cf. Hume's emphasis on habit, as discussed in his essays "Of the Origin of Government" and "Of the Original Contract."

24. *Institutes*, pp. 239-61; *Principles*, II, 420-56.

25. *Institutes*, pp. 261-94.

26. Ferguson's biographer advances the theory that kinship with Dr. Black's family and the Blacks' friendship with Montesquieu was one of the reasons for Ferguson's being a disciple of Montesquieu. Not to have quoted Montesquieu, however, would have called for an explanation by any Scottish philosopher of the period. See John Small, *op. cit.*, p. 663.

27. We might pause for a moment in our tracing of Ferguson's scheme to note the change in emphasis which the social sciences have adopted since their emergence from moral philosophy. Instead of following in detail the above pattern, each of the social sciences has abstracted for itself one of the typical human relations or sets of situations, such as the political, and has ramified the discussions of the intricacies of such relationships. Ordinarily any such treatment is prefaced by a preliminary discussion of the place of this subject matter within the classification of the sciences, and a statement of the aims and methods of the study. Often as basic material the "facts" of human nature are postulated or assumed, and viewed as affording the motives or drives to the kind of behavior under consideration. Both the preliminary methodological discussion and the detailing of the psychological bases have, however, been much shortened; the psycho-genetic fallacy is still sometimes committed. What is left out usually is the positing of a general ethical principle, though often such a one works its way into the discussion unobserved.

28. Stewart, *Works*, x, 38, 261; Small, *op. cit.*, pp. 609, 613; Sir Leslie Stephen, *History of English Thought*, II, 214-15. David Hume, apparently, was not so much impressed by it. Before it was in print, he wrote Dr. Hugh Blair that the work was unworthy of publication, because of defects in style and reasoning, and urged Blair to use his influence to have Ferguson withdraw it. After it was published, Hume wrote both Ferguson and Blair in congratulatory spirit, generously passing on to Ferguson the many compliments he had heard on the book, but saying privately to Blair that, though he had tried, he could not revise his opinion of it; see Greig (ed.), *Letters of David Hume*, II, 11 ff., 120 ff., 125 ff., 131 ff., 136. Lord Woodhouselee, the biographer of Kames, judged this essay of Ferguson's "the most complete, and incomparably the most elegant specimen" of theoretical history; see his *Life of . . . Kames*, I, 201.

29. *Civil Society*, pp. 1, 105, 107, 220-21, 280-82, 338, 359, 367, 395, 472, 475; cf. *Principles*, II, 252, 270-71, 279, 285. [The references throughout this book are to an edition of the *Civil Society* frequently available in this country, the 8th, published in Philadelphia, 1819.]

30. See Lois Whitney, *Primitivism and the Idea of Progress in English Popular Literature of the Eighteenth Century*, Ch. 2. Professor Whitney's book is, throughout, a most valuable interpretation of the thought of the century with respect to ideas of progress and degeneration. In speaking of the century's fondness for adversely criticizing luxury, one should not forget Mandeville's defense of it.

31. The quotations in this and the following seven paragraphs are

scattered through the first seventeen pages of the *Civil Society*. It scarcely needs to be pointed out that this emphasis on the group as the unit of investigation is one of the chief reasons for sociologists' notice of Ferguson today.

32. *Principles,* i, 174-75; *Civil Society,* p. 135.

33. *Civil Society,* pp. 146-47.

34. *Ibid.,* pp. 221-23. Huth says of Ferguson's criticism, "Ferguson findet so starke Tone wie keiner vor ihm."—*Op. cit.,* pp. 45-46. See also Sombart, *op. cit.,* pp. 14-19.

35. *Civil Society,* pp. 221-22, 233, 241-44.

36. *Ibid.,* pp. 36, 41-43, 264-65, 280-81, and all of Part iii, sec. v, and Part i, sec. iv.

37. *Ibid.,* pp. 108-9, 267-70, 275-77, 346, 385, esp. 112 and 371. This emphasis which Ferguson gives to conflict is what made Gumplowicz, with his theory of the role of conflict in the formation of groups and states, accord Ferguson the title of "Father of Sociology."

38. *Ibid.,* pp. 373-75, 378, 403, esp. 386-88, and Part v, sec. ii-iv incl.

39. *Ibid.,* Part vi.

40. *Ibid.,* p. 151. Earlier in this essay Ferguson had written: "When I recollect what the President Montesquieu has written, I am at a loss to tell, why I should treat of human affairs; but I too am instigated by my reflections, and my sentiments; and I may utter them more to the comprehension of ordinary capacities, because I am more on the level of ordinary men."—P. 119.

41. *Ibid.,* p. 17.

CHAPTER III

1. Kames, *Essays on the Principles of Morality and Natural Religion* (Edinburgh, 1751), p. 147, and all of Essay iii; *Sketches of the History of Man* (2 vols., Edinburgh, 1774), ii, 300. Dugald Stewart reminds us that in the last edition of the *Essays,* appearing when Kames was eighty years old, he abandoned the doctrine of the deceitful sense of liberty and became a necessitarian.—Stewart, *Collected Works,* vi, 382. For Stewart's own discussion of the problems, see *op. cit.,* vi, 43, 340-41, 393-94, and Appendix, pp. 343-402; the Index, Vol. ii, gives long lists of references on free will, free agency, necessity.

2. Reid, *Intellectual Powers,* p. 52; *Active Powers,* pp. 511, 546-47, 615-16; cf. George Turnbull, *Observations upon Liberal Education* (London, 1742), p. 359.

3. Smith, *Theory of Moral Sentiments,* Vol. i of London ed. of *Works* (1812), 515-16; *Wealth of Nations,* i, as cited, 400.

4. Hutcheson, *A System of Moral Philosophy,* i, 205-6, 209-10; cf. *A Short Introduction to Moral Philosophy,* pp. 31-36; and Scott, *op. cit.,* Ch. 8, and pp. 168, 190-200, 226-27, 250-52. A useful summary of the theories of macrocosm and microcosm is George Perrigo Conger's book, *Theories of Macrocosm and Microcosm in the History of Philosophy* (New York, 1932).

5. Monboddo, *Antient Metaphysics,* iii, 4-13; iv, Preface, and pp. 1-5.

6. For an account of the remarkable work of this man, see M. F. Ashley Montagu, *Edward Tyson, M.D., F.R.S., 1650-1708* (American Philosophical Society, Philadelphia, 1943). It may be, as Professor Arthur O. Lovejoy remarks with reference to Monboddo's theories, that "orang-outang" was a generic term; see his "Monboddo and Rousseau," in *Modern Philology,* xxx (1932-33), 283; and Montagu, pp. 242 ff.

7. For a brief summary of the ideas of Maupertuis on the origin of new species and his theory of inheritance anticipatory of Mendel's, see

H. F. Osborn, *From the Greeks to Darwin* (new ed., New York, 1927), pp. 113-15; and the paper by Arthur O. Lovejoy, "Some Eighteenth-Century Evolutionists," in *Popular Science Monthly*, LXV (1904).

8. John Hunter, F.R.S., *Essays and Observations on Natural History, Anatomy, Physiology, Psychology, and Geology*, arranged and revised, with notes . . . by Richard Owen (2 vols., London, 1861), I, 39, 43.

9. *The Anthropological Treatises of Johann Friedrich Blumenbach*, tr. and ed. by Thomas Bendyshe (London, 1865), pp. 97-98, 209-10, 214-15, 227-37, 276.

10. Arthur O. Lovejoy, *The Great Chain of Being* (Harvard University Press, Cambridge, Mass., 1936), p. 184.

11. *Ibid.*, p. 59; by permission of the publishers. Chapters VI, VIII, IX of Lovejoy's discussion are pertinent here.

12. *Ibid.*, pp. 233-36, 244, and Ch. IX.

13. This scheme appeared in editions later than the first of 1735, and was the one followed in the first complete English edition, done by Dr. William Turton in 1806.

14. Richard Pulteney, *A General View of the Writings of Linnaeus* (2nd ed., London, 1805), p. 176.

15. Edward Lee Greene, *Carolus Linnaeus* (Philadelphia, 1912), p. 90.

16. Blumenbach, in Bendyshe, *op. cit.*, pp. 163-64.

17. Quoted by Charles Singer, *Greek Biology and Greek Medicine* (Clarendon Press, Oxford, 1922), pp. 29-31, as from Aristotle's *Historia animalium* and *De partibus animalium*, in *The Oxford Translation of the Works of Aristotle*, ed. by W. D. Ross (Clarendon Press): by permission of the publishers.

18. L. C. Miall, *History of Biology* (New York, 1911), p. 57. Miall notes that the reaction began to set in in 1766 in Germany when Pallas insisted that the scale is not linear, but is better represented by a branching tree. Cf. Lovejoy, *Great Chain of Being*, chs. cited in note 11.

19. Blumenbach, in Bendyshe, *op. cit.*, pp. 317-51. Cf. English and Scottish works in the same vein: John Gregory, *A Comparative View of the State and Faculties of Man with Those of the Animal Kingdom* (London, 1765), and Charles White, *An Account of the Regular Gradation in Man, and in Different Animals and Vegetables; and from the Former to the Latter* (London, 1799). The permeating influence of Leibniz' principle of continuity should not be forgotten, even though he himself disallowed "mediate species between man and beasts"; cf. his *New Essays Concerning Human Understanding*, Bk. IV, Ch. 16, ¶ 12.

20. *Essay on Man*, ll. 233-46, 267-68.

21. These quotations are from one of the American editions, published at Dover, N.H., in 1808. Smellie died before finishing the second volume of the first edition.

22. For a detailed account of the interplay of social theory and natural history in the 18th and 19th centuries, see Frederick J. Teggart, *Theory of History* (New Haven, 1925), Chs. 8-12 incl.; and cf. R. H. Murray's statement that the stimulus given to evolutionary studies came more from the moral philosophers than from scientists proper.—*Science and Scientists in the Nineteenth Century* (New York, 1925), p. 129.

23. Pope, *op. cit.*, Epistle I, "Of the Nature and State of Man with Respect to the Universe," ll. 47-50, 69-72.

24. Kames, *Essays*, pp. 365-66.

25. The salient points of Kames' discussion of races are found in the *Sketches*, Vol. I, Bk. I, Sketch I. In II, 75, Kames states a predicament still admitted by anthropologists: "We want data, I acknowledge, to determine with accuracy what effects can be produced by a climate."

26. Franklin Thomas, *The Environmental Basis of Society* (New York, 1925), pp. 269-70. Cf. Frank H. Hankins, *The Racial Basis of Civilization* (New York, 1926), *passim*; and Paul Radin, *The Racial Myth* (New York, 1932).

27. Note the sharp criticism of Kames' resort to Divine interference, offered by another John Hunter, a young physician, in his doctoral dissertation delivered at the University of Edinburgh in 1775, who said of Kames' method of arguing: "Now if we take up this mode of philosophizing, and attribute everything for which we can give no reason to the Divine interference, we shut the door and stop up all the sources from which all those things spring which adorn life, promote the arts, and finally increase the force and the faculties of the human mind."—Quoted by Bendyshe, *op. cit.*, p. 360. One of the sharpest critics was Samuel Stanhope Smith, Professor of Moral Philosophy at Princeton (then the College of New Jersey), later president of the same institution, and son-in-law of that John Witherspoon who introduced the Scottish system into this country. In a little book entitled *Essay on the Causes of the Variety of Complexion and Figure in the Human Species* (Philadelphia, 1787), Smith declared himself an environmentalist against Kames' racialism. Included in the volume is an essay, "Strictures on Lord Kames' Discourse on the Original Diversity of Mankind," a point-by-point refutation of Kames.

28. Henry Graham, *Scottish Men of Letters in the Eighteenth Century*, p. 188.

29. *Antient Metaphysics* (6 vols., Edinburgh, 1779-99), III, 337, 344-47, esp. 355-56. For comprehensive discussion of the favorite reference to the happy brutes, see George Boas, *The Happy Beast in French Thought of the Seventeenth Century* (Baltimore, 1933).

30. *Origin and Progress of Language* (6 vols., Edinburgh, 1773-92), I, 182-83. [All references to Vol. I are to a 1774 ed. of that single volume.] Cf. *Antient Metaphysics*, III, 5; VI, 130 and 142.

31. On this "principle of plenitude," see Lovejoy, *The Great Chain of Being*, p. 52 and *passim*.

32. *Origin and Progress of Language*, I, 220-24.

33. *Ibid.*, I, 396-98; II, 1-3; *Antient Metaphysics*, I, 138; III, 1-2.

34. *Origin and Progress of Language*, I, Bk. I, Ch. 10; *Antient Metaphysics*, VI, 138-47; cf. Whitney, *op. cit.*, pp. 281-91.

35. *Origin and Progress of Language*, I, 446-47, n.; *Antient Metaphysics*, III, Bk. II, esp. 282. Knight, Monboddo's biographer, *op. cit.*, pp. 276-77, tells us of a manuscript in the possession of the Burnet family, entitled *The Degeneracy of Man in the State of Society*. Throughout the printed works there are many references to Rousseau and indications of the influence of his *Discours sur l'inégalité*, which had been first printed in Amsterdam in 1755; but there is the classic touch, too, as for example: "Then shall Astraea visit the earth again, whose latest footsteps are now no longer to be seen."

36. For the most compact single discussion of these varieties of men, see *Antient Metaphysics*, Vol. VI, Bk. II, Chs. 11 and 12.

37. Chauncey Brewster Tinker, *Nature's Simple Plan* (Princeton, 1922), pp. 15-17. Since the anthropoids are tailless, Monboddo's preoccupation (in *The Origin and Progress of Language*) with men with tails inclines Professor Lovejoy to the belief that Monboddo really had some idea of descent of apes, monkeys, and man from a common ancestor which had a tail; see Lovejoy's "Some Eighteenth-Century Evolutionists," in *Popular Science Monthly*, LXV (1904), and his "Monboddo and Rousseau," previously cited. The chief evidence is a letter of Monboddo's, to Sir John Pringle, dated June 16, 1773, reproduced in Knight,

op. cit., pp. 82-85. Nowhere in the volumes of his two works, however, is there such a definite lead; cf. Joseph Patrick Blickensderfer, "A Study of Lord Monboddo and His Works," Ph.D. thesis, Harvard, 1925; and Whitney, *op. cit.*, pp. 281-91.

38. References to Peter are to be found throughout his works. For the true story of Wild Peter, see Blumenbach, in Bendyshe, *op. cit.*, pp. 325-40.

39. *Origin and Progress of Language*, Vol. I, Bk. I, Chs. 15 and 16; *Antient Metaphysics*, III, 41-44, 64 ff. and Appendix III; IV, 25-34, 403 ff.

40. *Antient Metaphysics*, III, 282.

41. Tinker, *op. cit.*, p. 14.

42. Blumenbach, in Bendyshe, *op. cit.*, p. 296; see also pp. 141 and 258.

43. Ramsay, *op. cit.*, I, 357.

44. Maillet, *Telliamed*, pp. 230, 246 ff., 268-69.

45. See Lovejoy's paper, "Monboddo and Rousseau," in *Modern Philology*, xxx (1932-33), 275-96.

46. *Antient Metaphysics*, III, 43-44.

47. Dunbar, *op. cit.* (2nd ed., London, 1781), p. 162.

48. *Origin and Progress of Language*, I, 270-313, esp. 289-90; *Antient Metaphysics*, IV, 26-33; III, 105, 133-37. The term "orang-outang" for Monboddo was apparently generic, applying also to gorillas and chimpanzees; so with a number of the authors.

49. *Origin and Progress of Language*, I, 269, and Bk. II, Chs. 4 and 5; *Antient Metaphysics*, III, 363. He makes it clear in at least one reference that his generosity does not extend to any monkey, ape, or baboon, with or without tails.—*Origin and Progress of Language*, I, 311. Cf. note 48 above.

50. *Antient Metaphysics*, IV, 20.

51. *Ibid.*, IV, 32; cf. III, 28, 282, 338-41, 363.

52. *Ibid.*, IV, 25-35, 61 ff., 96, 122.

53. This discussion will be rehearsed in Chapter VIII.

54. *Antient Metaphysics*, III, 363; cf. *Origin and Progress of Language*, I, 338-40.

55. But cf. the several Lovejoy papers cited.

56. Cf. Robert M. and Ada W. Yerkes, *The Great Apes* (New Haven, 1929), Ch. 3, "Progress of Acquaintance with the Anthropoid Apes During the 18th Century," esp. p. 23 for a laudatory comment on Monboddo.

CHAPTER IV

1. J. B. Black, *The Art of History* (Methuen & Company, London, 1926), pp. 14-15. On the popularity of history and other topics, see James Westfall Thompson, *A History of Historical Writing* (New York, 1942), II, xxxviii and xxxix.

2. Black, *op. cit.*, pp. 14-15.

3. *Ibid.*, pp. 15-22, 85. Gibbon had written: "History is for the philosophic mind what gaming was to the Marquis de Dangeau. He saw in it a system, connections, a sequence, while others discovered only the caprices of fortune."—Quoted from Gibbon's *Essai sur l'étude de la littérature*, xlviii, by Black, pp. 157-58. Cf. the discussion in Carl Becker, *The Heavenly City of the Eighteenth-Century Philosophers* (New Haven, 1932), pp. 19, 29, 96-99.

4. A fundamental analysis of history as a field of investigation is to be found in Frederick J. Teggart, *Theory of History* (New Haven, 1925).

5. A complete account of this idealization of a supposed original state of man is in preparation by Professors Lovejoy, Chinard, Boas

and Crane. It is to be called *A Documentary History of Primitivism and Related Ideas*. The first volume, *Primitivism and Related Ideas in Antiquity* (Baltimore, 1935), Ch. I, gives the orientation for the whole study and is pertinent here. It confirms Hume's saying, "The humour of blaming the present, and admiring the past is strongly rooted in human nature."—*Essays*, I, 443.

6. Sir Leslie Stephen, *History of English Thought* (John Murray, London, 1881), I, 57, 59; by permission of the publishers. Cf. Black, *op. cit.*, pp. 79, 85-86. An excellent discussion of the historiography of the period is given in Eduard Fueter, *Histoire de l'historiographie moderne*, tr. par Émile Jeanmaire (Paris, 1914), Livre IV, "L'historiographie du rationalisme." Cf. also Cassirer, *op. cit.*, Kap. V.

7. Goguet wrote: "The history of laws, arts, and sciences is, properly speaking, the history of the human mind. . . . I have followed, then, as far as I could perceive them, the footsteps of the human understanding."—Quoted from the Preface to Vol. I of the Edinburgh ed. of 1761.

8. Clarifying discussion of these influences is to be found in Teggart, *op. cit.*, pp. 81-82, 91-123, 209.

9. G. L. Van Roosbroeck, *Persian Letters before Montesquieu*, Publications of the Institute of French Studies, Inc. (New York, 1932), p. 17.

10. A convenient list of historians may be found in Harry Elmer Barnes, *History, Its Rise and Development*, reprinted from the *Encyclopedia Americana* (1922 ed.).

11. Turnbull, *Observations upon Liberal Education* (London, 1742), pp. 379, 382, 391-92.

12. *Inquiry*, p. 265.

13. *System*, I, 34-35; II, 146-47, 223-27, 231, 279-81, 286-87.

14. *System*, I, 1, 280-83, 293, and Bk. II, *passim*; II, 119-20, 128, 149, 223-28, 231-33; *Short Introduction*, Bk. II. W. R. Scott, in his *Francis Hutcheson*, pp. 249-53, suggests that the changes in the shades of meaning of the term "nature" and its derivations as used by Hutcheson may be due to the successive influences on Hutcheson of Shaftesbury, Butler, Aristotle, and the Stoics. See such passages as the *System*, I, 29; *Short Introduction*, 1-2, 256 ff. For a helpful listing, "Some Meanings of Nature," see Lovejoy, Chinard, Boas, and Crane, *op. cit.*, Appendix, pp. 447-56.

15. *Inquiry*, pp. 75, 83, 87-95, 200-11. Note the anticipations here of the concepts of ethnocentrism and the "we-group" as developed by William Graham Sumner in his *Folkways* (Boston, 1906), and of the notion of culture-pattern as found in Ruth Benedict, *Patterns of Culture* (Boston and New York, 1934), and others.

16. John Maurice Clark, "Adam Smith and the Currents of History," in Clark *et al*, *Adam Smith, 1776-1926* (Chicago, 1928), p. 73; and Smith, *Wealth of Nations*, Bk. III, Ch. 1.

17. A fresh analysis of Smith's relation to the theory and developments of the 19th century is to be found in Eli Ginzberg, *The House of Adam Smith* (New York, 1934).

18. Stewart, *Works*, X, 32-34, 37.

19. Bagehot, "Adam Smith as a Person," in his *Biographical Studies* (2nd ed., London, 1889), pp. 248-55.

20. *Works*, II, 247-48; cf. this judgment with the facts dealt with in the "Dissertation," in *Works*, I, entire. Dugald Stewart presents no original facets of thought for the modern reader. His service to us today is that of a man thoroughly versed in the knowledge of his time, able to interpret to us not only the regularities but many of the vagaries of his contemporaries. In his own day, however, his reputation and his influ-

ence were great; and for an American it is interesting to know that when Thomas Jefferson decided to recruit from Great Britain the faculty for the new University of Virginia, it was to Dugald Stewart that he sent his representative for consultation and advice; see Gilbert Chinard, *Thomas Jefferson, the Apostle of Americanism* (Boston, 1929), pp. 510-11.

21. *Works*, x, 35. Stewart goes on to speak of the excellent examples given by Kames, by John Millar, and by David Hume.

22. Paraphrased from Comte, by Teggart, *Theory of History*, p. 99; by permission of the publishers, Yale University Press.

23. *Op. cit.*, p. 87, and *passim*, but especially Chs. 7-10 incl.

24. *Sketches of the History of Man*, i, 39-43; see the whole of the "Preliminary Discourse, concerning the Origin of Men and of Languages," and Sketch viii, "Progress and Effects of Luxury." Cf. Whitney, *op. cit.*, pp. 277-81.

25. *Sketches*, i, 100, 103-5, 390-92. On this suggestion of a stimulus to the arts, cf. Professor Teggart's discussion of the psychological release and opportunity for exercise of initiative which have often accompanied conquest, and for which the modern world needs to discover an unwarlike equivalent.—*Processes of History* (New Haven, 1918), pp. 88-91, 98, 149-62.

26. *Historical Law Tracts*, pp. 25-26, 90-94, 104. See Woodhouselee's criticism of such theoretical or conjectural history in his *Life of . . . Kames*, i, 305-6, and iii, 110-53. But see the method still somewhat used in a recent series, *The Evolution of Law*, compiled by Kocourek and Wigmore (Boston, 1915), ii, 15 ff.

27. Quoted in Rae's *Life of Adam Smith*, p. 142, and Woodhouselee's *Life of . . . Kames*, i, 318.

28. *Sketches*, Vol. ii, Bk. ii, Sketch ix.

29. Whitney, *op. cit.*, pp. 277, 281-91.

30. *Antient Metaphysics*, v, 93, 235; vi, 107-9, 130, 135. Monboddo makes many references to the Chain of Being.

31. *Op. cit.*, vi, 138-47; cf. v, 3; iii, Appendix iii, and our discussion of Monboddo's judgment on Wild Peter, in Ch. iii.

32. *Ibid.*, vi, 148-57, 167 ff., 177 ff., 193, 219 ff.; v, 168 ff., 323; iv, 358; cf. *Origin and Progress of Language*, i, Bk. ii.

33. *Origin and Progress of Language*, vi, 177-78, 626 ff.; *Antient Metaphysics*, iv, 361-62.

34. *Antient Metaphysics*, v, 88, 321, and Bk. iii; vi, 192-95, 199-200.

35. *Ibid.*, v, 238-39, 319-22, and Bk. iv, *passim*.

36. Whitney, *op. cit.*, pp. 281-89. The three contradictions Miss Whitney emphasizes are those concerned with his interpretation (1) as to how a good God could have endowed man with a nature requiring him to sin and suffer; (2) as to the ennobling of the mind which should accompany the deterioration of the body of man but does not; (3) as to his defense of the civil state. A few of the passages in which these contradictions are exposed are *Antient Metaphysics*, iii, 103, 172-73, 269; iv, 32-33; v, 88.

37. *Op. cit.*, i, 8; v, 419, and Ch. 36. (References are to the Edinburgh ed. of 1805, 5 vols.)

38. Wilbur C. Abbott, *Adventures in Reputation* (Cambridge, Mass., 1935), pp. 126-27.

39. "Of the Populousness of Ancient Nations," in *Essays, Moral, Political, and Literary*, ed. by Green and Grose, i, 381-443.

40. *Treatise*, Bk. ii, Pt. i, Ch. 10; Bk. iii, Pt. ii, Chs. 2-4; *Principles of Morals*, sec. iii and Appendix iii; several essays, discussed later.

41. "Of the Rise and Progress of the Arts and Sciences," and "Of

Refinement in the Arts," in *Essays*, I, 174-97 and 299-309, respectively.

42. Quoted by Harold Laski, *Political Thought in England from Locke to Bentham* (New York, 1920), p. 156.

43. See, especially, "Of the Origin of Government," "Of the Original Contract," and "Of Passive Obedience."

44. In "Of the Rise and Progress of the Sciences," "Of Polygamy and Divorce," "Of Love and Marriage," "Of the Study of History," and "Of the Immortality of the Soul."

45. Teggart, *Theory of History*, pp. 76-84; see Hume's statements, *Essays*, I, 126, 292, 381-82; II, 334, and *History of England*, II, 441.

46. *Essays*, I, 113, 115, 174; II, 311.

47. *History of England*, I, 1-2; II, 446. Cf. Sally Daiches, *Über das Verhältnis der Geschichtsschreibung D. Hume's zu seiner Praktischen Philosophie* (Leipzig, 1903), pp. 20-22.

48. *Essays*, I, 170, 174, 244, 246, 249. See Teggart, *op. cit.*, pp. 174-78, 181, and George H. Sabine, "Hume's Contribution to the Historical Method," in *Philosophical Review*, 15 (New York, 1906), 19-26.

49. *History of England*, VI, 117. Cf. Voltaire's interest in cultures, as mirrored, for example, in his *Siècle de Louis XIV* (1751) and his *Essai sur les mœurs et l'esprit des nations* (1756).

50. Heinrich Goebel characterizes Hume's history thus: "Die Geschichte ist ihm die grosse Lehrmeister in der Menschheit, ein Spiegel, der die Bilder der Vergangenheit auffängt, um die Gegenwart zu unterhalten und zu belehren. Ihr Zweck besteht darin, dass sie nützlich und angenehm ist."—*Das Philosophische im Humes Geschichte vom England*, Inaugural Dissertation (Marburg, 1897), p. 2.

51. *History of England*, V, 7-8, 25-27, 198-99, 226, 388, 468-71; VI, 124.

52. Black, *op. cit.*, p. 98; cf. pp. 77-116. Cf. Sabine, *op. cit.*, pp. 35-38.

53. See Abbott, *op. cit.*, pp. 130 ff., with regard to Hume's scholarship. An anonymous writer in the *Quarterly Review* quotes the description by an old friend of Hume's of his method of work, which does not indicate a laboring Benedictine: "Why, mon, David read a vast deal before he set about a piece of his work; but his usual seat was on the sofa, and he often wrote with his legs up; and it would have been unco' fashious to have moved across the room when any little doubt occurred."—Vol. 73, p. 554; quoted also by Black, *op. cit.*, p. 91.

54. Quoted by Abbott, *op. cit.*, p. 133.

55. *Essays*, I, 113-17, 170, 411, 443-60; *Treatise*, pp. 484, 493-94, 520 ff., 543, 561, 567; *Principles of Morals*, pp. 189-90.

56. *Essays*, II, 296-300; I, 177-97; cf. the essay "Of National Characters," where the discussion turns on the power of imitation, sympathy, and contagion of manners.

57. *Essays*, I, 177, 178-87, 196, 244, 248-49, 250, 254; II, 289-305. On this whole discussion, see Teggart, *op. cit.*, pp. 178-81.

58. Teggart, *op. cit.*, pp. 84, 87; Sabine, *op. cit.*, p. 26.

59. Sir Grafton Elliot Smith, *The Diffusion of Culture* (London, 1933), Ch. III and pp. 119-20. Sir Elliot is prompted to this analysis by his position as spokesman of the "Diffusionist" school in anthropology, but one need not be an extremist in that view to agree with his criticisms here.

60. Teggart, *op. cit.*, Part I, "The Study of Events."

61. *Ibid.*, Ch. 7.

62. *Ibid.*, p. 79.

63. *Ibid.*, pp. 84-87.

64. *Ibid.*, Chs. 9-11 incl. give an understanding of the problems faced especially by sociologists and anthropologists, as a result of the adoption of this set of ideas by way of Comte and Tylor.

CHAPTER V

1. George Anderson, *Estimate of the Profit and Loss of Religion
. . . illustrated with References . . . to . . . Kames* (Edinburgh, 1753),
p. 1.

2. The term earlier in use was Pneumatics or Pneumatology; Ferguson, for example, was Professor of Pneumatics and Moral Philosophy.
Pneuma is, of course, the clue; recall how in the Middle Ages Christ
was spoken of by certain sects as the Great Pneumatic, and the Gospel
of John called the pneumatic gospel, the gospel of religious inspiration.
From Ferguson's definition we may gather that the eighteenth century
used the terms to cover the physical aspects of mental life; see *Institutes*, pp. 4-6, 10-13, 46-90, and *Principles of Moral and Political Science*,
I, 78. See also George Sidney Brett, *Psychology, Ancient and Modern*
(New York, 1928), pp. 23-26.

In the course of the century, "metaphysics" came to be the more
popular term, but toward the close of the century it was once again
applied more strictly to discussions of ontology, and "psychology" took
the field.

A good discussion of the psychology and theory of knowledge which
characterized the Enlightenment is to be found in Cassirer, *op. cit.*,
Kap. III.

3. Hutcheson, *A Short Introduction to Moral Philosophy* (1st ed.,
Glasgow), p. 2.

4. The outline offered here—for which thanks are expressed to Miss
Jane Henle, Smith '34—is drawn principally from the first chapter of
the *Short Introduction to Moral Philosophy*, the book which, following
Professor Scott's analysis, is accepted as giving Hutcheson's final
formulation of his philosophy.—Scott, *op. cit.*, Ch. 9. But cf. *Essay on the
Nature and Conduct of the Passions* (London and Dublin, 1728), *passim*,
and *System of Moral Philosophy* (London, 1755), Vol. I, *passim*.

5. *Inquiry*, pp. 1-3; cf. *System*, I, 6-7. Hutcheson also brings in
association, "a natural involuntary determination to associate or bind
together all such perceptions· as have often occurred together, or have
made at once a strong impression on the mind, so that they shall still
attend each other, when any object afterwards excites any one or more
of them."—*System*, I, 30.

6. *Essay on the . . . Passions*, pp. 3-4.

7. *System*, I, 5; cf. *Essay*, p. 2, for a different statement.

8. *Essay*, pp. 2-4; *System*, I, 4-6. Cf. Thomas Fowler, *Shaftesbury and
Hutcheson* (London, 1882), pp. 205-6.

9. *Essay*, pp. 3-4; *System*, I, 5-6.

10. *Essay*, pp. 4-10, 13 ff.

11. *Ibid.*, pp. 28-29. His quotation is from Malebranche.

12. *Treatise of Human Nature*, pp. 67-68, 252, 254, 634. See Alfred
North Whitehead's comparison of Hume's epistemological atomism with
the physical atomism of Democritus and Epicurus, in his *Adventures of
Ideas* (Cambridge, 1933), p. 159; and Jay William Hudson's *The Treatment of Personality by Locke, Berkeley and Hume*, University of Missouri
Studies, Philosophy and Education Series, Vol. I, No. 1 (Columbia, Mo.,
1911).

13. *Treatise*, p. 189; John Laird, *Hume's Philosophy of Human Nature* (Methuen & Company, London, 1932), p. 30.

14. *Treatise*, pp. 10, 11, 13, 164, 305; see the discussion of Hume's
type of associational psychology, in George Sidney Brett's *History of
Psychology* (London, 1921), II, 272-74.

15. *Treatise*, pp. 73-84, 96-97, 118-23, 130-43, 183, 223.

16. *Ibid.*, p. 183.

17. Laird, *op. cit.*, pp. 185-86; *Treatise*, pp. 182 ff., 267.

18. Brett, *op. cit.*, II, 276. Laird says Hume "meant . . . to become the Newton of the Human Mind."—*Op. cit.*, p. 20.

19. *Treatise*, pp. 366-68.

20. *Ibid.*, pp. 192-95, 271, 276, 296, 399, 414, 438-39, 574.

21. *Ibid.*, pp. 276-77, 399 ff., 438 ff. The listing in the first citation includes despair and security, but these are never discussed.

22. *Ibid.*, pp. 418-19.

23. *Ibid.*, pp. 399, 414-15, 438-39, 457-58.

24. *Ibid.*, pp. 305 ff., 366.

25. Laird, *op. cit.*, p. 201.

26. *Treatise*, pp. 316-19, 340, 354, 369.

27. See Laird, *op. cit.*, pp. 209-11, where these items are discussed as Hume's debt to Hutcheson; John J. Martin, *Shaftesbury's und Hutcheson's Verhältnis zu Hume* (Halle, 1905), esp. pp. 16-19, 66-69, 107-17; Scott, *op. cit.*, pp. 124-30.

28. *Works*, I, 100-3, 109. We make no distinction in these references between the *Inquiry* and the *Essays*; the text is that sponsored by Sir William Hamilton (6th ed., Edinburgh, 1863). Reid had earlier, he tells us, embraced the whole of Berkeley's system; see *Works*, I, 91, 283.

29. Andrew Seth, *Scottish Philosophy* (Edinburgh and London, 1885), p. 76.

30. *Works*, I, 95-99.

31. *Ibid.*, pp. 105, 194, 334-39; and Olin McKendree Jones, *Empiricism and Intuition in Reid's Common Sense Philosophy* (Princeton, 1927), p. 34.

32. *Works*, I, 182-83. Reid's loose use of the words "notion," "suggestion," "conception," have led some of his critics to say that all unconsciously he fell into a position of representative mediate perception, instead of immediate perception which he so much wanted to maintain; see Hamilton's notes, in *Works of Reid*, II, 819, note C; and Jones, *op. cit., passim.*

33. *Works*, I, 243.

34. *Ibid.*, pp. 442-43.

35. Seth, *op. cit.*, pp. 92-93; cf. Brett, *op. cit.*, III, 14 ff.

36. Reid, *Works*, I, 209.

37. Jones, *op. cit.*, Ch. 5 and p. 65.

38. *Works*, II, 524, 531.

39. *Ibid.*, II, 545-47, 550.

40. *Ibid.*, pp. 579-80.

41. *Ibid.*, pp. 587-90, 592. Reid uses henceforth, as almost synonymous terms, the expressions "moral sense," "moral faculty," "conscience."

42. *Principles of Moral and Political Science*, I, 78-79, 102.

43. *Ibid.*, pp. 85-86; cf. pp. 79-83 for other criticisms of Humean positions.

44. *Ibid.*, p. 91.

45. *Ibid.*, pp. 114-19.

46. *Ibid.*, pp. 68, 98, 102.

47. *Institutes*, pp. 81-90.

48. *Principles*, I, 120-28.

49. James, *Principles of Psychology*, II (1918 ed.), 383; James' first ed. was 1890. Note John B. Watson's criticism of James' definition in his *Behaviorism* (New York, 1924), p. 110.

50. *Energies of Men* (London, 1932), pp. 25-26, 49, 64, 78, 97, 99, 118, and Ch. 9. Note McDougall's earlier work, *Introduction to Social Psychology* (1st ed., 1908), in which he admits the anticipation of his posi-

tions by the Scottish School (19th ed., 1924, pp. 2-3), and in which he states that the task of social psychology is "to show how, given the native propensities and capacities of the individual human mind, all the complex mental life of societies is shaped by them and in turn reacts upon the course of their development and operation in the individual."— *Ibid.*, pp. 17-18.

51. *Principles*, ɪ, 123-26, 131, 137 ff., 221.

52. *Lehmann, op. cit.*, pp. 69 ff., and *Principles*, ɪ, 120, 137-39, 143-45, 151, 209, 222.

53. For the behaviorist attack, see John B. Watson's "What the Nursery Has to Say about Instincts," in the *Pedagogical Seminary*, xxxɪɪ, No. 2 (June, 1925), 293 ff.; almost any writing of Watson's gives the same account. For the sociologists' position, the works of Cooley, Mead, Park, Faris, are indicative.

54. Stewart, *Works*, x, xxxiv-xxxv; Hume, *Treatise*, Introduction.

55. Murphy, *An Historical Introduction to Modern Psychology* (Harcourt, Brace & Company, New York, 1929), p. 29; by permission of the publishers. Cf. Brett, *op. cit.*, ɪɪɪ, 256 ff.

56. *System*, ɪ, 30.

57. Cf. Howard C. Warren, *A History of Association Psychology* (New York, 1921), pp. 13 ff.; Laird, *op. cit.*, pp. 38-46.

58. *Works*, ɪ, 145 n.H., 252, 294, 433.

59. Murphy, *op. cit.*, pp. 103-4.

60. On this point cf. Torgny T. Segerstedt, "The Problem of Knowledge in Scottish Philosophy," in *Lunds Universitets Arsskrift*, N. F. Avd. 1, Bd. 31; 2, nr. 6 (Lund, 1935), where the rationalistic elements are traced to the Cambridge Platonists by way of Shaftesbury.

CHAPTER VI

1. These preferred conceptions of the 19th century are analyzed by Leopold von Wiese in *Sociology: Its History and Main Problems* (The Sociological Press, Hanover, N.H., 1928), p. 17.

2. Leopold von Wiese and Howard Becker, *Systematic Sociology* (New York, 1932), p. 78; cf. Earle Edward Eubank, *The Concepts of Sociology* (Boston, 1932), pp. 131-32. A convenient list of definitions of society may be found in Wilson D. Wallis, *Introduction to Sociology* (New York, 1927), Ch. 13.

3. An excellent brief statement concerning uniformitarianism with respect to human nature is to be found in Arthur O. Lovejoy, *The Great Chain of Being*, pp. 288-93.

4. *De officiis*, ɪ, ɪv, 12.

5. Shaftesbury, *Essay on the Freedom of Wit and Humour* (1709), later included in the *Characteristics of Men, Manners, Opinion, Times* (1711); reference is to the Robertson edition of the latter, ɪ, 74-75. There can be no overlooking Shaftesbury's great influence on the Scottish School, in general and on many particular points.

6. Dunbar, *Essays on the History of Mankind in Rude and Cultivated Ages* (2nd ed., London, 1781), p. 17 (the first edition appeared in the preceding year); Ferguson, *Essay on the History of Civil Society* (Edinburgh, 1767), pp. 4-10, 24, 28.

7. Aristotle, *Politics*, ɪ, ɪ, 9-12; here the well known sequence of family, village, city-state is presented. Aristotle points out that while the state differs generically from the family, "it exists by nature, inasmuch as the first partnerships so exist; for the city-state is the end of the other partnerships, and nature is an end, since that which each

thing is when its growth is completed we speak of as being the nature of each thing. . . . From these things . . . it is clear that the city-state is a natural growth. . . ."

8. Rutherforth, *Institutes of Natural Law* (Cambridge, 1754), I, 23.

9. Acknowledgment is here gladly made of a most helpful and clarifying letter of Professor Lovejoy to the writer, in which several of his consistent interpretations are brought to a focus on this topic.

10. Fuller treatment of discussions of the state are offered in Chapter VII.

11. *System of Moral Philosophy* (London, 1755), I, 34-35. Cf. Sombart, as cited in Ch. II, n. 34.

12. *Ibid.*, II, 212-13; cf. pp. 146-47, 220. His discussion of the deeds or steps in the forming of the contract is found on pp. 227-28; but it must be remembered that Hutcheson warns his readers that he is interested primarily in "inquiring into the just and wise motives to enter into civil polity, and the ways it can be justly constituted; and not into points of history about facts" (p. 224).

13. Ferguson, *Essay on the History of Civil Society*, p. 12.

14. This figure of the microcosm-macrocosm was a feature of Shaftesbury's thought which passed over into Hutcheson's; see W. R. Scott, *Francis Hutcheson* (Cambridge, 1900), pp. 168, 198-200, 226, 249-52. For the longer history of these philosophical concepts see Conger's work as cited in Ch. III, n. 4.

15. *Inquiry into the Original of Our Ideas of Beauty and Virtue* (2nd ed., London, 1726), pp. 121 ff., 173-77, 188; *Short Introduction to Moral Philosophy*, Bk. I, Ch. 1, and Bk. II, Chs. 1, 2, 3.

16. Ferguson, *op. cit.*, pp. 29-37, 94-95, 108, 124, 143, 151-52, 164, esp. 29, 36. Cf. Proesler, p. 106. On these points Ferguson consciously adopted the position of Socrates.

17. *Essays*, new ed. by Green and Grose (London, 1882), I, 113.

18. *Treatise of Human Understanding*, ed. by L. A. Selby-Bigge (Oxford, 1896), pp. 485-94.

19. *Ibid.*, pp. 316, 365, 575-76, 592. Many other references could be given, but it must suffice to say that much of pertinence will be found in Bk. II, Part I—sec. XI; II, II—v and VIII; III, II—I and II; III, III—I.

20. *Treatise*, p. 503.

21. In the letter to which reference is made above.

22. William Graham Sumner, *Folkways* (Boston, 1906), Ch. 1.

23. See, for example, *Treatise*, Bk. II, Part III, sec. v, and pp. 97, 104, 170, 556.

24. *Ibid.*, p. 490.

25. *Ibid.*, p. 352.

26. Georg Simmel, *Soziologie* (Leipzig, 1908), pp. 348-50, 488-90; for secondary exposition see, for example, Emory S. Bogardus, *A History of Social Thought* (2nd ed., Los Angeles, 1928), pp. 560-66.

27. *Treatise*, p. 318.

28. Franklin Henry Giddings, *Principles of Sociology* (New York, 1896), Preface. Much of Book II of Hume's *Treatise* is relevant to the concepts of social distance and consciousness of kind.

29. Giddings, *op. cit.*, Preface to 3rd ed.

30. *Treatise*, p. 537.

31. *Ibid.*, pp. 539, 542, 566, and Bk. III, secs. VIII, IX and X; cf. "Of the Original Contract," in the *Essays*.

32. *Treatise,* p. 489.

33. *Essays*, I, 248.

34. Smith, *Theory of Moral Sentiments*, Vol. I of ed. of *Works* (London, 1812), pp. 131-56, 188-94, 413-17, and Part I, sec. I, Chs. 1-4 incl.;

Wealth of Nations (Everyman ed.), pp. 12-15. Though the discussion would be somewhat irrelevant here, it might be noted that a compact treatment is offered in the *Moral Sentiments,* Part III, of the relation of praise and praiseworthiness to conduct.

35. L. A. Selby-Bigge, ed., *British Moralists* (Oxford, 1897), I, Introduction, lx; cf. Huth, *op. cit., passim,* and Proesler, *op. cit.,* p. 152.

36. *Lectures on Justice, Police, Revenue and Arms,* ed. by Edwin Cannan (Oxford, 1896), pp. 9-16.

37. *Principles of Moral and Political Science* (Edinburgh, 1792), I, 268-69.

38. *Essay on the History of Civil Society,* pp. 4-6, 8, 24, 86. A footnote reference, on p. 9, to Rousseau's *Discourse on the Origin of Inequality* suggests his criticism of Rousseau's "boldness of invention" and "suggestions of fancy" in tracing the progress of man from "a supposed state of animal sensibility." See Proesler, *op. cit.,* pp. 141 ff.

39. *Civil Society,* Part I, secs. III and IV; *Principles,* I, 18-20, 24, 30-31, 37, and all of Part I, Ch. I, sec. 3; *Institutes of Moral Philosophy* (2nd ed., Edinburgh, 1773), pp. 85-90.

40. *Civil Society, op. cit.,* esp. pp. 26, 28.

41. *Principles,* II, 232.

42. *Ibid.,* pp. 214-25, 230-35, 245. Cf. Hume's emphasis on habitual obedience as discussed in his essays, "Of the Origin of Government" and "Of the Original Contract."

43. *Civil Society,* pp. 186-88. Huth says of Ferguson's criticism of the contract theories, "Ferguson findet so starke Tone wie keiner vor ihm."—*Op. cit.,* pp. 45-46.

44. *Op. cit.*

45. Theodor Buddeberg, "Ferguson als Soziologe," in *Jahrbücher für Nationalökonomie,* Heft 123 (Jena, 1925), p. 627.

46. The quotations are from the *Works of Thomas Reid,* ed. by Sir William Hamilton (2 vols., Edinburgh, 1846-63), I, 244, and II, 566; cf. also II, 641, 663-70. The specific works from which the quotations come are the *Essays on the Intellectual Powers* (1785) and the *Essays on the Active Powers* (1788).

47. *Works,* II, 565-66, 641.

48. Stewart, *Collected Works,* ed. by Sir William Hamilton (11 vols., Edinburgh, 1854-60), II, 11; VIII, 20-29. The specific works to which reference is made are *Outlines of Moral Philosophy* (1793), *Lectures on Political Economy* (1855), delivered orally, 1800-10, in the University of Edinburgh. Incidentally, it may be noted that Stewart's *Dissertation Exhibiting the Progress of Metaphysical, Ethical and Political Philosophy Since the Revival of Letters in Europe* (1st part, 1815; 2nd part, 1821) is full of the history of ideas.

49. Kames, *Essays on the Principles of Morality and Natural Religion* (Edinburgh, 1751), pp. 82-86, 127-28; *Sketches of the History of Man* (Edinburgh, 1774), I, Bk. II, sketch I, 366-72.

50. *Sketches,* I, 356. The full account of animal government appears in Bk. II, sketch I.

51. *Origin and Progress of Language,* I, 220-24.

52. Treatment of Monboddo is rounded out in Chapters III, IV and VIII.

53. Monboddo, *Antient Metaphysics,* Vol. V, *passim,* esp. p. 321; cf. *Origin and Progress of Language,* Vol. I, Bk. II.

54. William C. ·Lehmann, *Adam Ferguson and the Beginnings of Modern Sociology* (New York, 1930), pp. 153-56.

55. Buddeberg, *op. cit.,* p. 627.

56. Sir Henry Sumner Maine, *The Ancient Law* (1861).

57. Ferdinand Tönnies, *Gemeinschaft und Gesellschaft* (1887).
58. *Civil Society*, p. 12.

CHAPTER VII

1. Ferguson, *Civil Society*, p. 14.
2. Beattie, *Elements of Moral Science*, in an American edition of his *Works* (Philadelphia, 1809), ix, 3.
3. An illuminating analysis of the *Encyclopédie* is to be found in René Hubert's "Les sciences sociales dans l'encyclopédie," in *Travaux et memoirs de l'Université de Lille*, novelle série, section Droit, Lettres No. 8 (Lille, 1923). (Published also in Paris in 1923.)
4. Preface to the *Short Introduction to Moral Philosophy*.
5. Ferguson, *Institutes*, 169-73, 212-38; *Principles*, ii, 168-90, 315-405.
6. See Edwin Cannan's edition of Adam Smith's *Lectures on Justice, Police, Revenue, and Arms* (Oxford, 1896).
7. *De officiis*, Bk. i, Ch. iii; cf. Pufendorf's *De Jure Naturae et Gentium* and his *De Officio Hominis et Civis* for the differentiation between theoretical and practical considerations.
8. *De Jure Naturae et Gentium*, Bk. vi, Ch. i. The three chapters of Bk. vi are headed "On Matrimony," "On Parental Power," "On the Power of a Master." Pufendorf was at many points a model to Scottish authors.
9. Hutcheson's discussion is found in the *Short Introduction*, Bk. iii, Chs. i-iii, and the *System*, Bk. iii, Chs. i-iii.
10. Smith's discussion is to be found under the heading "Domestic Law," a subheading of "Justice," in Cannan's ed. of the *Lectures on Justice, Police, Revenue, and Arms*, pp. 73-106.
11. By polygamy Hume means, in more careful terminology, polygyny, the marriage of one man to several women.
12. In his *Sketches of the History of Man*, Bk. i, sk. vi.
13. Jacob Bouten says that it was due to Fénelon that education came to be included among the topics of moral philosophy, but it was the diffusive power of Rousseau's writings that made it one of the most frequently discussed themes of the century; see his *Mary Wollstonecraft and the Beginnings of Female Emancipation in France and England* (Amsterdam, 1922), pp. 44, 64. Actual achievements in French society by women in the 17th and 18th centuries should not be overlooked; cf. Victor Cousin, *La société française au XVIIe siècle* (Paris, 1858).
14. Two interesting studies in this field have recently been published by Professor Katherine Gee Hornbeak, in the Smith College Studies in Modern Languages: *The Complete Letter-Writer in English, 1568-1800* (Northampton, Mass., 1933-34), and *Richardson's Familiar Letters and the Domestic Conduct Books* (Northampton, 1938).
15. Gregory, *op. cit.*, pp. 178 and 103.
16. Robert Palfrey Utter and Gwendolyn Bridges Needham, *Pamela's Daughters* (New York, 1936), pp. 24, 206-7.
17. John Ramsay, *Scotland and Scotsmen of the Eighteenth Century* (Edinburgh, 1888), i, 204, 207. Ramsay devotes the whole of Chapter 3 to Kames. One of his anecdotes runs as follows: "Lord Abercromby told me that one night after supper in his own house he [Kames] spoke in rapturous terms of a young lady's legs. In a vein of dignified irony, Mrs. Drummond said to him, 'I thought, my lord, you had never gone so *low* as a lady's legs, contenting yourself with her head and heart.'"
18. No. 1328 in the Watson Collection, National Library of Scotland. The letter is dated October 31, 1780, from Blair-Drummond.

19. These letters are preserved in the British Museum, Add. 40635.

20. Woodhouselee, *op. cit.*, I, 363.

21. *Elements of the Philosophy of the Human Mind*, Part III, sec. v.

22. See his essay, "Of the Study of History."

23. For background of the discussions of family relationships and education, good material is offered in C. L. Powell's *English Domestic Relations, 1487-1653* (New York, 1917); L. L. Schücking's *Die Familie im Puritanismus* (Leipzig und Berlin, 1929); and, of course, *The Whole Duty of Man*, either a complete or an abridged translation of Pufendorf's *De Officio Hominis et Civis*.

24. Harold Laski, *Political Thought in England from Locke to Bentham* (London, 1920), pp. 9-18, 100.

25. For fuller discussion on this point, see Chapter VI.

26. Paul Janet, *Histoire de la science politique dans ses rapports avec la morale* (4e ed., Paris, 1913), p. lxxv.

27. Dugald Stewart, *Works*, I, 174. Cf. Cassirer, *op. cit.*, Kap. VI, for full discussion of "Recht, Staat und Gesellschaft."

28. Smith, *Theory of Moral Sentiments*, Part VII, sec. IV, esp. p. 610. Cf. Stewart, *op. cit.*, I, 26, 171, 174-75, and VII, 257 ff.

29. Laski, *op. cit.*, p. 203; Ernest Barker, *Political Thought in England from Herbert Spencer to the Present Day* (New York, 1915), pp. 40, 120-27, 165-67; Kocourek and Wigmore, *Formative Influences of Legal Development* (Boston, 1918), Preface, p. vi. Cf. Franz Oppenheimer, *The State* (Vanguard Press ed., New York, 1922), Preface, and pp. 10, 15, 103. For fuller and more favorable discussion of these concepts, see the work of Otto von Zierke, tr. by Bernard Freyd as *The Development of Political Theory* (New York, 1939), in which the significant thought of Johannes Althusius (1557-1638) and its later modifications are set forth.

30. Ferguson, *Institutes*, pp. 131-33, 170-71.

31. Adam Smith, *Lectures*, p. 1.

32. *Ibid.*, pp. 1, 3-4.

33. Smith, *Moral Sentiments*, pp. 608-9.

34. Cicero, *De officiis*, Bk. III, ¶ XVII.

35. Cf. Ferguson's definition of adventitious rights: Those that require to be supported by evidence in which the manner of their acquisition is to be cited and considered.—*Principles*, II, 198.

36. Hutcheson, *Short Introduction*, Bk. II; cf. his *System*, Bk. II, and Ferguson, *Principles*, II, Chs. III and IV. Cf. Shaftesbury's *Characteristics*, ed. by Robertson, I, 73-74, and II, 81-84.

37. Hutcheson, *Short Introduction*, Bk. III, Chs. IV-x, incl. Cf. his *System*, Bk. III.

38. Kames, *Sketches*, Bk. II, "Progress of Men in Society."

39. *Elucidations respecting the Common and Statute Law of Scotland* (Edinburgh, 1776), Preface.

40. *Essays*, pp. 146-47.

41. *Principles*, I, 256-63.

42. This note is especially strong in the *Essay on the History of Civil Society*, Part I, secs. 4 and 9; Part III, secs. 1, 2, 4; Part IV, secs. 2, 3, 4. See Harry Elmer Barnes' comments on Ferguson as an anticipator of Gumplowicz on these points; *Sociology and Political Theory* (New York, 1924), pp. 11 and 52-53; *The New History and the Social Studies* (New York, 1925), pp. 312-13. Note the similarity to Franz Oppenheimer's theory in *The State*, Ch. 1.

43. *Principles*, II, 409, 419, 459, 509, 511, and Ch. VI, secs. 8-10 incl.

44. *Treatise*, Bk. III, "Of Morals," Part II, especially secs. II and VIII, and p. 490.

NOTES

NOTES   271

45. *Op. cit.*, Bk. III, Part II, sec. VII, esp. pp. 537, 539.
46. *Ibid.*, secs. VIII, IX, and X, esp. p. 566.
47. These appeared first in 1741 as *Essays, Moral and Political,* and were enthusiastically received. In 1742 a second edition was published to which a second volume was added, and the title eventually became *Essays, Moral, Political and Literary.*
48. A very good, though brief, discussion of Hume's political theory appears in Mary Shaw Kuypers' *Studies in the Eighteenth-Century Background of Hume's Empiricism* (Minneapolis, 1930), Ch. VI. Janet, *op. cit.*, livre 3e, Ch. VIII, gives attention not only to Hume, but to Hutcheson, Smith, and Ferguson. Halévy's *Growth of Philosophical Radicalism,* tr. by Mary Morris (London, 1928), Part I, Ch. III, offers good material on Hume and Smith; see also Laird, *op. cit.*, Ch. IX.

CHAPTER VIII

1. John K. Ingram, *History of Political Economy* (London, 1915), pp. 40-86; Gide and Rist, *A History of Economic Doctrines* (New York, n.d.), pp. 50-66; Lewis H. Haney, *History of Economic Thought* (New York, 1911), pp. 132 ff.
2. Merz, *History of European Thought in the Nineteenth Century* (Edinburgh, 1896-1914), IV, 127-28; cf. James Bonar, *Philosophy and Political Economy* (London, 1893), Bk. II, Chs. VIII and IX.
3. Jacob Viner, "Adam Smith and Laissez-Faire," in John Maurice Clark *et al., Adam Smith, 1776-1926* (University of Chicago Press, Chicago, 1928), p. 116; by permission of the publishers. The whole of this volume is very pertinent to our discussion of Smith.
4. Ruggiero, *The History of European Liberalism,* tr. by R. G. Collingwood (Oxford, 1927), p. 49.
5. Adam Smith, *Lectures,* pp. 3, 154. Note the distinction in Johnson's *Dictionary* between "police" and "policy," *ibid.*, p. 154 n., and Cannan's note in the Introduction, p. xxvi.
6. *Wealth of Nations,* Bk. IV, Introduction and Ch. IX.
7. *Ibid.* (Everyman ed.), I, Bk. I, Ch. II, 13. For Smith's extension of the results of the division of labor beyond the economic realm, see Roy Pascal, "Property and Society: The Scottish Historical School of the Eighteenth Century," in *The Modern Quarterly* (London, 1938), pp. 171 ff.
8. *Ibid.*, Bk. III, Chs. I, III-IV.
9. *Ibid.* (Everyman ed.), II, Bk. IV, Ch. IX, 180.
10. Cf. Gide and Rist, *op. cit.*, pp. 61-102. References to other commentators would be too numerous to be mentioned here.
11. Wilhelm Hasbach, *Untersuchungen über Adam Smith und die Entwicklung der Politischen Ökonomie* (Leipzig, 1891), pp. 421, 439.
12. "Anecdotes of the Late Dr. Adam Smith," in the London *Oracle* of July, 1790; found among the Chambers papers, Laing, II, 45½, University of Edinburgh.
13. Edwin Cannan, "Adam Smith as Economist: The Gospel of Mutual Service," in *An Economist's Protest* (London, 1927), pp. 424, 426, 430.
14. Quoted by E. R. A. Seligman, in the Introduction, *The Wealth of Nations* (Everyman ed.), p. vii.
15. Eli Ginzberg, *The House of Adam Smith* (New York, 1934), p. 7 and *passim.* Some passages in the *Wealth of Nations* supporting this contention may be found in Bk. I, Chs. II, VIII, IX, X. Cf. Proesler, *op. cit.*, p. 153.

16. Cannan, in the Introduction to the *Lectures*, pp. xxii-xxiv; Dugald Stewart, "Account of the Life and Writings of Adam Smith," in *Collected Works*, x, 66-67; Gide and Rist, *op. cit.*, pp. 347-55; Ingram, *op. cit.*, pp. 86-88; Henry Higgs, *The Physiocrats* (London, 1897), pp. 46, 79, 93, 125-44.

17. A. W. Benn, *The History of English Rationalism in the Nineteenth Century* (London, 1906), ii, 209-10. See *The Republic*, tr. by Benjamin Jowett (3rd ed., Oxford, 1921), i, 368-75; cf. A. A. Trever, *A History of Greek Economic Thought* (Chicago, 1916), pp. 26-37. Of course, what appears at first to be a discussion of economics in Plato turns out to be a moral discussion as to the criteria of justice. Another point of difference is that Plato's division of labor roots in the diversity of man's abilities, which Smith neglects, preferring to rest his principle on the universal propensity to barter.

18. Smith, *Moral Sentiments*, pp. 545-55.

19. Cf. the *Wealth of Nations* (Everyman ed.), i, 10-11, with Mandeville's *Fable of the Bees*, ed. by F. B. Kaye (2 vols., Oxford, 1924), i, 169-70 and 355-58. Mr. Kaye points out that Dugald Stewart credited Mandeville with having been Smith's inspiration; see Kaye's Introduction, i, xcviii-ciii, cxxxiv ff., and 109-16, 299-300; ii, 352. Cf. Proesler, *op. cit.*, p. 144, where the theory of the division of labor is attributed, and justly, to Ferguson earlier than Smith.

20. Hans Vaihinger, *The Philosophy of "As If,"* tr. from 6th German ed. by C. K. Ogden (London, 1924), pp. 19-20, 184-87. It must be noted that Buckle was one of the first to interpret Smith's method as so completely deductive, even while he recognized that Smith used a great deal of history; see Buckle, *History of Civilization in England* (World's Classics ed.), iii, 331, 341-42. For early discussion of Smith's method, cf. Walter Bagehot, *Economic Studies* (London, 1880), p. 21, and T. E. C. Cliffe Leslie, *Essays on Political and Moral Philosophy* (Dublin, 1879), pp. 148-66, 216-42; John Rae, *The Sociological Theory of Capital* (New York, 1905), pp. 1, 328 ff.

21. Friedrich Albert Lange, *History of Materialism*, tr. by Ernest Chester Thomas (London, 1925), pp. 235-37.

22. *Inquiry*, pp. 284-85; cf. *Short Introduction*, pp. 141-42, and *System*, i, 317-24.

23. On this point see John Rae, *Life of Adam Smith* (London, 1895), pp. 11-15; Cannan's Introduction to Smith's *Lectures*, pp. xxv-xxvii; W. R. Scott, *Francis Hutcheson* (Cambridge, 1900), Ch. xi, Part ii; Henry Laurie, *Scottish Philosophy in its National Development* (Glasgow, 1902), p. 33. Both Cannan and Scott list a startling number of parallel passages in Hutcheson and Smith, and call attention especially to the "germ" chapter in Hutcheson's *Short Introduction*, Bk. ii, Ch. xii. Back of that we have noticed Pufendorf's "germ" chapter in the *De Officio*, Bk. i, Ch. 14.

24. Albert Schatz, *L'Œuvre économique de David Hume* (Paris, 1902), p. 232.

25. Laski, *op. cit.*, p. 112; Stewart, *Works*, x, 66-67.

26. Laski, *op. cit.*, pp. 151-53; by permission of the publishers, the Oxford University Press. For discussions of similarities between Hume and Smith, and for their agreements and disagreements with Physiocrats and Mercantilists, see Ingram, *op. cit.* (new and enl. ed.), pp. 68 n., 81-84, 98-99, 103-4, 113, 125; Gide and Rist, *op. cit.*, pp. 50 n., 53, 64 n., 85, 106-20, 165, 273; Halévy, *op. cit.*, Part i, Ch. iii; Bonar, *op. cit.*, Bk. ii, Ch. vi; Laird, *op. cit.*, Ch. ix; Wilhelm Hasbach, *op. cit.*, and *Die allgemeinen philosophischen Grundlagen der von F. Quesnay und Adam Smith begründeten politischen Oekonomie*, in Staats- und Sozialwissenschaftliche Forschungen, Bd. x, Heft 2 (Leipzig, 1890).

W. R. Scott points out Hutcheson's influence on Hume; *op. cit.*, pp. 124 ff.

27. See his *Works*, x, li-lii; and note the enlarged bibliography, suggested to his students, which will carry them beyond the "code" of Smith; *Works*, ix, 458.

28. Quoted by Stewart's biographer, John Veitch, in Stewart's *Works*, x, l-li. Veitch notes that Stewart was for years under suspicion because of his espousal of political economy.

29. Stewart, *op. cit.*, Vols. viii and ix; esp. viii, pp. 9-17, 20-24; ii, 231-38; x, xliv, l, li.

30. Gide and Rist, *op. cit.*, p. 103.

31. By John Maynard Keynes (London, 1926).

32. Albert E. Baker, *Bishop Butler* (London, 1923), p. 22.

33. A. E. Taylor, *The Faith of a Moralist* (Macmillan Company, New York and London, 1930), p. 1; by permission of the publishers. Cf. Cassirer, *op. cit.*, Kap. iv.

34. A. E. Taylor, *The Laws of Plato* (London, 1934), Introduction, p. li. As a matter of fact, many of the 18th-century discussions are prefigured in *The Laws*.

35. Benn, *op. cit.*, i, 110.

36. *Ibid.*, p. 60.

37. In addition to such standard references as Benn, *op. cit.*, and Sir Leslie Stephen, *English Thought in the Eighteenth Century*, G. V. Lechler's older discussion, *Geschichte des Englischen Deismus* (Stuttgart, 1841), should be consulted. Leland's *View of the Deistical Writers* (1754) is the oldest commentary. It is worth remembering that Locke was not a Deist, though his *Reasonableness of Christianity* (1695) led many to think he was. The titles of some of the books significant in the controversy of the century are very telling:

Herbert of Cherbury, *De Veritate, prout distinguitur a Revelatione Verisimili, Probabili et a Falso* (1624).
Arthur Bury, *The Naked Gospel* (1690).
John Locke, *The Reasonableness of Christianity* (1695).
John Toland, *Christianity Not Mysterious* (1696).
Thomas Halyburton, *Natural Religion Insufficient* (1714).
William Wollaston, *The Religion of Nature Delineated* (1722).
Anthony Collins, *Discourse of the Grounds and Reasons of Christian Religion* (1724).
Matthew Tindal, *Christianity as Old as the Creation* (1730).
Bishop Butler, *The Analogy of Religion, Natural and Revealed* (1736).
Henry Dodwell, *Christianity Not Founded upon Argument* (1742).
William Paley, *Natural Theology* (1802).

38. Hutcheson, *System*, i, 35-36. Again, recall Shaftesbury's discussion of Natural Religion in *The Moralists* (1709).

39. *Essays on Philosophical Subjects* (London, 1795), p. 107.

40. Ramsay, *op. cit.*, i, 463, n. 1.

41. Ferguson, *Principles*, i, 164-67.

42. Stewart, *Works*, vi, 111-12.

43. Quoted from Locke's *Essay*, Bk. iv, Ch. xix, sec. 4.

44. Kames' discussions are found in the *Essays on the Principles of Morality and Natural Religion*, esp. Part ii, Essays i, ii and vii.

45. *Ibid.*, pp. 327, 393-94. The authorship of this prayer was by some ascribed to Kames' friend, Hugh Blair.

46. Charles William Hendel, Jr., *Studies in the Philosophy of David Hume* (Princeton, 1925), pp. 399, 414. Cf. Stephen, *op. cit.*, Vol. i, Ch. vi,

and Laird, *op. cit.*, Ch. x; Felix Müller, *David Hume's Stellung zum Deismus* (Borna-Leipzig, 1906), and André Leroy, *La critique et la religion chez David Hume* (Paris, 1931); A. E. Taylor, *David Hume and the Miraculous* (Cambridge, 1927), pp. 3-5, 50-54; Norman Kemp Smith, *Hume's Dialogues Concerning Natural Religion* (Oxford, 1935), pp. 1-56, esp. 13, 15, 25, 30.

47. This essay, never published separately, was inserted as Section x into the *Enquiry Concerning Human Understanding* and is completely irrelevant to that discussion. Mr. Selby-Bigge assumes that it was one of Hume's efforts to gain notoriety at any cost. For the logical inadequacies of the argument see A. E. Taylor, *op. cit., passim*, and Norman Kemp Smith, *op. cit.*, pp. 57-64.

48. For the history of these essays see "History of the Editions," Green and Grose ed. of the *Essays*, Vol. I.

49. In a footnote Hume deals with the question of the prohibition of suicide in the Christian scriptures and announces that it is as lawful under Christian dispensation as under the unchristian.

50. Published first in *Four Dissertations* (1757). This is the essay which contains Hume's ribald attack on the Catholic doctrine of the Real Presence.

51. Norman Kemp Smith, *op. cit.*, Preface, pp. vi-vii, and 25 ff. See Appendix C for evidences bearing on dates of revision and Hume's evident intentions of making more negative the outcome of the argument. Quotations hereinafter will be from Smith's edition of the *Dialogues*, pp. 167, 184-85, 202, 211, 221, 222, 235, 237, 240-48, 262.

52. Stewart, *Works*, x, "Account of the Life and Writings of Adam Smith, LL.D.," 33-37.

53. *Antient Metaphysics*, IV, 35 ff., 61 ff., 96, 121 ff., 358; VI, 150-57, 167 ff., 171 ff. Cf. *Origin and Progress of Language*, Vol. I, Bk. II.

54. *Origin and Progress of Language*, I, 2.

55. *Ibid.*, Vol. I, Bk. III; *Antient Metaphysics*, Vol. IV, Bks. II and III.

56. See Ch. I; and cf. Woodhouselee, *op. cit.*, Vol. I, Bk. II, Ch. I, and Cassirer, *op. cit.*, Kap. VII.

57. See a recent study by Helen W. Randall, *The Critical Theory of Lord Kames*, Smith College Studies in Language and Literature.

CHAPTER IX

1. See the author's papers: "The Emergence of the Social Sciences from Moral Philosophy," *International Journal of Ethics*, XLII (April, 1932), 304-23; "The Comparable Interests of the Old Moral Philosophy and the Modern Social Sciences," *Social Forces*, XI (October, 1932), 19-27; "Sociology Considered as Moral Philosophy," *Sociological Review*, XXIV (January, 1932), 26-36.

Principal Works of the Scottish Authors
under Discussion

This list is for convenient reference. In most cases it gives the bare facts of initial publication and does not include detailed information on the history of editions. Fugitive papers are included only when they are pertinent to the discussions of this book. Citations to particular editions are indicated at appropriate places in the Notes.

~~~~~~

ADAM FERGUSON

A Sermon Preached in Erse Language to His Majesty's First Highland Regiment of Foot on December 18, 1745. Eng. tr. London, 1746.

The Morality of Stage Plays Seriously Considered. Edinburgh, 1757.

The History of the Proceedings in the Case of Margaret, Commonly Called Peg, Only Sister to John Bull, Esq. London, 1761.

Analysis of Pneumatics and Moral Philosophy for the Use of Students in the College of Edinburgh. Edinburgh, 1766. (Enlarged and published as *Institutes of Moral Philosophy*, 1769.)

An Essay on the History of Civil Society. Edinburgh, 1766; 7th ed., Edinburgh, 1814; Leipzig, 1768; Basil, 1789; Jena, 1904.

Institutes of Moral Philosophy. Edinburgh, 1769; 1772; 1773; 1785 enl.; new ed. at Basil, 1800; German tr. at Leipzig, 1772; Russian tr., etc.

Remarks on a Pamphlet Lately Published by Dr. Price, Entitled "Observations on the Nature of Civil Liberty," etc. 1776, published by the Government. (Anon.)

The History of the Progress and Termination of the Roman Republic, illustrated with maps. London, 1783. French tr., Paris, 1784-91. German tr., Leipzig, 1784-86; abridged ed., 1 vol., New York, 1873.

Principles of Moral and Political Science, being chiefly a retrospect of lectures delivered in the College of Edinburgh. 2 vols., Edinburgh, 1792; French tr., 1821.

"Minutes of the Life and Character of Joseph Black, M.D." Read August 3, 1801. (*Transactions of the Royal Society of Edinburgh*, 1805.)

DAVID HUME

A Treatise of Human Nature: Being an attempt to introduce the experimental method of reasoning into moral subjects. Vols. 1, 2, London, 1739; Vol. 3, London, 1740.

Essays, Moral and Political. Edinburgh, Vol. 1, 1741; 2nd ed., 1742; Vol. 2, 1742; 3rd ed., in 1 volume, 1748.

Three Essays, Moral and Political: Of National Character; Of the Original Contract; Of Passive Obedience. London, 1748.

Philosophical Essays Concerning Human Understanding. London, 1748; 2nd ed., 1751.

The Enquiry Concerning the Principles of Morals. London, 1751.

Political Discourses. Edinburgh, 1752.

Essays and Treatises on General Subjects. 4 vols. Edinburgh and London, 1753-54.

The History of England. 6 vols. London, 1754-62.

Four Dissertations: I—The Natural History of Religion; II—Of the Passions; III—Of Tragedy; IV—Of the Standard of Taste. London, 1757.

Two Essays: On Suicide; The Immortality of the Soul. London, 1757.

Life of David Hume Written by Himself. London, 1777.

Dialogues Concerning Natural Religion. London, 1779.

Private Correspondence of David Hume with Several Distinguished Persons Between 1761-1776. London, 1820.

The Philosophical Works of David Hume, including all the essays, and exhibiting the more important allusions and corrections in the successive editions published by the author. 4 vols. Edinburgh, 1826.

Letters of David Hume and Extracts from Letters Relating to Him. (Edited by T. Murray. Edinburgh, 1841.)

Philosophical Works of David Hume. (Edited by T. H. Greene, and T. H. Grose. 4 vols. London, 1874-75.)

Letters of David Hume to William Strahan. (Edited by G. Birkbeck Hill, with notes, index, etc. Oxford, 1888.)

A Treatise of Human Nature. (Edited by L. A. Selby-Bigge. Oxford, 1888.)

An Enquiry Concerning the Human Understanding and an Enquiry Concerning the Principles of Morals. (Edited by L. A. Selby-Bigge. Oxford, 1894.)

FRANCIS HUTCHESON

An Inquiry into the Original of Our Ideas of Beauty and Virtue: in two treatises. In which the principles of the late Earl of Shaftesbury are explained and defended, against the Author of the fable of the bees: and the ideas of moral good and evil are established, according to the sentiments of the antient moralists. With an attempt to introduce a mathematical calculation in subjects of morality. London, 1725; 2nd ed., 1726; 3rd ed., 1729; 4th ed., 1738; 5th ed., 1753; Glasgow, 1772; French tr., Amsterdam, 1749; German tr., Frankfurt, 1762.

An Essay on the Nature and Conduct of the Passions and Affections, with illustrations on the moral sense. London and Dublin, 1728; 2nd ed., 1742; 3rd ed., Glasgow, 1769.

De naturali hominum socialitate. (Inaugural Lecture delivered at University of Glasgow, 1730.) Glasgow, 1756.

Considerations on Patronages, addressed to gentlemen of Scotland. n.p. 1735.

The Meditations of M. Aurelius Antoninus (with Professor Moor). *Newly translated from the Greek, with notes and an account of his life.* Glasgow, 1742; 2nd ed., 1749; 3rd ed., 1752.

Metaphysicae synopsis: Ontologiam et Pneumatologiam complectens. Glasgow, 1742; 2nd ed., 1744; 3rd ed., 1749; 4th ed., 1756; 5th ed., 1762; 6th ed., 1774; Strasburg, 1772. (Anon.)

Philosophiae moralis institutio compendiaria ethices at jurispridentiae naturalis elementa continens. Glasgow, 1742; 2nd ed., 1745; 3rd ed., 1755; Rotterdam, 1745; Strasburg, 1772; Dublin, 1787.

A Short Introduction to Moral Philosophy in Three Books; containing the elements of ethics and the law of nature. Glasgow, 1747; 2nd ed., 1753; 3rd ed., 1764; 4th ed., 1772; 5th ed., Philadelphia, 1788.

Reflections upon Laughter, and Remarks upon the Fable of the Bees. Glasgow, 1750.

A System of Moral Philosophy, in three books. 1755. 2 vols., published by son. (William Leechman's account of life, etc., prefixed.)

Logicae compendium. Glasgow, 1756. 2nd ed., 1759; 5th ed., Glasgow, 1764; Strasburg, 1772.

LORD KAMES (HENRY HOME)

Remarkable Decisions of the Court of Session, from 1716 to 1728. Edinburgh, 1728.

Essays upon Several Subjects in Law. Edinburgh, 1732.

Decisions of the Court of Session from Its First Institution to the Present Time, abridged and digested under proper heads, in the form of a dictionary. 2 vols. Edinburgh, 1741.

Essays upon Several Subjects Concerning British Antiquities. Edinburgh, 1747; 3rd ed., 1763.

Essays on the Principles of Morality and Natural Religion. Edinburgh, 1751 (Anon.); London, 1758 (Anon.); 3rd ed. (Not anon.); German tr., Braunschweig, 1768; Leipzig, 1772.

The Statute Law of Scotland, abridged, with historical notes. Edinburgh, 1757.

Historical Law Tracts. Edinburgh, 1758; 4th ed., 1792; French tr., 1766.

Principles of Equity. Edinburgh, 1760; 2nd ed., Edinburgh, 1767; 3rd ed., 2 vols., 1778.

Introduction to the Art of Thinking. Edinburgh, 1761; 5th ed., Edinburgh, 1810.

Elements of Criticism. Edinburgh, 3 vols., 1762; 8th ed., Edinburgh, 1807; New York ed., 1830; German tr., Leipzig, 1763-66.

Progress of Flax-Husbandry in Scotland. 1766.

Remarkable Decisions of the Court of Session, 1730-1752. Edinburgh, 1766.

"Essay on the Laws of Motion." (*Transactions of Philosophical Society of Edinburgh,* 1771, under title "Essays and Observations, Physical and Literary.")

The Gentleman Farmer; being an attempt to improve agriculture by subjecting it to the test of rational principles. Edinburgh, 1776; 6th ed., 1815.

Sketches of the History of Man. Edinburgh, 1774; 2 vols. (Anon.), Glasgow, 1802.

Elucidations Respecting the Common and Statute Law of Scotland. Edinburgh, 1777.

Select Decisions of the Court of Session (1752-1768). Edinburgh, 1780. (Supplement to *Remarkable Decisions.*)

Loose Hints upon Education, chiefly concerning the culture of the heart. Edinburgh, 1781.

An Essay on the Hereditary and Indefeasible Right of Kings. Edinburgh, 1797. Composed in the year 1745.

LORD MONBODDO (JAMES BURNET)

Of the Origin and Progress of Language. Edinburgh, 6 vols., 1773-92 (Anon.); German tr., Vols. I-III, with foreword by Herder, Riga, 1784-85.

Antient Metaphysics. Edinburgh, 6 vols., 1772-99. (Anon.)

"The Degeneracy of Man in a State of Society." 80 folio pages. (Ms. in possession of his family.)

THOMAS REID

"An Essay on Quantity, on the occasion of reading a treatise in which simple and compound ratios are applied to virtue and merit." (*Philosophical Transactions of the Royal Society of London for 1748*, Vol. XLV.)

An Inquiry into the Human Mind on the Principles of Common Sense. Edinburgh, 1764; 2nd ed., 1765; 3rd ed., 1769; 4th ed., London, 1785; French tr., 1768.

"A Brief Account of Aristotle's Logic." (*In Kames' Sketches of the History of Man*, Vol. II. Also, in Vol. II, *Works of Thomas Reid*.)

Essays on the Intellectual Powers of Man. Edinburgh, 1785. (Also incorporated in *Works*, Vol. I.)

Essays on the Active Powers of Man. Edinburgh, 1788. (Also incorporated in *Works*, Vol. II.)

Account of the University of Glasgow. (Statistical Account of Scotland, published by Sir John Sinclair, Glasgow, 1799. Also in Vol. II, Hamilton ed., *Works of Thomas Reid*.)

The Works of Thomas Reid. (Edited by Sir William Hamilton. 2 vols., Edinburgh, 1846-63.)

Œuvres complètes de Thomas Reid. (M. T. Jouffroy, avec des fragments de M. Royer-Collard et une introduction de l'éditeur. 6 vols., Paris, 1828-36.)

ADAM SMITH

The Theory of Moral Sentiments. London, 1759; French tr., 1764.

Dissertation on the Origin of Languages. (Published with 2nd ed. of *Moral Sentiments*, 1761.)

Lectures on Justice, Police, Revenue and Arms . . . reported by a student in 1763. (Edited by Edwin Cannan. Oxford, 1896.)

An Inquiry into the Nature and Causes of the Wealth of Nations. London, 1776, 2 vols.; French tr., 1779-80; Danish tr., 1779-80; German tr., 1776-78; Italian tr., 1780; Spanish tr., 1792; Dutch tr., 1796.

Essays on Philosophical Subjects. London, 1795.

The Works of Adam Smith. With an account of his life and writings. (Edited by Dugald Stewart. 5 vols., London, 1811-12.)

DUGALD STEWART

Elements of the Philosophy of the Human Mind. 3 vols., 1792-1827.

"Account of the Life and Writings of Adam Smith, LL.D." (*Transactions of the Royal Society of Edinburgh*, 1793.)

Outlines of Moral Philosophy. 1793; 4th ed., 1818. French tr. by Jouffroy, 1826.

"Account of the Life and Writings of William Robertson, D.D." (*Transactions of the Royal Society of Edinburgh*, 1796.)

"Account of the Life and Writings of Thomas Reid, D.D., F.R.S.E." (*Transactions of the Royal Society of Edinburgh*, 1802.)

Philosophical Essays. Edinburgh, 1810; 3rd ed., 1818.

Biographical Memoirs. Edinburgh, 1811.

"Dissertation exhibiting a general view of the progress of metaphysical, ethical, and political philosophy, since the revival of letters in Europe." (1st part, 1815; 2nd part, 1821. Supplement to 4th and 6th eds. of *Encyclopedia Britannica*.)

Philosophy of the Active and Moral Powers of Man. Edinburgh, 1828. 2 vols.

"Lectures on Political Economy." (First published in *Works*, Vols. VIII and IX, Edinburgh, 1855.)

Collected Works of Dugald Stewart. (Edited by Sir William Hamilton, 11 vols., Edinburgh, 1854-60.)

INDEX

Names of persons appearing in the Notes only are not included in this index.

Green, John Richard, 102
Green, T. H., 145
Gregory, David and James, 7
Gregory, Dr. John, 186-87
Grotius, Hugo, 83, 169, 191, 193

Habit: in Hume, 103; in Hutcheson, 117; in Ferguson, 140-41
Hamilton, Sir William, 66, 143, 145
Hankins, Frank H., vii
Hartley, David, 144, 145
Harvey, William, 56
Hasbach, Wilhelm, 211
Hedonism, 28; in Ferguson, 36 ff.; in Hutcheson, 115 ff.; in Hume, 126 ff.; in Smith, 209 ff.
Helvetius, Claude Adrien, 23
Herbert, Edward, Lord Herbert of Cherbury, 220
Herder, Johann Gottfried von, 12
Herodotus, 156, 183
History, Ch. IV, *entire*; missing: in Ferguson, 41 ff., 100-1, in Reid, 84, in Hutcheson, 85-86, in Smith, 86-88, in Stewart, 89-92, in Kames, 92-95, in Monboddo, 95-100, in Hume, 102-9; as literature, 78; as philosophy, 78-80, 94; as science, 80, 110-13; 18th-century passion for, 83 ff.; "natural" history and criticism of it, 87-92, 105-13; and psychology, 101, 108-9; and climate, 105; timelessness, 113
Hobbes, Thomas, 11, 26, 53, 114, 122, 138, 144, 149, 191, 214
Homo Sapiens, 34, 56, 58-60, 64, 67 ff., and Ch. III, *passim*
Hooke, Robert, 56
Hooker, Thomas, 13
Hornbeak, Katherine G., viii, and Ch. VII, n. 14
Human Nature, *see* Psychology
Hume, David, 2, 3, 10, 67, 78, 85, 114, 184, 213; pivot of the Scottish group, 11; Newton of the human mind, 19; his empirical psychology, 19, 56, 121-30; criticism of Kames' *Law Tracts*, 94; his discussion: of history, 102-9, 142-43, of politics, 159, 198-205, of marriage, 181-83, of education for women, 189-90, of political economy, 215-16, of religion, 220, 221, 224-35; resemblances of his psychology to Hutcheson and Reid, 129, 135; anti-individualis-

tic interpretation of society, 155 ff.; sway of custom, 156
Hunter, John, 57
Hutcheson, Francis, 2, 3, 10, 11; called "New Light," 8-9; lecturing in English instead of Latin, 9; his empirical aims, 19, 115; his fervor for mathematical methods, 22, 27; his doctrine of the moral sense, 55, 85, 116, 120, 194-95; macrocosm-microcosm, 55; man as animal, 56; discussions of: history, 85-86, psychology, 115-21, 144-45, society, 153-55, marriage, 177-80, government, 194-95, economics, 213-15, religion, 221; scope of moral philosophy, 176
Hutton, James, 6, 8

Individualism: rationalistic, 13, and Ch. V, *passim*; ethical, 26 ff.; anti-individualistic theories of society, 105-6, 171, and Ch. VI, *passim*; as method, 145-46; economic, 212 ff.
Ingram, John Kells, 206
Instincts: in Ferguson, 34, 139 ff., 197; in Hume, 56, 125 ff.; in Smith, 56, 209-15; in Hutcheson, 213-15, and Ch. V, *passim*
Ionian natural philosophers, 73

James, William, 141
Janet, Paul, 191
Johnson, Samuel, 15, 70, 211
Jones, Olin McKendree, 131 (quoted without being named), 134
Jouffroy, Théodore Simon, 3
Jurisprudence: in Ferguson, 38, 192-93, in Smith, 191 ff., 208; natural jurisprudence and individualism, 149 ff.
Justin, 183

Kames, Henry Home, Lord, 2, 10, 12, 62, 95, 114, 238; as farmer, 6; his empiricism, 19; on man's freedom, 54, 257, Ch. III, n. 1; on Chain of Being, 63-64; on races of man, 64-66; on diversity of language, 65-66; Monboddo's rival, 66, 73; on history, 92-95; on society, 166-69; on marriage, 183-84; on education, 187-89; on politics, 195-96; on religion, 223-25
Kant, Immanuel, 2, 12, 145